INTERNALLY DISPLACED PEOPLE

Global IDP Survey is a project of the Norwegian Refugee Council.
The objectives of the project are to:

- collect and disseminate information on the plight of IDPs;
- produce regular publications analysing trends and figures on IDPs;
- keep a database of country and regional information;
- promote and host regional and international workshops;
- encourage debate with international institutions;
- develop a network for information exchange on IDPs.

Global IDP Survey Project

Project Director: Jon Bennett
Managing Editor: Janie Hampton
Database Coordinator: Christophe Beau
Administration: Gry Sando

Norwegian Refugee Council, Oslo and Geneva

Secretary-General: Ola H. Metliaas
Geneva Representative: Brita Sydhoff
Head, Overseas Division: Oddhild Gunther

For further information contact:
Global IDP Survey
Chemin Moise-Duboule 59
CH-1209 Geneva
Switzerland
Email: idpsurvey@nrc.ch

Internally Displaced People
A Global Survey

Edited by Janie Hampton

Norwegian Refugee Council

Global IDP Survey

Earthscan Publications Ltd, London

First published in 1998 by
Earthscan Publications Limited

Citation: Internally Displaced People: A Global Survey
Global IDP Survey of the Norwegian Refugee Council
Ed: Hampton, J

A catalogue record for this book is available from the British Library

ISBN: 1 85383 521 8

Design and typesetting by Oxford Publishing Services, Oxford
Cover design by Andrew Corbett
Printed and bound in Great Britain by Biddles Ltd, Guildford and King's Lynn

For a full list of publications please contact:

Earthscan Publications Ltd
120 Pentonville Road
London N1 9JN
Tel: 0171 2780433
Fax: 0171 2781142
Email: earthinfo@earthscan.co.uk

Earthscan Publications Limited is an editorially independent subsidiary of Kogan Page Limited and publishes in association with WWF-UK and the International Institute for Environment and Development.

Contents

Part 1: Issues and Perspectives

Part 2: Regional Profiles

List of Maps

Acknowledgements

The Global IDP Survey and the Norwegian Refugee Council are grateful for financial contributions from the following donors:
Department for International Development, UK
European Community Humanitarian Office
Individuell Manneskiohjalp, Sweden
International Development Research Center, Canada
Ministry of Foreign Affairs, Norway
Ministry of Foreign Affairs, Netherlands
Ministry of Foreign Affairs, Denmark
Ministry of Foreign Affairs, Switzerland
Norwegian Church Aid
Radda Barnen, Sweden
Red Barna, Norway
Swedish International Co-operation Agency
United Nations Children's Fund
United Nations Development Programme
World Food Programme
World Vision International

Contributions in kind were gratefully received from:
Brookings Institution Project on Internal Displacement, USA
Community and Family Services International, Philippines
Ecumenical Commission for Displaced Families and Communities, Philippines
Feinstein International Famine Center, Tufts University, USA
Human Rights Watch, London and New York
International Rescue Committee, New York
International Organization for Migration, Geneva
Jesuit Refugee Services, Thailand
Overseas Development Institute, London
Refugee Studies Programme, University of Oxford
UN Centre for Human Rights, Geneva
United Nations Children's Fund
United Nations High Commissioner for Refugees
School of Politics, University of New South Wales, Australia

The following people kindly commented on the manuscript:
Sam Ath, Cambodia Red Cross
Peter Carey, University of Oxford
Jeff Crisp, UNHCR, Geneva

Sarah Graham-Brown, Gulf specialist, Oxford
Virginia Hamilton, United States Committee for Refugees
S H Hasbullah, University of Peradeniya, Sri Lanka
Erin Mooney, Centre for Human Rights, Geneva
Naila Nauphal, Wolfson College, Oxford
Jenny Pearce, University of Bradford, UK
Mohammed Sekkoum, Algerian Refugee Council
John Taylor, University of the South Bank, London
Kevin Watkins, Oxfam Policy Department, Oxford

The following people contributed their time and expertise:
Barbara Harrell-Bond, University of Oxford
David Mosse, School of Oriental and African Studies, University of London
Teresa Thompson, Oxford Christian Institute of Counselling
Nicholas Lea, Oxford Economic Modelling
Nicola Russell, Centre for Advanced Studies, France
Margaret Okole of Oxford assisted with the editing

All those associated with the Global IDP Survey would like to thank the many people in
Geneva, the USA and Oslo who gave so generously of their time and advice.

Statistics and country reports are based on many sources of information, cross-checked by the
authors and the editorial staff. These include reports of the UN, governments, NGOs, human
rights organizations and academic institutions. Much of the information was obtained in the
countries concerned. To avoid overcrowding of the text, specific references are omitted. Key
reference materials, however, are listed in the Bibliography.

Acronyms and abbreviations

ABSU	All Bodo Students Union (India)
ACF	Action internationale contra la faim
ACPD	Consultative Assembly of the Displaced Population (Guatemala)
ADF	Allied Democratic Forces (Uganda)
AFDL	Alliance des Forces démocratiques pour la Liberation (Congo)
AFRC	Armed Forces Revolutionary Council
ANC	African National Congress (South Africa)
APRA	American Popular Revolutionary Alliance
ARMIF	Central American Regional Association of NGOs Working with Refugees, Displaced Persons amd Forced Migrants
ASEAN	Association of Southeast Asian Nations
ATTF	All Tripura Tiger Force (India)
AVANSCO	Asociación Para el Avance de las Ciencias Sociales
BLF	Bodo Liberation Front (India)
BSPP	Burma Socialist Programme Party (Myanmar)
Cáritas	Catholic Church
CBIHA	Coordination Bureau for International Humanitarian Aid (Georgia)
CCJ	Colombian Commission of Jurists
CEA	National Commission for Attention to Refugees, Returnees and Displaced People (Guatemala)
CHRLA	Centre for Human Rights Legal Action
CHT	Chittagong Hill Tracts (Pakistan)
CIREFCA	International Conference on Central American Refugees, Repatriates and Displaced People
CIS	Commonwealth of Independent States (former USSR)
CISPF	CIS peacekeeping force
CNDD	Conseil national pour la défence de la démocratie (Burundi)
CNF	Chin National Front (Myanmar)
CODHES	Consultancy on Human Rights and Displacement
CONAI	National Commission of Intermediation (Mexico)
CONAVIGUA	Guatemalan widows' coordinator
CONDECOREP	National Coordination of Displaced People and Communities in Reconstruction (Peru)
CONDEG	National Council of Displaced Persons (Guatemala)
CONPAZ	Coordination of Chiapas NGOs for Peace (Mexico)
CPDIA	Permanent Consultation on Displacement in the Americas
CPP	Cambodian People's Party
CPR	Communities of Population in Resistance (Guatemala)
CRC	Convention on the Rights of the Child
CTEAR	Technical Commission for the Resettlement Accord (Guatemala)
DHA	Department of Humanitarian Affairs
DMC	disaster management committee
DPRK	Democratic People's Republic of Korea
DRC	Democratic Republic of Congo

DRC	Danish Refugee Council
EC	European Commission
ECHO	European Community Humanitarian Office
ECOMOG	Economic Community of West Africa Monitoring Group
ECOWAS	Economic Community of West African States
ELN	National Liberation Army (Colombia)
EPICA	Ecumenical Program on Central America
EPR	Popular Revolutionary Army (Mexico)
ERC	Emergency Relief Co-ordinator
ERRP	emergency rehabilitation and reconstruction plan
EZLN	Zapatista Army of National Liberation (Mexico)
FALANTIL	Forcas Armadas de Libertacao Nacional de Timor-Leste (Armed Forces of National Liberation for East Timor)
FAR	Forces armées de Rwanda
FARC	Revolutionary Armed Forces of Colombia
FAZ	Forces armées de Zaire
FIS	Islamic Salvation Front (Front islamique du salut)
FMS	Federation Migration Service (Russia)
Fodigua	Indigenous Fund (Guatemala)
Fonatierra	Land Fund (Guatemala)
FPS	Flood Protection Sector (Pakistan)
Frelimo	Mozambique Liberation Front
FRETILIN	Frente Revolucionaria do Timor Leste Independente (Revolutionary Front for an Independent East Timor)
FRODEBU	Front democratique du Burundi
FUNCINPEC	Front uni national pour un Cambodge indépendent neutre pacifique et coopératif (United National Front for an Independent, Neutral, Peaceful and Co-operative Cambodia)
GAD	Group in Support of Displaced Persons' Organizations
GAM	Mutual Support Group for Relatives of the Disappeared (Guatemala)
GIA	Armed Islamic Group (Groupe islamique armée)
GSP	general system of preferences
GURN	Government of Unity and National Reconciliation (Angola)
HACU	Humanitarian Assistance Coordination Unit (Uganda)
HCG	Humanitarian Coordination Group
IASC	Inter-Agency Standing Committee
ICRC	International Committee of the Red Cross
ICVA	International Council of Voluntary Agencies
IDP	Internally Displaced Person
IEBL	inter-entity boundary line (Bosnia-Hercegovina)
IFOR	NATO peace implementation force
IFP	Inkatha Freedom Party (South Africa)
IIDH	Inter-American Institute for Human Rights
ILO	International Labour Organization
IOC	Integrated Operations Centre (Rwanda)
IOM	International Organization for Migration
IPKF	Indian Peace Keeping Force (Sri Lanka)
JLP	Jamaica Labour Party
KANU	Kenya African National Union
KDP	Kurdish Democratic Party (Iraq)

KDPI	Kurdish Democratic Party of Iran
KNU	Karen National Union (Myanmar)
KNPP	Karenni National Progressive Party (Myanmar)
LNM	Lebanese National Movement
LRA	Lord's Resistance Army (Uganda)
LRRRC	Liberia Refugee, Repatriation and Resettlement Commission
LTTE	Liberation Tigers of Tamil Eelam (Sri Lanka)
MFDC	Mouvement des forces démocratiques de Casamance
MINARS	Ministry of Social Assistance
MINUGUA	UN Mission to Guatemala
MIRA	Indigenous Revolutionary Antizapatista Movement (Mexico)
MNDP	National Platform on Displacement in Peru
MPLA	Movement for the Popular Liberation of Angola
MRTA	Tupac Amaru Revolutionary Movement (Peru)
MSF	Médecins sans frontières
NATO	North Atlantic Treaty Organization
NGO	non-governmental organization
NLD	National League for Democracy (Myanmar)
NLFT	National Liberation Front of Tripura (India)
NMSP	New Mon State Party
NOM	National Office for Migration (Haiti)
NRC	Norwegian Refugee Council
OAU	Organization of African Unity
OCHA	Office of the Coordinator of Humanitarian Affairs
OHR	office of the high representative (Bosnia-Hercegovina)
OLS	Operation Lifeline Sudan
OPEC	Organization of Petroleum Exporting Countries
OSCE	Organization for Security and Cooperation in Europe
PAR	Programme to Support Repopulation (Peru)
PAR in AC	UNHCR-NGO Partnership in Action
PBI	Peace Brigades International
PCS	Project Counselling Service
PDS	public distribution system (North Korea)
PKK	Kurdistan Workers' Party (Iraq)
PLO	Palestine Liberation Organization
PNP	Peoples National Party (Jamaica)
PoK	Pakistan-occupied Kashmir
PPP	Pakistan People's Party
PRD	Party of the Democratic Revolution (Mexico)
PRI	Party of the Institutional Revolution (Mexico)
PRODERE	UNDP Programme for Refugees, Repatriates and Displaced People
PUK	Patriotic Union of Kurdistan (Iraq)
Renamo	Mozambique National Resistance
RPA	Rwandan Patriotic Army
RPF	Rwandan Patriotic Front
RRAN	Resettlement and Rehabilitation Authority for the North
RSK	Republic of Serbian Krajina (Croatia)
RUF	Revolutionary United Front
SACB	Somalia Aid Coordinating Body
SADC	Southern African Development Community

SELF	Special Emergency Life Food (Liberia)
SFOR	peace stabilization force (Bosnia-Hercegovina)
SLORC	State Law and Order Restoration Council (Myanmar)
SLPP	Sierra Leone People's Party
SNM	Somali National Movement
SPLA	Sudan People's Liberation Army
SWANAME	South West Asia, North Africa and the Middle East
UNAMIR	UN Assistance Mission in Rwanda
UNDMT	United Nations Disaster Management Team
UNDP	United Nations Development Programme
UNHCR	United Nations High Commissioner for Refugees
UNHRC	United Nations Commission on Human Rights
UNICEF	United Nations Children's Fund
UNITA	União Nacional para a Independência Total de Angola (National Union for the Total Independence of Angola)
UNITAF	United Nations Task Force
UNOHCI	UN Office of the Humanitarian Co-ordinator for Iraq
UNOMIG	UN monitors (Georgia)
UNOSOM	United Nations Operations in Somali
UNP	United National Party (Sri Lanka)
UNPROFOR	United Nations Protection Force
UNREO	UN Rwanda Emergency Office
UNTAES	United Nations transitional authority (Croatia)
URNG	Guatemalan National Revolutionary Unity
USAID	United States Agency for International Development
USC	United Somali Congress
USCR	US Committee for Refugees
USSR	Union of Soviet Socialist Republics
WFP	World Food Programme
WNBF	West Nile Bank Front (Uganda)
WWF	Worldwide Fund for Nature

Foreword

Francis Deng
Representative of the UN Secretary-General on Internally Displaced Persons

Since the end of the cold war, increasing numbers of people have been forced to leave their homes as a result of armed conflicts, internal strife and systematic violations of human rights. Nearly always, they suffer from conditions of insecurity and destitution, acutely in need of protection and sources of survival. Whereas refugees have an established system of international protection and assistance, those who are displaced within their national borders fall within the domestic jurisdiction and under the sovereignty of the state concerned, without legal or institutional bases for the international community to provide protection and assistance.

Accurate information is critical to the development of an international system for addressing this worldwide problem of people who suffer internal displacement. As regularly emphasized in my reports to the United Nations, a pool of information is needed on the various dimensions of internal displacement: its causes and manifestations, the degree of access of the displaced to basic services, their protection concerns, the capacity and willingness of governments to address their needs, and the response of the international community.

The Global IDP Survey launched by the Norwegian Refugee Council is an important step in this direction. The consolidation of worldwide information on internal displacement into a single report will provide an invaluable reference towards understanding the plight of displaced people and encouraging solutions for them. By documenting all known situations of internal displacement, the Global IDP Survey can also help safeguard against situations being overlooked or forgotten. In raising awareness of the specific needs of displaced people, it should assist in ensuring that situations are addressed in a comprehensive manner, inclusive of strategies for prevention, protection, and reintegration and development. Furthermore, the Survey should help fill the information gap that currently exists for vulnerable groups, in particular displaced women and children and the need for special strategies to address their needs effectively.

Most significantly, the development of a worldwide information system on internally displaced people should help create a global constituency for them. Although there are a growing number of actors at the national, regional and international level involved with displaced people, they are often unaware of each other's existence and activities.

Identifying and bringing together the different players should help promote a global effort to enhance protection, assistance and solutions for displaced people as well as encourage steps to prevent the conditions that cause their displacement. I wholeheartedly endorse this initiative and look forward to collaborating closely with its efforts.

Conflict-induced internal displacement, 1997/8

Afghanistan	1.45 million
Algeria	unknown
Angola	1.2 million
Armenia	75,000
Azerbaijan	550,000–612,000
Bangladesh	50,000–100,000
Bhutan	50,000–100,000
Bosnia-Hercegovina	450,000
Burundi	551,000
Cambodia	26,500
China	500,000 (usually as a measure against political dissents; figures highly speculative)
Colombia	500,000–1 million
Congo-Brazzaville	240,000
Croatia	174,000
Cyprus	265,000
Dem Rep Congo	1 million
East Timor	unknown
Eritrea	unknown
Ethiopia	15,000
Georgia	280,000
South Ossetia	13,000
Ghana	20,000
Guatemala	250,000
India	390,000
Iraq	1.2 million
Iraqi Kurdistan	700,000
govt controlled	500,000
Kenya	100,000
Lebanon	500,000–800,000
Liberia	725,000
Mali	100,000 (+ 10,000 demobilized soldiers)
Mexico	6,000
Mozambique	30,000–50,000
Myanmar	800,000–1 million
Nigeria	470,000
North Korea	unknown
Pakistan	50,000
Peru	250,000
Philippines	189,000

Russian Federation	
Chechnya	350,000
Krasnodar	60,000
Russia	90,000
Stravropol	100,000
Rwanda	180,500
Senegal	5,000
Sierra Leone	200,000
Somalia	250,000–350,000
South Africa	20,000 +
Sri Lanka	790,000–1 million
Srpska	416,000
Sudan	4 million
Syria	200,000
Tajikistan	600,000 (but almost all returned by October 1997)
Turkey	330,000 (government figure). Most international organizations estimate +- 2.5m, which includes economic migrants
Uganda	400,000

Internal displacement caused by development projects, natural disasters, or economic migration (selection only)

Bangladesh	750,000–1 million
China	2–4m (natural disasters) 400,000 (development programmes) 120m (economic migrants)
Haiti	1 million
India	21.3 million
Mauritania	200,000
Nepal	150,000
Nigeria	800,000
Pakistan	200,000
Vietnam	48,000

Introduction

One of the world's most acute and growing problems is the increasing number of internally displaced people, or internal refugees. Unlike refugees who cross international borders, those who stay within their own country must rely upon their own governments to uphold their civil and human rights. If the state chooses not to invite external assistance, then the international community has limited options to protect these people. In many countries it is the government or its military forces who have caused the displacement or prevent access to their citizens.

There are an estimated 20–22 million people internally displaced by conflict throughout the world. Many live in appalling conditions with little security. People are forced to leave their homes because of civil or international war, political conflict, 'ethnic cleansing' or human rights violations. Many more millions of people flee from natural disasters or economic development projects. Most people want to flee as far as possible from conflict, but refugees are becoming increasingly less welcome, so the number of internally displaced people has been steadily growing. Some governments are reluctant to discuss the situation and little official information is available. Occasionally governments exaggerate a problem in order to secure more international aid.

This global survey provides the most comprehensive and contemporary information available. It gives the background, figures and trends in 56 countries on five continents where internally displaced people are known to exist in large numbers. This book is an essential reference work for all people involved in international politics, humanitarian aid, human rights, development studies and international relations.

We have used the definition for internally displaced people (IDPs) used by the United Nations:

> *Persons or groups of persons who have been forced to flee or to leave their homes or places of habitual residence as a result of, or in order to avoid, in particular, the effects of armed conflict, situations of generalized violence, violations of human rights or natural or human-made disasters, and who have not crossed an internationally recognized state border.*

This is a cumbersome definition, but it tries to encompass all aspects of internal displacement. It assumes that the international aid community will become concerned, particularly where violations of human rights occur.

There is an ongoing debate on the definition of IDPs. People may be forced to flee from their homes because of war (civil or international); disasters (natural or man-made); development (construction of dams or urban clearances); and changes in the economy (industrialization or famine). Although some mention is made of economic migrations (in China, for example) this survey generally excludes those who move for economic, cultural or social reasons. The writers have highlighted the specific problems of their countries – in Chechnya displacement is caused by armed conflict; in Nigeria 'development' is a greater problem. A person forced to migrate from war in Afghanistan is no more or less desperate than a family displaced at less speed by drought in Haiti. However, if everyone who ever fled their homes for whatever reason was included, then the global figure for IDPs would probably exceed 100 million.

Information is rarely neutral and there are vested interests in withholding or exaggerating facts and figures related to IDPs. Most of the figures in this book have to be qualified by the word 'estimated'. In some countries, such as East Timor and North Korea, even an estimate is impossible. Information is often disputed, even by those agencies closest to the situation. Discerning which source is the more reliable is always difficult: a community health worker may be more accurate than a university statistician. Politicians from one party may want high figures, whereas their opponents want smaller ones. The Global IDP Survey's figures differ slightly from those of the US Committee for Refugees's *World Refugee Survey*, which uses some different sources. But the variation in figures is not the important issue; it is the plight of individual people and families that needs to be addressed.

To support internally displaced people, information must be compiled and exchanged. Documentation is currently still a top-down process. The facts and figures are mostly collected by international aid agencies. The information is rarely disaggregated by gender or age, and IDPs are rarely themselves involved. Improvements in the methods of collection and dissemination are required.

The Global IDP Survey aims to disseminate knowledge of internally displaced people and advocate for them through this book, journals, seminars, training, a database and the internet. Key information on IDPs will appear on the internet on the Norwegian Refugee Council's web site at: http://www.sol.no/nrc-no. Knowledge of the *gaps* in information and in assistance is as important as the known facts. One purpose of this book is to identify those gaps. Readers are invited to share information relating to IDPs.

Over forty academics and development workers from all over the world have researched the latest information from a wide range of official and unofficial sources. The internet has been used to assemble the information from all corners of the world at short notice. Nearly two hundred references are included in the bibliography.

Leading specialists in forced migration have contributed original chapters describing the trends and issues current in international fora relating to internally displaced people. They analyse and discuss relevant concerns such as the rights of IDPs and the responsibilities of the international community towards them.

The book is sponsored by the Norwegian Refugee Council through its project the Global IDP Survey. Six governments, more than twenty universities and research centres, a dozen aid agencies and four UN departments from all over the world have contributed finance, time and expertise, for which they are heartily thanked.

This book highlights the urgency of the crisis and challenges the international community to find durable solutions for the millions of internally displaced people worldwide.

Janie Hampton, Editor

Part 1
Issues and Perspectives

Recent trends in protection and assistance for internally displaced people

Roberta Cohen

Over the past decade, the plight of people forcibly displaced within their own borders has become, for the first time, a subject of international concern. In the growing debate on how best to enhance protection and assistance for internally displaced people, many proposals have been put forward. Although most generally pale in the face of the magnitude and severity of the problem, it is important to identify those that can be built upon, and to seek to enhance their prospects for success.

Guiding principles on internal displacement

One of the more promising initiatives at the international level to promote protection and assistance for IDPs is a body of principles tailored specifically to their needs. Entitled the Guiding Principles on Internal Displacement, they were presented to the UN Commission on Human Rights in 1998 by Francis M Deng, Representative of the UN Secretary-General on Internally Displaced Persons.

The Guiding Principles fill a major gap in the international protection system for the internally displaced. They set forth the rights of IDPs and the obligations of governments and insurgent forces in all phases of displacement. They offer protection before internal displacement occurs (that is, protection *against* arbitrary displacement), during situations of displacement, and in post-conflict return and reintegration. They are the first attempt to articulate what protection should mean for IDPs and to establish an explicit right not to be arbitrarily displaced, by specifying the impermissible grounds for displacement and the guarantees that should be afforded when displacement takes place. They further affirm the right of IDPs to request international humanitarian assistance, the right of international actors to offer such assistance, and the duty of states to accept such offers.

Although not a binding instrument, the Guiding Principles have immense practical value in providing a yardstick for monitoring the treatment of IDPs. They can be expected to strengthen the advocacy work of humanitarian, human rights and development organizations on behalf of the displaced and can also be of use to governments in drafting laws to protect internally displaced people. By offering an authoritative statement of the rights of internally displaced people, they should raise international awareness of their plight. Over time, they could contribute to the creation of a moral and political climate in which they might attain the force of customary law.

The Guiding Principles are the result of many years of work by a team of international legal experts collaborating with international organizations, regional bodies and NGOs, under the direction of the Representative of the UN Secretary-General. When the legal team first compiled and analysed the international norms applicable to IDPs, it found substantial grey areas and gaps in the law. While it also found extensive coverage for the displaced, it recommended a specific body of principles that would consolidate into one document existing norms which at present are dispersed in many different instruments of human rights law, humanitarian law and refugee law by analogy. The Guiding Principles not only restate existing laws but make key provisions more explicit and address the gaps identified. For instance, they provide explicit guarantees against the forced return of IDPs to places of danger, and they provide for compensation for property lost during displacement.

Various humanitarian organizations such as UNHCR and ICRC have testified to the value of principles specific to IDPs. NGOs in particular have called for one 'compact, usable document' for better protection of displaced people. Further, the UN General Assembly and Commission on Human Rights have encouraged the development of a normative framework to enhance protection for IDPs.

Concerns have nonetheless been expressed about whether the development of new standards would undercut efforts to implement existing standards of human rights and humanitarian law, and whether a normative framework specifically tailored to IDPs would discriminate against other groups. The purpose, however, of developing a normative framework for IDPs is to reinforce and strengthen existing protections. The focus of the Guiding Principles on a particular group accords with other international initiatives to draw attention to disadvantaged groups, whether refugees, minorities, or indigenous peoples. Moreover, because the needs of IDPs are so frequently overlooked, principles specific to them are essential to ensuring that, in a given situation, they like others are protected and their unique needs

acknowledged and addressed.

The wide acceptance and dissemination of the principles should be encouraged so that they are used by relevant actors at all levels. Most significantly, the Guiding Principles could prove an important means of encouraging affected populations themselves to mobilize and develop strategies to increase protection. The challenge of securing protection for IDPs is one that requires a concerted effort not only by the international community but at the national and local levels as well.

Quest for a definition

The Guiding Principles apply to people or groups of people 'who have been forced or obliged to flee or to leave their homes or places of habitual residence in particular as a result of, or in order to avoid the effects of, armed conflict, situations of generalized violence, violations of human rights or natural or human-made disasters, and who have not crossed an internationally recognized state border.'

This definition is the broadest one in use at the international or regional level. It contains the two crucial elements of internal displacement: coerced or involuntary movement and remaining within one's national borders. It also includes the major causes of displacement, but its use of the qualifier, 'in particular', makes clear that internal displacement is not limited to these causes alone, so as not to exclude future groups that might need special attention. At the same time, the definition does not encompass those who migrate because of economic causes. People forced from their homes because of economic injustice and marginalization tantamount to systematic violation of their economic rights would come under the definition. But in most cases of economic migration, the element of coercion is not so clear, and development programmes generated by national and international agencies are the most appropriate means of addressing their problems.

The definition focuses in large part on people who, if they were to cross a border, would qualify as refugees, both under the OAU Convention and the Cartagena Declaration and arguably, in many cases, under the narrower definition of the Refugee Convention as well. But it also includes people who would not qualify as refugees, for example those uprooted by natural and human-made disasters. The argument for including natural disasters is based essentially on cases where governments respond to such disasters by discriminating against or neglecting certain groups on political or ethnic grounds or by violating their human rights in other ways. For example, when drought and famine ravaged Ethiopia in the mid-1980s, the government forcibly relocated hundreds of thousands of Tigrayans it regarded as political opponents, under the pretext of responding to a natural disaster. In other countries people have been displaced because of a combination of natural causes and racial, social or political reasons. Maintaining natural disasters in the definition highlights that people subjected to such disasters may have special protection needs.

The same reasoning applies to the inclusion of human-made disasters, such as nuclear or chemical accidents. Whereas in many instances, people displaced by such disasters receive assistance from their governments and the international community, other cases may be complicated by persecution and systematic violations of human rights, necessitating international protection. The same would be true for development projects that cause displacement. Should, for example, the Three Gorges Dam currently under construction in China, entail the forcible displacement of one million people without adequate resettlement, compensation or respect for human rights, it could qualify as a human-made disaster whose displaced populations require attention under the definition.

What distinguishes IDPs and should make them of concern to the international community is the coercion that impels their movement, their subjection to human rights abuse emanating from their displacement, and the lack of protection available within their own countries. The definition's importance lies in identifying people who should be of special concern to the international community, raising awareness to their plight, and facilitating the work of governments and private organizations seeking to increase protection and assistance for IDPs.

Institutional arrangements

Over the past decade, a multitude of humanitarian, human rights and development organizations have come forward to provide protection, assistance, reintegration and development support to IDPs. Many have shown themselves remarkably flexible in interpreting their mandates broadly to encompass IDPs and in developing special expertise and skills to reach displaced people. Nonetheless, the overall response has been highly uneven, poorly coordinated and characterized by neglect of protection and human rights.

These inadequacies have prompted a wide-ranging debate both within and outside the United Nations about how to improve the international response to emergency situations. Among the options put forward for IDPs are whether a new agency should be created, whether an existing agency should be assigned the responsibility or whether the strengthening of collaborative arrangements among agencies whose mandates and activities relate to IDPs is the most practical alternative.

The first option has already proved unrealistic. Neither the political will nor the resources exist to create a new agency. In any event, it would duplicate the many existing resources and capacities that have already been deployed to assist IDPs. A more persuasive alternative is to enlarge the mandate of an existing agency such as UNHCR, which has already developed special expertise in working with displaced people. Yet, in 1993 when the Netherlands proposed that the UN assign general competence for IDPs to UNHCR, neither UNHCR nor its executive committee endorsed the idea. In 1997, UNHCR was again queried about taking over responsibility for IDPs prior to UN Secretary-General Kofi Annan's announcement of UN reforms. While appearing more willing to expand its role, it did not express readiness to shoulder the entire responsibility.

The choice has thus fallen on the residual option, that of strengthening and better coordinating existing collaborative relationships. In his July 1997 reform programme, the UN Secretary-General endorsed this option by assigning responsibility to the emergency relief coordinator (ERC) for ensuring that IDP protection and assistance are addressed. To be effective, however, the ERC, who has been coordinating the UN's overall response to humanitarian emergencies since 1992, will have to assume a more active leadership role than in the past, allocating responsibility for IDPs and taking steps to improve the current system's response to the problem.

One step the ERC could take would be to assign principal responsibility for IDPs to one operational organization in each acute emergency. The organization chosen would be expected to monitor the IDPs' situation, take a lead in developing strategies to ensure that their protection, assistance, reintegration and development needs are addressed, and directly address some of these needs itself, in collaboration with other agencies. Case studies of various countries show that when one agency is designated with responsibility for IDPs, greater attention is paid to their needs.

The designation of a principal agency

should be done by the ERC with the approval of the Inter-Agency Standing Committee (IASC), a body composed of the heads of the world's major assistance and development organizations. Resident humanitarian coordinators in the field who report to the ERC should then be expected to help mobilize the support of other agencies on behalf of the organization chosen: the needs of IDPs are, after all, varied and may require the expertise of different organizations. The extent to which the assistance, protection and reintegration and development needs of IDPs are being met should then be monitored by the IASC. Particular attention should be paid to avoiding past practice of focusing on the provision of assistance with almost no attention paid to protection.

Finally, the ERC should call the IASC's attention to situations of internal displacement that are neglected either because governments do not acknowledge the problem or request assistance, or because donors fail to respond effectively. As the reference point for IDPs, the ERC should be expected to play a leadership role in seeing that *all* situations of internal displacement are identified and addressed. The recent inclusion of the Representative of the UN Secretary-General in IASC meetings as a standing member should help raise visibility of IDPs. So too should the UN Secretary-General's reform programme which explicitly identified IDPs as falling between the gaps of the different UN agencies. NGO advocacy will be strongly needed to press the ERC and the UN Secretary-General to ensure that the inter-agency collaborative system now in place for IDPs works effectively.

New approaches to protection

Providing humanitarian assistance, the UN Secretary-General pointed out in 1997, requires not only an efficient relief system but 'a capacity to protect vulnerable populations to survive in a hostile environment'. While many humanitarian and development organizations have long interpreted protection to mean the provision of food, medicine and shelter, in more recent years, measures to ensure respect for the human rights and physical safety of the affected population are being emphasized as an integral part of protection.

For both the International Committee of the Red Cross (ICRC) and UNHCR, humanitarian action has always been about ensuring the basic human rights and security of the victims as well as the delivery of relief. ICRC, for example, makes representations to governments and non-state actors when violations of humanitarian law occur, and in certain circumstances issues public statements. It also undertakes activities such as evacuating civilians from situations of danger, creating protected areas, gaining access to and securing the release of detainees, establishing tracing networks, and facilitating arrangements for the creation of humanitarian space and cease-fires.

UNHCR likewise has undertaken extensive protection activities on behalf of IDPs. These include monitoring the treatment of threatened minority groups, intervening with the authorities to request protective action, investigating and prosecuting specific cases, and assisting governments to provide personal documentation. In situations of armed conflict or massive violations of human rights, UNHCR identifies its activities as assisting the safe passage of civilians through front lines, relocating and evacuating civilians from conflict areas, assisting besieged people unable or unwilling to move from their homes, intervening with local authorities to prevent the involuntary return of IDPs to areas of danger, and alerting governments and the public to human rights abuses. UNHCR also has participated in mediation and reconciliation efforts between returning displaced people and local residents.

ICRC and UNHCR, however, are not present in all situations and even when they are, they may not have the capacity or mandates to deal with all protection problems, necessitating the involvement of others. UNHCR, in particular, has called upon the UN human rights system to increase its involvement. Although traditionally not involved with humanitarian emergencies, the Office of the UN High Commissioner for Human Rights has begun in recent years to deploy field staff to enhance protection. In Rwanda, human rights field staff, in collaboration with UNHCR, facilitated the return of IDPs. In Abkhazia, Georgia, human rights field staff have also contributed to the safe return of IDPs. But the existence of so many other cases of internal displacement would make it valuable for the High Commissioner's office to set up a corps of UN human rights protection officers to be activated in situations of internal displacement. Working together with humanitarian and development organizations, they could serve in safe areas and camps, monitor and assist with returns, and help to make areas of return more secure. While the international community has long accepted the field protection activities that humanitarian organizations such as UNHCR and ICRC provide, similar acceptance needs to be extended to the protection activities of human rights bodies.

NGOs have also begun to shoulder greater protection responsibilities in situations of internal displacement. Médecins sans frontières (MSF), for example, has a policy of *temoignage* or witnessing which includes establishing a presence near people in danger, reporting on their condition and engaging in public condemnation when there are massive and repeated violations of human rights and humanitarian law. The policy of the World Council of Churches also calls for a wide range of protection activities for uprooted people, including advocacy, the provision of sanctuary and legal aid, conflict resolution activities, and the monitoring of returns.

Many international organizations and NGOs have been reluctant to raise or become involved in protection issues, for fear of provoking restrictions on their access and attacks on their personnel, or because they lack experience or expertise in these issues. Yet, when the physical security and fundamental human rights of the people benefiting from their assistance are threatened, ignoring such concerns could render their assistance programmes meaningless.

At a minimum, international organizations and NGOs could take steps to enhance the security of their beneficiaries by designing assistance programmes to enhance protection. Providing fuel to women so that they do not have to walk into unsafe areas to gather firewood is one way of increasing protection. The provision of adequate lighting in camps and settlements is another. This kind of preventive protection has for its source UNHCR's guidelines on the protection of refugee women and children, which some organizations are beginning to apply to IDPs. The Women's Commission for Refugee Women and Children in particular has begun to monitor the extent to which these guidelines are being carried out by international organizations and NGOs in the case of IDPs.

Another means of providing protection is by reinforcing presence when protection problems arise. Although presence to be truly effective must be combined with some form of action, in some situations substantial numbers of outside representatives watching and listening can deter abuse. Organizations unwilling to engage in direct protection activities should at least report violations to those who can. Humanitarian and development agencies are often the first to become aware of protection problems, but because they do not consider protection or human rights a central concern or function, it has not been their practice even to communicate these problems to those who could do something.

Increasingly, however, it is being argued that humanitarian and development organizations should forward information on human rights violations to human rights groups and others who are prepared to act upon it.

Protection can further be advanced by working directly with the displaced and with local communities and local authorities in finding solutions. In Central America, NGOs have been involved in campaigns to promote legal recognition for IDPs. One NGO has established a neighbour warning system that watches routes and fields at night in the Andean region of South America. Multiethnic programmes to encourage contact and trust among different groups also help increase protection for IDPs. The World Council of Churches, for example, in an effort to integrate displaced people into local communities, has been encouraging its member churches to examine and challenge negative portrayals of the displaced. International Alert has identified four ways in which NGOs can increase protection in the CIS countries: helping governments to revise national legislation and practices that may jeopardize the security of IDPs; supporting local NGOs working with IDPs; supporting national reconciliation efforts; and helping governments to create viable mechanisms to cope with crisis situations.

One way that international agencies and NGOs alike can effectively manage the risks of engaging in protection work is by banding together and taking joint stands. The adoption of joint positions can strengthen the overall impact of an initiative and at the same time reduce the risks involved for each participating organization. For, while one vocal NGO can be easily singled out by a government for expulsion, it is much harder and more costly for a government to take punitive measures against all NGOs.

Better training in protection problems needs to be provided to the staff of humanitarian and development agencies and to those

Improving protection for internally displaced women

UNHCR guidelines for the protection of refugee women and its guidelines against sexual violence should be applied to internally displaced women and girls, combined with the steps listed below:

- Make the collection of gender-specific information a routine part of assessments made by humanitarian and development agencies.
- Design assistance programmes to enhance protection, with attention paid to placement of latrines, lighting, and how far women have to go for firewood.
- Designate women as food distribution points to prevent their having to trade sexual favours for food or simply receive inadequate portions.
- Maintain regular contact with internally displaced women to provide them with a sense of security and reassurance and develop with them preventive measures as well as protection strategies.
- Increase presence in the field when serious protection problems, such as sexual violence, are reported.
- Recognize that rape is a criminal offence, requiring punishment and exposure; these steps may also serve as a preventive measure.
- Provide counselling and psychological and medical treatment to those who have been raped or subjected to other serious human rights abuse.
- Engage in advocacy on behalf of displaced women with local and national authorities, initiate joint statements and positions, and bring cases to the attention of the UN Special Rapporteur on Violence against Women, donor governments and the media.

in human rights field operations. Training should cover international standards, in particular the Guiding Principles on Internal Displacement and the compilation and analysis of legal norms upon which the principles are based. It should include instruction on how to identify human rights issues, how to report them, and whom to alert at headquarters and in the field when displaced people are endangered. It also should include instruction in the practical measures for enhancing physical safety in the field. This could be by accompaniment, protective custody, neighbourhood patrols, protection watches, safe houses, interventions with the authorities, or evacuations of life-threatening cases. As women and children comprise the vast majority of IDPs, their protection needs should be emphasized. In particular, field personnel should be aware that the way international assistance programmes are planned and implemented has direct bearing on the protection of these groups. The Office of the UN High Commissioner for Human Rights, together with UNHCR, could play a valuable role by organizing such training; so too could ICRC and NGO umbrella groups.

Conclusion

The resistance of governments and non-state actors will continue to be a serious obstacle to international involvement with IDPs. But the human rights and protection gap will also remain wide as long as human rights field staff are absent from most humanitarian emergencies and humanitarian and development agencies do not concern themselves with physical safety. Substantial numbers of IDPs are clearly in need of international protection and assistance, which their own governments are unwilling or unable to provide. A combination of legal, institutional and practical measures will be needed to address situations of internal displacement effectively. The steps outlined above, if reinforced and strongly supported, should prove an important first step toward achieving that goal.

Problems and opportunities of displacement

Jon Bennett

There is a small village called San José de Apartado in the war-torn region of Urabá in northwest Colombia. Most of the original residents fled the village when armed gangs swept through in 1996. When for a brief period the area was relatively quiet, people displaced from another part of the region entered San José de Apartado and took up residence in the abandoned homes. It was not long before their presence again attracted armed groups. This time, however, they took a stand. In March 1997, 300 or so residents declared themselves a 'community of peace'. They collectively decided not to carry arms and not to support or associate themselves with any armed group. Their stand for peace was particularly courageous in a region notorious for its widespread intimidation, drug dealing, arms trafficking and illegal land appropriation. In this rich banana-producing district, paramilitary groups forge alliances with wealthy landowners and drug barons in return for protection against guerrilla insurgents. Victimized by all sides, peasant farmers fleeing from the conflict often find their land being sold at minimal cost to wealthy landowners able to buy protection from the various armed groups.

For the community of 300, declaring neutrality has not been without major risks: within three months, 37 members were killed. The key to the safety of the remainder lay in the support given by international NGOs. Not only were emergency supplies offered, but also protection in the form of accompaniment, registration and the 'witness' function of international agencies. Here, as elsewhere in Colombia, such work has for the most part gone unnoticed by the media. This is low-intensity warfare without the headline appeal of mass displacement such as that in central Africa. Colombia's internally displaced people (*desplazados*) flee in small clusters, gradually crowding shanty towns around major cities, or drifting for months around the countryside.

The story of San José de Apartado is important for several reasons (Loughna, 1998). First, it illustrates that local initiative and coping mechanisms will always be a most effective barrier to human rights abuses. Organized communities can be a powerful force for peace, even amidst the squalor of a seemingly endless war. Second, we should not underestimate the value of international support for such initiatives and how the presence of aid agencies can enhance protection for people under threat.

Colombia is the latest in a catalogue of countries that have succumbed to violent internal war resulting in mass internal displacement. In this decade alone there have been more than 90 conflicts in 64 locations across the world, only four of which were classic interstate conflicts. In 1995, 38 million people fled civil conflict and more than 160 million were affected by natural disasters (Walker, 1997). One of the chief characteristics of internal war (and its aid corollary, the 'complex emergency') is the strategic use of citizens themselves as shields for combatants, as the target of 'ethnic cleansing', or simply as expendable individuals in a fiercely contested resource war. The nature of the conflict, its intensity and duration will determine the choices available to citizens forced to leave their homes. These choices are also determined by a host of other factors: the proximity of international borders, urban centres; the location of family, clan and community members; financial resources; the kind of help available from national or international bodies; and so on. In many instances, flight is not an individual choice, but one made by community leaders. Women, children and the elderly are often the first to flee, leaving behind able bodied men to protect home and property. This was the case in Bosnia, for instance. Alternatively, the family breadwinners may move first to seek a relatively safe area to move the family, as in Afghanistan.

This chapter briefly examines how displacement changes people's perceptions of their environment and how new circumstances determine local coping mechanisms and power relations. A broader analysis of displacement requires indicators not simply restricted to physical circumstances; some areas of research required for a better understanding of how people adapt to forced migration are suggested. Very little field research has been undertaken that begins with the assumption that IDPs are social actors rather than categories of need. An anthropological perspective may yield some practical suggestions for how external agents should approach the social, psychological and physical needs of displaced communities and how assistance packages could more readily reflect the aspirations of the communities concerned. Displacement might then be regarded as a transformation – a process – rather than a fixed (and temporary) reality in people's lives.

Migration is necessarily disruptive for individuals and communities alike. It can, however, become an impetus for personal or political gain as well as loss. It redefines one's own, and others', perceptions of nation, community and even family. Using examples drawn from recent and well documented situations of internal displacement, some of the variables that demand greater research and integration into aid policy are examined.

Perceptions of displacement

Even though displacement may be understood as context-specific, the resource-driven and technical demands of relief programmes have tended to group IDPs under one 'problem' category without giving due attention to people's own perception of their plight and the kind of coping mechanisms they use to allay further hardship. A look at how people live amidst upheaval and strive towards some degree of control over unfolding events may challenge the conceptual limitations of terms such as 'vulnerable groups', beneficiaries', 'target groups' and the like (Sørensen, 1998). Within the political, economic and physical constraints of war, people create social networks and may still shape their own present and future.

Aid workers, journalists and policy makers tend to present displacement as a series of linked events – from war to flight, refuge, return, and resettlement. The catalogue of international responses are geared towards these perceived experiences – transport, shelter, resettlement packages, and so on. For those caught up in social upheaval, however, the experience of displacement may be punctuated by more fundamental changes. For example, one of the major results of the 1994 Rwanda genocide was widowhood. This was not only a matter of personal loss but also a challenge to a whole set of social and political mores for the people concerned. In the post-trauma period, women emerged as community leaders; landrights were challenged, and women increasingly sought work outside the home (Bennett, 1997). In Afghanistan, the opposite occurred; displaced women became increasingly confined within camps, reinforcing the radical conservatism of the mainly Pushtun menfolk and arguably resulting in a cultural dislocation that will take generations to remedy. In Sudan, perhaps the single most destructive consequence of the last 15 years' war has been the stripping of the Dinka asset base (that is cattle) in Bahr el Ghazal and southern Kordofan. Where social and economic identity is so closely linked with cattle ownership, displacement itself may not be the enduring legacy of war. A few innovative approaches to assisting internally displaced people in south Sudan include, for instance, crossing battle lines with cattle vaccine and ensuring a degree of protection for cattle camps around major towns. For example, Oxfam UK undertook such programmes with the Mundari people in and around Juba from 1986 onwards.

Self-help

Internal conflict and the resulting displace-ment is typically an evolving process involv-ing the collapse of essential support structures at individual, communal and national levels. The response to social trauma is as varied as it is culture specific. Self-help can involve co-counselling groups which sometimes involve external agents in psychosocial rehabilitation. In Rwanda, women's 'survivor' groups such as AVEGA–AGAHOZO, formed in January 1995, built a national network of mutual support for those suffering family loss and dislocation. In its first year, the network had about 10,000 registered members, from an estimated total of 30,000 widows inside Rwanda and an unknown number in exile (Bennett and Kawatesi, 1996).

In 1996/7, research was carried out among female-headed households in several villages in Sri Lanka and Cambodia to

---

Somali women as peacekeepers

In a society steeped in traditional patri-archal clan structures, it has been a great challenge for Somali women to take on new roles in a postwar society as sole providers to their families and as those responsible for reconstruction of their communities. Breaking the mould implies re-examining women's roles in perpetuating the culture of violence. Boy children, for example, are given names such as Kalashnikov and clan lineages, including ancient animosities, are taught to their children by womenfolk. Women did, in fact, have a traditional 'passive' role in peace keeping when, for example, daughters were offered as wives to ex-enemies to seal the peace by bonding old antagonists with blood ties. Nevertheless, this was beyond the control of women who are now searching for more proactive roles they might play.

From 1988 to 1990 during the civil war in the breakaway Republic of Somali-land, a group of displaced women formed a group called Allah Amin. Its aim was to facilitate and provide support to about ten thousand inhabitants who were displaced inside Somaliland. The activities of these women included fund-raising, running makeshift hospitals for the wounded, sup-porting war widows, standard health-care provision and running children's schools. When the civil war ended in Somaliland, women returnees set up market stalls and played a crucial economic and social role in the rebuilding process.

---

understand how conflict had changed the lives of these women and what impact it had on their sense of identity. In Cambodia, the Khmer Rouge's deliberate policy to destroy family bonds has heightened levels of mistrust among those displaced for long periods, made worse by the 'culture of silence' about individual experiences. In Sri Lanka, the conflict has led in particular to increased prejudice among ethnic communities. The research sought to understand women's coping strategies through their own eyes, using participatory rural appraisal tools, plus drawings, role plays and group exchanges.

A key conclusion of the research was that aid agencies should look more readily at providing both economic and emotional support to those displaced by conflict, though with less emphasis on the individualistic Western model of counselling. Using participatory group activities as a means of self-help and understanding of coping strategies was particularly welcomed by participants. Oxfam UK, the sponsoring agency for the research, is now incorporating some of the findings into its field-level approaches to post-conflict rehabilitation (van der Wijk, 1997).

Defining power relations

Ethnic warfare, particularly the kind that involves the state opposing an ethnic group deemed to be a threat, includes routine techniques of social dominance, many of which predate the eruption of violence but prefigure in all official explanations of the war. The terms 'terrorist' and 'illegal migrant' carry obvious negative meanings, but other seemingly neutral terms such as 'ethnic minority' or 'opposition group' are also politically charged, depending on who is using the term. Displacement is rarely an apolitical process for citizens caught up in the struggle for power. Social identity and power relations are reformulated in the process of flight. One person's terrorist is another person's freedom fighter.

The notion of 'nationhood' has been reconstructed by people in exile in countries such as Eritrea, Jammu-Kashmir and, most recently, the Baltic States. Aside from political movements *per se*, we could look more closely at how people draw upon their experiences of migration to generate alternative forms of

---

Targeting vulnerable groups in Mozambique

With support from an international NGO, a life-skills building programme was established through a local community association in a rural village in one of Mozambique's northern provinces. The programme included basic numeracy and literacy, recreation, access to viable trade skills and 'mentor' relationships with adult role models. The programme was opened to a wide range of economically marginalized adolescents, including those who had been internally displaced, returning refugees, original local residents and, more recently, demobilized child soldiers. As the long-term goal was to promote genuine reintegration into the local community, special programmes were not established for particular subgroups such as former child soldiers or separated children. There was a conscious effort to address common problems and issues with support being reflective of individual needs rather than being tied to membership of a special subgroup.

---

organization based upon a new political reality. In Eritrea and Somalia, gender relations may have been positively affected; in south Sudan the role of the church has radically changed as a result of war; and in eastern Sri Lanka the breakdown of traditional social structures caused by internal displacement has, for some, resulted in new opportunities for individual entrepreneurship.

Many local cultural traditions have more established ways of dealing with the loss associated with displacement. These may involve religious ritual or communal rein-forcement of a shared 'struggle'. Disruption in social relations not only involves personal loss; it dismantles existing power structures and decision-making processes (Sørensen, 1998). New forms of collaboration may emerge or be strengthened by the shared experience of displacement. In Tigray, Ethiopia, throughout the 1980s, the Tigray People's Liberation Front ensured that peasant, women and youth associations remained intact during the mass movement from war and famine. Collective works were undertaken and national identity asserted through, for example, political and cultural rallies, even in the refugee settlements of Sudan.

Forced migration

In studying the plight of IDPs we take for granted the concept of 'forced migration', the involuntary movement of (usually) a large group of people due to external pressure. However, even in situations of extreme violence some people remain within their local community or at least within the immediate surroundings. The decision to stay might be simply a question of resources, or it might indicate an active resistance against migratory pressure, encouraging new forms of collective action, as seen in the case of San José de Apartado in Colombia. Alternatively, temporary displacement might be a pragmatic solution to social violence, especially in the early stages of a conflict. Thus, in Uganda 'nocturnal displacement' is common, whereby people fearing attack leave their homes during the night and return during the day to farm the land. In the town of Gulu, for example, as many as 15,000 people were reported in 1996 to be sheltering in the town's public buildings fearing the atrocities of the Lord's Resistance Army.

The concept of 'voluntary' displacement is problematic in societies where political conformity is particularly acute. In China, thousands of the dominant ethnic majority, the Han Chinese, have been forcibly sent as 'civilizing envoys' to outlying areas in the People's Republic. Local ethnic conflicts over the years are closely related to these Han Chinese migrations where one officially sanctioned ethnic group challenges existing power relations, even in areas where they are now a minority (Stolen, 1998). In Myanmar (Burma), tens of thousands of people have been told to move to the outskirts of the capital, Yangon, to make way for new construction projects. In the absence of any effective judicial or compensatory process, military threat is the ultimate sanction for those refusing to move. Given the oppressive nature of the current Myanmar regime, it is understandable that resistance is minimal and that the letter of request issued to these town dwellers is 'voluntarily' adhered to. Notwithstanding crude cultural relativism ('human rights is a Western concept', or 'they don't experience oppression in the same way because they're Burmese'), condemnation of these actions should, at the very least, be accompanied by more thorough research into viable alternatives and a greater understanding of the motivations towards resistance or compliance.

Conceptual difficulties also arise in the distinction between 'spontaneous' and 'organized' population displacements. In January 1998, in a Catholic church in the trading centre of Survey in the Rift Valley of Kenya, about 400 Kikuyu took shelter from attacks by Pokot and Samburu tribesmen who attacked their villages using guns and spears, torching homes, raping women and killing all who did not flee. This might have been a simple case of traditional cattle rustling had it not become clear that the police stood by and allowed the raiders to destroy homes. A more likely explanation is an orchestrated campaign to drive the Kikuyu out of the Rift Valley and to change the political geography of the region in favour of President Arap Moi's own ethnic group. The manipulation of age-old ethnic antagonisms to bolster contemporary political ambitions is not unique to Kenya. The Baggara tribesmen of western Sudan, for instance, were armed with sophisticated weaponry in the 1980s to turn traditional cattle raiding against the Dinkas into a geopolitical strategy of the government, resulting in mass displacement of the Dinka people.

Integration with local population

The location in which displaced people are allowed to live will form the basis of their survival strategy and dictate, to a large extent, their ability to integrate with the local population and economy. Too often, aid agencies providing temporary shelter for large numbers of displaced people fail to take into account the longer term impact on the environment and local resource base. 'Planning for' human settlement, rather than 'planning of' camps or sites would involve the assessment of a 'target area' as opposed to a 'target group' (Chalinder,1998). Many of today's emergencies no longer fall into the category of temporary and short-lived. In settlement areas in Africa in particular, there are numerous examples of ragged and crowded dwellings that bear witness to the fact that when originally planned, more priority was given to technical and engineering issues than to the social and economic rights of the inhabitants.

Ethnic or religious affiliations are often the prime determinants of the success with which a displaced population integrates with a local population. This can present particular problems for locating pastoralists, as in Somalia, but accounted for the large-scale absorption of Mozambican refugees into Malawi in the 1980s. Family and ethnic ties can also determine where people choose to flee – across borders or to major towns. In Liberia, about 500,000 IDPs fled to the capital, Monrovia, during the fighting from 1990 onwards. The Liberian population is very mobile and many upcountry families have relatives in the city. With only a few

exceptions, protection was effectively ensured by the presence of ECOMOG forces. In the summer of 1990 a newly formed local NGO, Special Emergency Life Food (SELF) was assisted by the World Food Programme in feeding Monrovia's population regardless of displaced status. Through local committees to count people and oversee distribution, the programme continued until early 1996 when general distribution to some 750,000 people was eventually phased out.

There are countless examples of governments themselves being resistant to integrative approaches to settling displaced people. Countering fears of environmental decay, strains on local resources and the like requires a more sustained approach by aid organizations and donors including, for instance, the linking of humanitarian assistance with longer term local capacity building. More research into the benefits to be derived from a less restrictive policy might persuade governments to alter their approaches.

Conclusion

Humanitarian interventions can be legitimate only when those dismissed as 'victims' become the agents of their own regeneration. It ought to be a matter of common sense that helping people 'at risk' to harness their often well-developed skills in survival and recuperation is the most effective kind of intervention. But participation is inherently a political – and politicizing – process: it implies a fundamental review of the roles of giver and receiver. The political economy of war and the fear of adding to, rather than abating, conflict has led many aid agencies to guard jealously their own resources and to hold partners increasingly accountable for aid disbursements. Attention to detail, however, is precisely the aim of the kind of research advocated in this chapter. The quest is to get beyond widespread conditions such as 'forced displacement' to the particular vulnerabilities that people face.

As well as the usual physical and macro-political considerations that determine and define the limits of movement of forced migrants in all phases of displacement, a provisional list of indicators most likely to determine the choices made by, or for, IDPs in determining where they settle and for how long, might include:

- demographic profiles, including pre-displaced populations as well as 'host' communities;
- ethnic profiles – locals and pre-displaced;
- land and tenure issues;
- economic profiles – general and sectoral, local and national;
- the impact of a swelling population on the local population;
- documentation issues relating particularly to women and children;
- community leadership – how collective and individual decisions are made with respect to migration; and
- generational and gender priorities – whether displacement restricts or opens up possibilities for an individual's economic, educational or political advancement.

In a camp for displaced people near Khartoum in 1993 aid workers were puzzled by the lack of motivation and low morale of teenagers who in most respects – nutrition, educational facilities, etc – were fairly well catered for. Truancy and petty theft were increasing and camp elders were at a loss over what to do. A small enterprising NGO cleared a deserted area, constructed a football pitch and volleyball court and hired out equipment in exchange for tokens earned through street postal deliveries (a youth employment scheme sponsored by a number of NGOs). Various sporting leagues were created and within 12 months a significant improvement in teenage behaviour was noted by all concerned. The story is anecdotal but not untypical; in planning aid interventions for displaced people a fundamental criterion of success is often overlooked – the human spirit.

References

Bennett, J (1997) 'NGOs and a New Government in Rwanda', in Bennett, J (ed), *NGOs and Governments: A Review of Current Practice for Southern and Eastern NGOs*, INTRA/ ICVA, Oxford

Bennett, J and Kawatesi, M (1996) *Beyond Working in Conflict: Understanding Conflict and Building Peace*, Relief and Rehabilitation Network Paper 18, Overseas Development Institute, London

Chalinder, A (1998) 'Temporary Human Settlement Planning for Displaced Populations in Emergencies', *Good Practice Review*, no 6, RRN, Overseas Development Institute, London

Stolen, K (1998) 'Research on Displacement', in Wendy Davies (ed) *Rights Have No Borders*, Oxford: Global IDP Survey/ Norwegian Refugee Council

van der Wijk, D (1997) *The Human Side of Conflict: Coping Strategies of Women Heads of Household in Four Villages in Sri Lanka and Cambodia*, Paper, Oxford: Oxfam UK/I

Internally displaced children: just scratching the surface

James Kunder

Esmerelda does not know the word for 'artillery,' but she remembers clearly the night her hamlet exploded. In drawings, she pictures the ground littered with pieces of bodies. She remembers running through dense forest for days, where it was always cold and wet, and where horrible insects crawled at night. Her younger brother, she recalls, coughed constantly until he died. Now she lives in a place called a 'camp'. The adults who guided her through her eight years cry a lot now, and strange men come in the evening to issue orders. . .

Dimitri, twelve, had never heard of a foundry, although he and a dozen families from his community now live in one that has been abandoned and stripped of its machinery. Everyone fled when the enemy approached, and came to this town where his kinsmen live. Two years have passed without school, without a job for his father or mother, with no resolution of the 'ethnic cleansing'. Local cousins long ago tired of the novelty of his visit; they now mock his clothing and accent. Many boys his age no longer return at night to the squalor, sewer stench and depression of the foundry, and Dimitri is spending more time with teenagers who steal to buy cigarettes. . .

Kita has returned to the village she left as a younger girl, although everything seems to have changed. When she became separated from her parents during the flight, and fell in with strangers, she felt forced to accept the protection the young soldier offered. She is now back with her mother, brothers and sister, but often fights with them, and with other girls who whisper about her. Many in the village hate her for living with one of the 'bandits'. Her brothers argue constantly about how to reclaim the family's farmland, but Kita knows that it will be impossible, with their father dead, to evict the neighbours cultivating the land.

Esmerelda, Dimitri and Kita have two things in common: they have been internally displaced from their homes and they are children. All their lives have been permanently altered by fleeing their homes.

This chapter describes practices by international organizations that effectively benefit displaced children, while pointing out the significant needs that still need to be met. This chapter argues that the international community has yet to organize itself effectively on behalf of displaced children, their families and communities.

Children and displacement

At one level, making a special case for displaced children within general issues of internal displacement makes little sense. Since children make up an estimated 50 per cent of many displaced populations, these issues are of course children's issues. Yet, it makes sense to focus on the special perspectives and needs of displaced children for three reasons: first, the experience of displacement during childhood comes at a delicate time in life,

---

Meeting the full range of displaced children's needs: Mozambique

Effective programmes for displaced children must meet a complex range of needs: psychosocial, educational, legal, physical health, cultural and vocational. In Mozambique, following the horrifically brutal civil war, Save the Children Fund focused on the reintegration of displaced children, including those who had been separated from their families. They helped establish community schools, health care, vocational centres, and other essential services in home villages. Emphasis was also given to psychosocial and cultural issues. Traditional ceremonies of reunification and thanksgiving, as well as purification rituals and cathartic song and dance – all targeted at rebuilding social, cultural and family identity – were studied, encouraged and supported.

A network of community volunteers was mobilized to follow the progress of returned and reunited children. These volunteers assisted with registration documents, school enrolment, and similar legal issues. Children were introduced to community leaders, who formally welcomed them and promised to assist the family. Special care was given to building linkages between the children's birth family and families who may have helped the children during displacement or separation.

---

when children are constructing their personal, family and community identities; second, conditions of modern conflict and displacement target children in particularly harmful ways; and third, internal

displacement raises issues of children's rights and legal standing.

All children and families affected by conflict, violence, human rights abuses or disaster suffer. IDPs, because of their extreme vulnerability associated with separation from support systems, face particularly acute problems. Lacking the structure and nurturing environments of their home communities, displaced children are more vulnerable to arbitrary action by those claiming authority, more liable to suffer forced conscription or sexual abuse, and more regularly deprived of food, water and health care.

As Graça Machel's (1996) study on *The Impact of Armed Conflict on Children* makes clear, 'in the course of displacement, millions of children have been separated from their families, physically abused, exploited and abducted into military groups, or they have perished from hunger and disease.' Surveys cited in the Machel study indicate that mortality rates among displaced children can be as much as 60 per cent higher than rates for conflict affected, non-displaced children in the same country.

The internal conflict in the post-Cold War period, with its frequent ethnic and religious overtones, places a special burden on children. In the eyes of opposing fighters motivated by group membership rather than political ideology, children are rarely viewed as innocents. Rather, young boys and girls are future soldiers, potential parents of enemies, leaders of the next round of vendettas. Targeting them accomplishes two purposes: sowing terror among current enemies and reducing the number of future opponents. Moreover, the informal, non-professional military cadres characteristic of this type of warfare value girls and boys as compliant recruits, plentiful porters who consume little food, and providers of sexual services. In short, they are prime targets for abuse.

Displaced children are uprooted during a

particularly crucial and vulnerable period of their lives. Research indicates that the act of displacement itself – its disruption, insecurity, the loss of role models, the experience of seeing adult protectors rendered powerless – can impair a child's capacity for normal development. As social mechanisms are disrupted by displacement, as community, family and personal identities are profoundly challenged, the continuity of experience necessary for normal development can be undermined.

Children's rights guaranteed by the Convention on the Rights of the Child (CRC) are nearly all put at risk by the poor conditions of displacement. These include rights to survival, protection, and development without discrimination. Displaced children may also suffer violations of rights by those who perpetrate violence, exploitation, sexual abuse, neglect, cruel or degrading treatment, or recruitment into military forces. They may also, especially if members of minority or opposition communities, face challenges to their citizenship, inheritance, cultural and linguistic rights. Lack of birth registration or other documents during the displacement period may provoke discrimination in efforts to obtain schooling, employment, or participation in civic functions. Displaced children's rights to maintain cultural traditions or use their primary language may be challenged directly by authorities bent on political goals, or simply by the circumstances of being displaced in radically different surroundings.

Some groups of children may confront especially traumatic conditions, and may require extra attention. These include children separated from their families, child combatants and other children who have been required to perform military duties, sexually abused children, children who have witnessed traumatic levels of suffering, and children with disabilities.

Children in long-term displacement: UNHCR in Georgia

Long-term, static displacement crises are common, and take a harsh toll on children who face extended uncertainty. Following the bitter breakaway struggle in the Abkhazia region of Georgia, which displaced large numbers of ethnic Abkhaz and ethnic Georgians, the country has settled into a long-term crisis in an atmosphere of armed political hostility. More than 200,000 displaced ethnic Georgians from Abkhazia no longer face emergency needs, but live in dire poverty – many in old factories, warehouses, or crowded, unhealthy apartment buildings – pending negotiations on the future of their home region. Some have begun a tentative, voluntary return to the Ghali region bordering Georgia proper, even though Ghali remains a hostile environment of burned homes, mined crossroads, and 'partisan' ambushes, all under the tenuous control of UN and CIS peacekeepers, and Abkhaz militia.

The UNHCR, recognizing the detrimental effects of long-term, static displacement on children, initiated a creative, community-based school rehabilitation campaign that helps both Georgian and Abkhaz children. In Ghali, despite pressure from Abkhaz authorities wary of the return of ethnic Georgians, UNHCR provides building material to voluntary returnees to rehabilitate gutted school buildings. To assist equally needy Abkhaz children, the UNHCR is supporting the rehabilitation of school buildings damaged by fighting in Abkhazia, despite opposition from Georgian government officials who fear implied recognition of Abkhaz independence claims. While a political stand-off continues, UNHCR has begun a risky but creative attempt to build for children a 'zone of peace' amidst conflict.

What have we learned to do right?

The guiding principle for all approaches to tackling this issue is that displaced children have precisely the same rights to survival, protection and development without discrimination as other children in the nation.

Locating, assessing, understanding, listening to, immunizing, protecting and advocating for displaced children may be especially complex, difficult, costly or even dangerous. Displacement crises in Rwanda, Bosnia, Cambodia, Colombia, Angola, Tajikistan and dozens of other emergencies around the world illustrate the complexity of guaranteeing children's rights amidst conflict and chaos. Yet the condition of displacement itself should not diminish children's fundamental rights under the Convention on the Rights of the Child, under international humanitarian law, and under international human rights law.

With this principle as a starting point, what programmatic approaches and best practices have we learned to meet the needs of internally displaced children? Essential operational approaches include these seven:

1. **Understand displaced children in the world in which they live:** Children are not sacks or warehouses to be filled with food. They are human beings living within culturally unique families, community and national environments, with individual goals, individual understandings of their surroundings, and enormous coping capacities that can be built upon. The disruption that accompanies displacement makes it especially crucial that outsiders take the time accurately to assess and evaluate the social context: beneficial and harmful programmes; priorities of the people themselves; and what the community can do for itself. Children must be asked their opinions, and their strengths and vulnerabilities understood. Local NGOs and community groups can be valuable partners.

2. **Design and implement comprehensive approaches to meeting the needs of displaced children:** Clearly, life saving steps always come first during a displacement crisis. But displaced children are likely to face a range of other challenges in relation to both their physical well-being, and their psychosocial health, their educational opportunities, their cultural traditions and their legal rights. A total picture of displacement and what it means to children is required. Work on behalf of displaced children includes care and advocacy as well as protection.

3. **Whenever possible, prevent the displacement:** The most important way of minimizing the impact on children of a crisis is by keeping the community together in its home area. Although violence or fear of abuse may challenge the best efforts, creative attempts to support communities – advocacy efforts with authorities, deployment of security forces, presence of international staff, strategic location of emergency services, support for community-based reporting systems – may prevent or at least diminish displacement.

4. **Hold authorities accountable for children:** The Representative of the UN Secretary-General, Dr Francis Deng, has pointed out that national governments, by definition, have primary *authority* and *responsibility* towards their internally displaced citizens, including children and their families. Almost every nation on earth has ratified the Convention on the Rights of the Child. It is this and other powerful advocacy tools that can be used in persuading controlling authorities to attend to the needs of children.

5. **Focus on durable solutions:** If it is

impossible to prevent large-scale displacement, the international community should focus immediately – as soon as life-threatening conditions are stabilized – on steps to assist the displaced in *voluntary* return to their home communities. The longer the period of displacement, the greater the likelihood that children will suffer long-term harm.

6. **Ensure the survival and well-being of children by supporting the community:** Two axioms that relate to all emergency settings are particularly compelling during displacement. First, the total contribution by the world community to children's well-being will pale in comparison with what families and communities can provide. Second, family and community structures under stress should be assisted as whole units.

7. **Demand that gender issues receive careful attention:** The chaos and social disruption of displacement greatly increase the likelihood that girl children will suffer sexual assault. Cultural factors may make girl children less likely to participate equitably in programme benefits, including nutrition, education or health care. Understanding these risks and involving displaced women and girls are effective steps to minimize them.

Action at multiple levels

The heads of state who signed the 1990 World Declaration on the Survival, Protection and Development of Children declared: 'The well-being of children requires political action at the highest level. We are determined to take that action.' To reach millions of displaced children effectively – and to close the gaps in capacity and resources – this determination demands real action at high political levels, at the national level, and locally.

The first gap is in comprehensive data and knowledge. In the absence of a global 'lead agency' for displaced children, attempts to locate displaced children, enumerate them, disaggregate the data by gender and other important factors, assess their condition and monitor their status over time have been disjointed. A serious commitment of staff, resources and organizational dedication is needed to redress this situation.

A second weakness is in the rapid response capacity of international agencies. Most children die or are subject to abuse during the early stages of displacement. When time is of the essence, the international community should anticipate resource requirements and agency responsibilities. The absence of an international pre-emptive or 'stand-by' capacity effectively denies the prevention of displacement – the most cost-effective approach.

Third, there is a 'protection gap' facing internally displaced children. International organizations and the donor community, even when they meet emergency needs like health care and food, provide no systematic barrier to widespread abuse of displaced children. Although the International Committee of the Red Cross (ICRC) deserves great credit for its efforts to extend the protection of international humanitarian law to all victims of war, there is no agency or combination of agencies that fills the role played by UNHCR for refugees. Nascent efforts by the UN Commission for Human Rights to build field-based protection capabilities should be supported. Without a focused, systematic effort to prioritize protection on the ground, displaced children will continue to be prime targets of abuse.

A fourth shortfall is in programming and funding support for durable solutions to displacement crises. The emergency phases of displacement are usually relatively well supported, but often contributions fall off precipitously as a displacement crisis drags

Resources within displaced communities in Guatemala

'Scorched earth' policies during the Guatemalan civil war led to displacement of hundreds of thousands of indigenous Guatemalans during the 1980s as rural families fled burning villages and military 'sweeps' through their hamlets. In certain areas, rural communities were relocated *en masse* to controlled sites, consistent with the forced, strategic displacement common in internal conflicts. Displaced children suffered deprivation of basic needs and loss of schooling, as well as psychological trauma and disruption of cultural traditions. Yet, displaced communities retained strengths and coping capacities. Displaced children were not only victims but, in the words of Dr Remedios Ortaliz of the Bulig Foundation, 'active survivors'.

UNICEF and other organizations working in the Guatemalan highlands built on these community strengths to improve opportunities for displaced children. Outside organizations undertook extensive community assessment, including statistical data and meetings with villagers. First clear, measurable priorities were set by the displaced people – including improvement of opportunities for teenagers, increased school enrolment for younger children, and rebuilding the community's cultural identity and self-esteem. Then community youth promoters were recruited from among displaced teenagers. These promoters eventually reached more than 64 communities, spurring progress in each of the community goals. School attendance, for example, improved dramatically. Moreover, these teenage promoters served as a constant source of accurate, grassroots feedback for external agencies seeking to assist the displaced.

Gender and displacement in Angola

With over a million IDPs spread across its vast territory, Angola in 1996 faced difficult issues of care, protection and return. Angolan and international institutions working with these people had only fragmentary data on their location and condition.

In an attempt to fill this gap and improve programmes, UNICEF and UNDP supported a multi-province socio-demographic study of the displaced population, conducted by the government's National Institute of Statistics, in cooperation with UNITA. The design and results of the survey were especially significant for the 55 per cent of Angolan IDPs who are women or girls.

By disaggregating IDP data by gender and age, the study alerted agencies to concentrations of women, teenagers and girls who were vulnerable. The study looked at heads of households, occupations, educational level, marital status and attitudes toward return. The findings permitted much more precise targeting of programme efforts to ensure that women's status and views were considered.

In one province, researchers found that 63 per cent of households were headed by women, underlining the need to include them in decision-making processes. Overall, more than 6 per cent of household heads were widows, suggesting the need for attention to property rights after return.

on, even though conditions for return of IDPs to their homes may improve. As open conflict subsides, the demobilization and reintegration of factional fighters often draws donor financing. This can produce the bitterly ironic result that combatants who perpetrated displacement may receive larger benefit packages than the children who were driven from their homes. By the time displaced children and families actually return to their homes, with or without international assistance, seldom does international interest or funding remain for reintegration or follow-up activities.

In sum, the international community has only scratched the surface in its response to displaced children. Although our understanding and field-level practices have improved, assuring that the Convention on the Rights of the Child has meaning for all displaced girls and boys, and organizing ourselves to provide that assurance, remain distant objectives.

References

Machel, Graça (1996) *UN Study on the Impact of Armed Conflict on Children*, URL: http://www. unicef.org/graca/women.htm

Comparative trends in forced displacement: IDPs and refugees, 1964–96

Susanne Schmeidl

Despite the difficulties associated with measuring forced migration in general and internal displacement in particular, an attempt is made in this chapter to discuss the trends of internal displacement from 1964 to 1996 and to contrast them with refugee migrations. While such a general approach does not allow for a detailed discussion of the causes of forced displacement, it allows for a summary of comparative trends across time and space.

Who are the IDPs?

The definition of refugees is well established in international law but there is still no consensus about the notion of internally displaced persons. IDPs are 'a very disparate and ill-defined group of people' (UNHCR 1997: 116). This definition problem has a tremendous impact on how accurately we are able to estimate their size and duration of displacement. Therefore, we need to keep in mind that some of the trends discussed here are biased by potential over, but more likely under, estimates.

The counting of migrating people in general, and people who are forcibly displaced, presents particular challenges. We are dealing with people on the move who in some cases may not even wish to be counted as people with needs. Refugees (and other international migrants) are more likely to be

accurately estimated since in crossing international borders they invariably come to the attention of the host government and/or international agencies. IDPs, by contrast, remain within the borders of their own country and under the jurisdiction of their own government. Their movement is far less likely to be traced for a variety of reasons: government incapacity; failure to recognize minorities or insurgents formally; or a simple denial of the problem. The exception here might be internal displacement due to natural disasters, which does not always point to government failure.

Volatile situations make accurate estimates difficult. While refugees flee to a safe haven abroad, IDPs often stay in areas of conflict not necessarily accessible to international organizations. While some IDPs may receive assistance from various organizations (and their numbers can be estimated) many are often beyond the reach of third parties and do not benefit from assistance or protection.

People frequently move within their own country to find employment or seek education. It is possible that IDPs, albeit forced to move, follow traditional (rural to urban or seasonal) migration routes and thus remain undetected. Furthermore, while it might be feasible to estimate the initial displacement of internal refugees by tracing their movement from areas of origin to another part of the country, it is far more difficult to assess when they cease to be IDPs. Refugees loose their status when they return home, integrate into the local host country or resettle into a third country. In counting IDPs, however, we must determine whether they have settled permanently or are still awaiting an opportunity to return to their original domicile.

Finally, numerical estimation of IDPs is difficult due to a lack of clear international institutional responsibility for their plight. Displacement due to internal aggression rarely reaches the attention of the international community unless it occurs on a significant scale; and those displaced by localized violence often go unrecorded.

UNHCR's mandate for IDPs

UNHCR's mandate traditionally applies to refugees displaced across international borders. The organization systematically collects information on refugees, but IDP numbers are confined to those 'peoples of concern' within its operational mandate. Until the 1990s, UNHCR's involvement with IDPs was unsystematic and *ad hoc*. Due to changing circumstances, UNHCR has more recently redefined its mandate to allow for the inclusion of IDPs in certain situations, resulting in a new set of guidelines. The 1997 guidelines indicate that UNHCR will take responsibility for IDPs under the following general conditions:

- 'when such people are present in or going back to the same areas as returning refugees' (like Guatemala, Mozambique);
- 'if they are living alongside a refugee population and have similar needs for protection and assistance' (for example, Afghanistan and former Zaire);
- 'where the same factors have given rise to both internal and external population movements, and where there are good reasons for addressing those problems by means of a single humanitarian operation' (for example, Bosnia); and

- 'where there is a potential for cross-border movement and where the provision of assistance to the internally displaced may enable them to remain in safety in their own country' (UNHCR, 1997: 117).

Another set of criteria include 'a specific request from the UN Secretary-General or the General Assembly; the consent of the state concerned and other relevant parties; the availability of funds, as well as adequate institutional capacities' (UNHCR, 1997: 117–18).

These guidelines, however, still do not allow UNHCR universally to aid IDPs and each involvement needs to be decided on a case by case basis. IDP information provided by UNHCR will, therefore, vary depending on their actual involvement in the situation and the ability of staff on the ground to estimate their numbers.

Data issues

The data used here come from official sources where attempts have been made to estimate refugee migration and internal displacement in a consistent fashion over a number of years. Lack of consensus over definition and methodological inconsistency has a tremendous impact on existing official estimates. Therefore, we have to be cautious when interpreting trends and be critical of their ability to reflect the reality of internal displacement. Nevertheless, at this point official estimates are our only opportunity to obtain a glimpse at comparative long-term trends across multiple countries and regions.

Officially published data on forced displacement in some form of a 'time series' can be obtained from:

1. UNHCR, which publishes country summaries in its report to the Executive Committee and, since 1993, a comprehensive annual *Statistical Overview of Refugees and Others of Concern*;

2. the US Committee for Refugees (USCR), which publishes annual refugee statistics in the *World Refugee Survey*;
3. the US Department of State, which published the *World Refugee Report* between the early 1980s to the early 1990s when it was terminated; and
4. the Global IDP Survey, which has produced this volume and from 1998 will compile a database on IDPs.

While the basis of most refugee data is the estimates of UNHCR, the only consistent source of estimating internal displacement to date has been USCR. UNHCR tends only to provide information on IDPs if field offices have the ability to obtain estimates or are involved in some form of assistance. For our purposes here, USCR estimates are used for internal displacement and a combination of UNHCR (80 per cent) and USCR (20 per cent) statistics for refugee movements. Information from the State Department survey was not used since it focused largely on refugees and did not provide much additional information. In addition, the time series was much shorter than those of UNHCR and USCR.

USCR uses a variety of listed sources for its estimates of IDPs such as international organizations, governments, newspaper accounts and field trips. Due to differences between some sources, it tends to present numbers in the form of ranges. In this chapter, the mean of those ranges is used, which introduces another possibility of over- or underestimation. Before the USCR began to emphasize the plight of IDPs and improve its estimation techniques, its figures were very crude. Thus, an initial increase in internal displacement in the early 1980s may reflect as much an improved coverage of this phenomenon as an actual increase in its magnitude. Due to the number of countries and time covered, IDP estimates provided by the USCR were not corroborated with other sources. The assumption is that the USCR provides its best guess of the number of IDPs and that it is unlikely that another source has better systematic estimates at present.

All data are annual stock numbers that are reported at the end of each calendar year. This means they are similar to census-type counts rather than actual flow estimates. The numbers are non-cumulative: they reflect neither new *additions* of refugees and IDPs, such as inflows and births, nor *decreases* due to deaths, repatriation or (re)settlement and reintegration. So far, none of the sources have provided exact information on the flow of forced migrants, either internally or externally.

Five main regions are discussed over a time period of 32 years, 1964 to 1996: Africa, Latin America, the region of Southwest Asia, North Africa and the Middle East (SWANAME), Asia/Oceania and the former eastern bloc. This last region has only recently become a major area of internal displacement and refugees. Due to the nature of how Western industrialized nations count refugees, the data (with the exception of information on refugees from the former eastern bloc) are derived from host countries in the developing world, which leads to an omission of about 5–10 per cent of all refugees in the world (Hein, 1993; UNHCR, 1993).

Duality of displacement

There are fewer countries reporting IDPs than reporting refugees, and most countries with IDPs also produce refugees. Thus, internal displacement seems to occur simultaneously with refugee flight and not instead of it. It is possible that internal displacement is more likely to be reported in countries that also produce refugees due to the international focus on the situation. Unless of significant magnitude, IDPs in countries with no refugee migration may remain unnoticed.

Out of 57 countries with internal displacement throughout this period, only five did not also have refugees at some point: Egypt (1970–72), Cyprus (1973–96), Tanzania (1980–81), Panama (1991) and Syria (1970–73, 1986), although Syria had new internal and external displacement in 1996. In most of these countries, internal displacement did not necessarily lead to external displacement due to very targeted violence (Tanzania, Panama), strong border controls (Syria, Egypt), or obstacles to exit (Cyprus being an island). Tanzania's short-term internal displacement was due to a border conflict with Uganda, which uprooted residents of the disputed territory. In Panama, the US invasion displaced part of the population and in the Russian Federation the conflict in Chechnya led to internal dispersion.

Comparative trends of forced displacement

Figure 1 contrasts the trend of estimates of IDPs with those of refugees. While there are some similarities in the growth of the two groups, internal displacement is more variable. This phenomenon can be attributed to shorter displacements and estimation problems particularly prior to the mid-1980s. Nevertheless, a clear upward trend of internal displacement becomes visible from 1982 until 1994 (ignoring a short decline in 1988 and 1989). After an initial decline in the early 1970s, refugee migration also began to grow constantly until 1990, with the largest increases between 1989 and 1990.

More specifically, in 1970 there were about 5 million IDPs from five countries and 9 million refugees from 25 countries. By 1980, IDP estimates increased to 7 million from ten countries. Refugee numbers were slightly more than 6 million from 38 countries in the same year. Between 1980 and 1990, estimates for both types of displacement almost tripled with 22 million IDPs from 23 countries and about 17 million refugees from 50 countries.

From 1990 significant demographic changes took place between the two groups. While the estimated numbers of refugees declined from 1990 onwards (despite a continuous increase of refugee-sending countries from 50 in 1990 to 63 in 1994), internal displacement increased sharply, peaking at 27 million in 32 countries in 1994.

However, after 1995 estimates of IDPs also dropped markedly, even though the number of countries reporting IDPs was still increasing. The decline of IDPs is largely accounted for by lower estimates reported for South Africa, Angola, Ethiopia and Rwanda. The simultaneous decline in refugee numbers can be attributed to two factors: the repatriation of refugees to Afghanistan, Ethiopia/Eritrea and Mozambique; and the end of a temporary addition of new refugee-producing countries from the former Warsaw Pact region, some lasting only a few years.

In 1996, the downward trend of IDP estimated numbers continued, with Turkey reporting 750,000 fewer displaced Kurds; and Rwanda, Mozambique and the Philippines providing no further estimates at all. Nevertheless, the number of countries with IDPs continues to grow with new displacements in Nigeria, Papua New Guinea, Algeria and Armenia. Similarly, although global refugee figures are still declining, the number of countries producing refugees is again on the rise (65) through various new refugee flows from Syria, Khzakhstan, Kyrgyzstan, India and Nigeria.

The drop in estimates for IDPs and refugees has actually increased the gap between the two, with almost twice as many internally displaced (19 million) as refugees (around 10 million) in 1996. The refugee estimates, however, exclude some Palestinian refugees and some refugees in Western industrialized countries. A similar undercount is also likely to be present in IDP estimates. With the exception of Afghanistan, when countries experience concurrent internal and

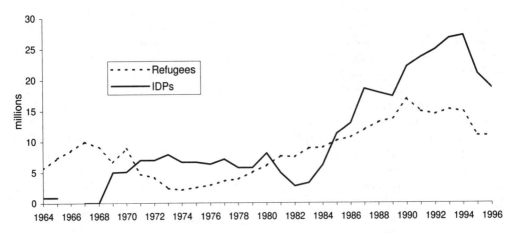

Fig 1   Comparative forced displacement: IDPs and refugees, 1964–96

international displacement, the numbers of the internally displaced are greater than refugees. The possibility that smaller populations of the internally displaced may not be reported because they are not noticed, blend with the not-displaced population or do not seek out camps for assistance, does not diminish the relative size and immense problem of internal displacement. Yet this trend seems to show that in general only part of a population fleeing from internal turbulence is fortunate enough to be able to cross international borders.

Taking into account the 'non-visibility' of small numbers of IDPs, the trend indicates that only part of a population fleeing from internal turbulence is able to cross international borders. Nevertheless, while estimates for IDPs are generally higher than those of refugees, it is often the same countries that report the highest numbers for both kinds of displacement.

Timing and duration of displacement

In terms of timing, international migration typically precedes internal displacement. There are rare cases of simultaneous displacement (for example, Bosnia 1992–96, Turkey 1991–96, and Syria 1996), but generally internal displacement lags behind refugee migration for a minimum of one, but usually several, years. This reinforces the possibility that the heavy international focus on refugees may diminish the official reporting of IDPs until their numbers soar into the millions.

During this study period, in 45 of the 55 countries with concurrent internal and external displacement, refugee migration preceded internal displacement. The exceptions were East Timor, Cambodia, Croatia, Laos, Peru, Kenya and Russia. In each of these cases there were either real or perceived obstacles to exit (East Timor an island with only one internal border, Peru with the Andean mountains); fighting in neighbouring countries (Cambodia, Croatia and Laos); or targeted violence (Russia) that initially deterred flight across international borders. In two other cases internal dis-placement occurred years after external flight: Honduras (1986–91) and India (1987–94). This suggests the emergence of a different kind of conflict or the addition of a new obstacle to international flight.

Internally displaced populations are increasing not only in size but also in duration. Prior to 1990, 25 per cent of internal displacement lasted only one or two years and only eight populations were displaced for ten or more years. Today about 61 per cent lasts five years or less and 21 per cent have been in place for ten years or more. The comparative figures for refugee migration are 53 per cent and 27 per cent respectively. This shows that in the 1990s, internal displacement is far more common and the duration of such displacement can be no longer considered short term. Yet again, this may also show that official sources are increasingly noticing IDPs and thus are more likely to report their displacement.

Regional overview

Figures 2 and 3 provide an overview of the regional distributions of IDPs and refugees. There are some general similarities in that in Africa, Latin America and SWANAME there was little to no internal displacement during the early 1970s, while there were already millions of refugees. Due to the wars in Indo-China, Asia hosted nearly all the developing world's IDPs during the 1970s, but was surpassed by Africa and SWANAME in the 1980s. Latin America did not enter the picture until the mid-1980s and was the region least affected by forced displacement. The newest region with both refugees and IDPs is the former eastern bloc. Estimates of IDPs in this region rose above those for Asia and Latin America after 1993.

Africa

In Africa there were no significant numbers of IDPs until 1976 and only since 1983 did they outnumber those for refugees (Figure 4). The reason for forced displacement (internal and external) in Africa was largely due to countries with brutally repressive regimes, ethnic conflict (including both communal confrontations and separatism), and external destabilization campaigns and interventions.

In contrast to the internal displacement, however, refugee migration seems far longer with the average displacement lasting 11 years as opposed to six years for IDPs.

In the 1990s, IDPs and refugees emerge from a new set of countries without much displacement in the past: Djibouti, Kenya, Liberia, Mali, Nigeria, Sierra Leone and Togo. Also, there are estimates for IDPs in countries that previously only reported refugees: Burundi, Rwanda and Congo (Zaire).

Asia

In contrast with Africa, internal displacement was very common in Asia during the 1970s (see Figure 5). After initial large-scale refugee migrations due to the suppression of Tibetan autonomy (1956–59), the Cultural Revolution in the late 1960s, and the East Pakistan conflict in 1971, internal displacement took over the picture of forced displacement in the region. Similar to refugee migration, internal displacement was reported mainly in the three countries linked to the Indochinese conflict – Vietnam, Kampuchea and Laos.

During most of the 1980s, estimates for IDPs dropped below that for refugees and only began to rise again when separatism in Sri Lanka (early 1980s to the present) and the southern Philippines (1972–87) and regime repression, separatism and ethnic warfare in Myanmar (beginning in the mid-1980s) created large numbers of IDPs and refugees. Ethnic tensions in India have also led to internal displacement in recent years.

The average length of displacement in Asia is similar to Africa, about 11 years for refugees and six years for IDPs. In this study period, there were 11 countries with 'chronic' refugee migrations and four with 'chronic' internally displaced populations. Joint displacement was reported in Cambodia, Laos, Indonesia, the Philippines, Sri Lanka and Vietnam. Newcomers in this region are Papua New Guinea for both types of displacements, and Bhutan for refugee migration.

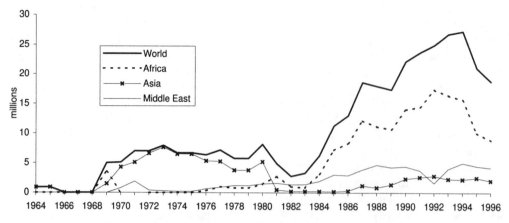

Fig 2   Regional comparison of IDP estimates, 1964–96

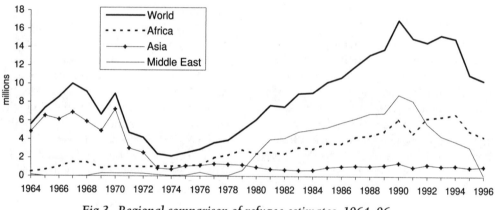

Fig 3   Regional comparison of refugee estimates, 1964–96

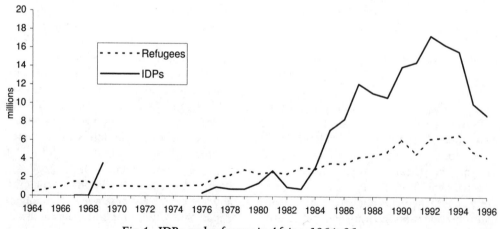

Fig 4   IDPs and refugees in Africa, 1964–96

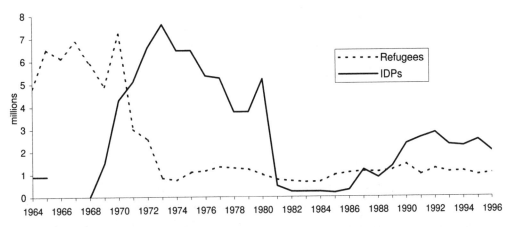

Fig 5   IDPs and refugees in Asia, 1964–96

Southwest Asia, North Africa and the Middle East (SWANAME)

Southwest Asia, North Africa and the Middle East are the only regions where estimates of IDPs are lower than those for refugees (Figure 6). This is due to the Afghan exodus, which at times contributed as much as 60 per cent to the total refugee population in the world. Nevertheless, after 1993 ensuing internal conflict in Afghanistan (after the defeat of the Soviet-backed government) and increasing violence in Iraq and Turkey against Kurdish separatists raised the estimates of IDPs above those for refugees.

Unlike Africa and Asia, the duration of both types of displacement lasted only about six years (excluding the long-standing Palestinian refugee population). Cyprus heads the list for duration with 24 years, followed by Lebanon with 21 years. A notable newcomer to refugee migration and internal displacement in the mid-1990s is Algeria with its intensifying political and religious confrontation.

Latin America

Latin America has overall been the least affected area with low estimates of forced displacements (Figure 7). Except for a short-peak of one million refugees fleeing authori-

tarian regimes in Bolivia (1966–69) and Paraguay (1966–69), estimates for refugee migration tended to stay well below one million. Estimates for IDPs did not appear until 1981 and reached one million in 1986. However, Latin America is also characterized by significant underestimation of refugees. For example, the USA failed to recognize El Salvador's displaced population as refugees.

The average displacement in Latin America is nine years for refugees and seven years for IDPs. El Salvador, Guatemala and Peru have all experienced chronic displacement. Colombia is the most notable new case with both refugees and significant numbers of IDPs.

The Soviet bloc and its aftermath

In this region, no significant forced displacement was reported until the break-up of the Soviet Union, when the collapse of communist regimes in the region suddenly lifted draconian border controls (Figure 8). Any displacement prior to this period is not well documented. The majority of refugee displacements in this region, however, were short lived, and only the protracted conflicts in former Yugoslavia and the former Soviet Union produced large-scale internal and external displacements. Therefore, the average time for displacement in the region

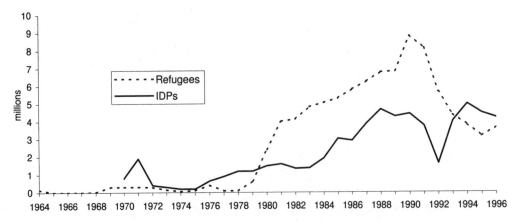

Fig 6   IDPs and refugees in Southwest Asia, North Africa and the Middle East, 1964–96

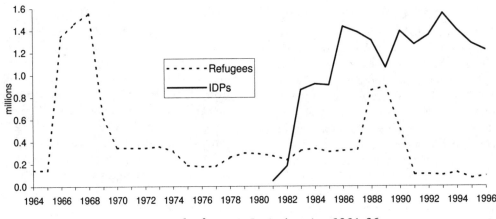

Fig 7   IDPs and refugees in Latin America, 1964–96

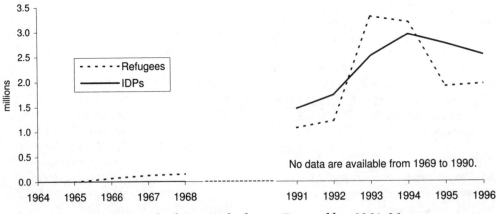

Fig 8   IDPs and refugees in the former Eastern bloc, 1964–96

was actually slightly longer for IDPs (three years) than for refugees (2.8 years).

Conclusion

In the light of the above discussion and taking estimation problems into account, the following general conclusions can be drawn. While a few large refugee and internally displaced populations have been reduced, there is a continuous rise in the countries reporting such displacement. In addition, taking both size and duration into account, the 1990s is seeing a shift from large-scale refugee displacements to increasing internal displacement. Forced migrants seem to have far fewer opportunities of escaping across borders in the 1990s. The containment of forced displacement within countries is due to a number of factors including:

- an increase in the number of internal conflicts in potential countries of asylum that might work as a deterrent;
- donor fatigue among traditional countries of asylum and resettlement (including 'Fortress Europe' and the new emphasis by Western countries on the 'right to remain';

- protracted civil wars creating impassable border areas; and
- a more diverse uprooted population including those people less equipped to travel long distances.

In other words, a major difference between IDPs and refugees might be the conditions that allow (or discourage) exodus across international borders.

References

Hein, Jeremy (1993) 'Refugees, Immigrants, and the State', *Annual Review of Sociology*, vol 19, pp 43–59

Sørensen, Birgitte Refslund (1998) 'Self Help Activities Among Internally Displaced People', in Wendy Davies (ed) *Rights Have No Borders*, Oxford: Global IDP Survey/Norwegian Refugee Council

UNHCR (1993) *The State of the World's Refugees 1993–95: The Challenge of Protection*, Harmondsworth: Penguin Books

—— (1997) *The State of the World's Refugees 1997–98: A Humanitarian Agenda*, Oxford: Oxford University Press

Recent literature on IDPs

Louise Ludlam-Taylor

Recent publications from academic and operational institutional sources are briefly summarized in this bibliographic essay to highlight the main issues in the ongoing IDP debate.

The end of the Cold War heralded the dawn of a new international order and the potential for a more united world. However, increased polarization between the rich and poor nations has emerged with internal conflicts ravaging disintegrated states. As non-government organizations play an increasingly important role in international affairs, the nature of humanitarian assistance in these complex emergencies has changed. NGOs, whose new operational tools have facilitated unprecedented access to conflict areas, have become key players – for better or for worse – in the conflict management strategies of the international community.

The converging interests of academics and aid practitioners are reflected in the substantial body of literature on complex emergencies, including the role and effect of NGOs – see *Mercy Under Fire: War and the Global Humanitarian Community* (Minear and Weiss, 1995); *The Politics of Humanitarian Intervention* (Harris ed, 1995); *Humanitarian Intervention in Contemporary Conflict* (Ramsbotham and Woodhouse, 1996); *World in Crisis: The Politics of Survival at the End of the 20th Century* (Médecins sans frontières, 1996) and *World Disaster Report 1997* (International Federation of the Red Cross, 1997). Long-term projects are being undertaken to study complex emergencies. These include the Humanitarianism in War

Project – a joint project of the Thomas Watson Jr Institute for International Studies and the Refugee Policy Group – and the War-torn Societies Project – a joint project between the United Nations Research Institute for Social Development and the Programme for Strategic and International Security Studies of the Graduate Institute of International Studies in Geneva. The publications and research both highlight the inability of the international community to prevent or to respond adequately to these conflicts, whose root causes can be traced to historical as well as contemporary economic and political relations. The new aid paradigm is characterized by the international community's strategy of selective intervention, whereby rich governments use humanitarian assistance as a palliative measure rather than implementing tough political solutions in conflict areas – see Duffield's (1997) article entitled 'NGO Relief in War Zones: Towards an Analysis of the New Aid Paradigm'.

Key components of the current conflicts are negative ethnic politicization and manipulation leading to the displacement of people. This reflects the political reality in Kenya, Burundi and Bosnia, as illustrated in *Ethnic Clashes, Displaced Persons and the Potential for Refugee Creation in Kenya: A Forbidding Forecast* (Abdullahi, 1997), *Burundi: Forced Relocation: New Patterns of Human Rights Abuses* (Amnesty International, 1997) and *Going Nowhere Fast: Refugees and Internally Displaced People in Bosnia* (International Crisis Group, 1997). The 1990s have witnessed a dramatic increase in the number of IDPs worldwide and a concurrent relative decline in the number of registered refugees – see the *World Refugee Survey 1997* (US Committee for Refugees, 1997). A combination of factors has led to this increase: the changed nature – moving from interstate to internal conflicts – and the proliferation of conflicts; the desire of the international community to contain refugee flows by providing assistance in the countries of origin, where the conflicts rage; the reluctance to open their doors to refugees and to finance the stay of refugees in third countries as well as their support of early repatriation programmes.

Recent interest in the plight of IDPs is reflected in the growing body of literature; the publications primarily focus on IDPs in conflict situations and the protection gap. Few publications cover the major problems facing IDPs in the post-conflict period or self-help programmes illustrated in *Refugee and Internally Displaced Women: A Development Perspective* (Cohen, 1995) and *Participatory Basic Needs Assessment with the Internally Displaced Using Well-being Ranking* (Hamilton et al, 1997). Larger projects on IDPs include the Brookings Institution/Refugee Policy Group Project on Internal Displacement and the Forced Migration Projects of the Soros Open Society Institute. Literature on regional initiatives, include *CIREFCA: At the Crossroads Between Uprooted People and Development in Central America* (Gallagher et al, 1990) and *The CIS Migration Conference: A Chance to Prevent and Ameliorate Forced Movements of People in the Former Soviet Union* (Helton, 1996). Given the magnitude and the complexity of the IDP problem, many issues remain unresolved and are likely to remain so in the current political climate.

Definition

No international agreement has been reached on an acceptable definition of IDPs and many question the utility of defining them as a separate category. The working definition the Brookings Institution and the Global IDP Survey use is that IDPs are 'persons or groups of persons who have been forced to flee or to leave their homes or places of habitual residence as a result of, or in order to avoid, in particular, the effects of armed conflict, situations of generalized violence, violations of human rights or natural or human-made disasters, and who have not crossed an internationally recognized state border'.

The words 'in particular' denote that the list of causes of displacement is not exhaustive. This definition is an improvement on the original working definition used by the Special Representative of the UN Secretary-General on Internally Displaced Persons, which included the limiting notion of 'forced to flee suddenly or unexpectedly in large numbers'. In *Protecting the Displaced*, Roberta Cohen (1996) emphasizes that the definition must include the following elements: coercion, which induces the displacement, human rights violations as a result of the displacement and the lack of protection provided by national governments. Some argue that displacement caused by natural disasters and development-induced displacement as discussed in *Understanding Improvishment: The Consequences of Development-Induced Displacement* (McDowell, 1996) and *Relocated Lives: Displacement and Resettlement within the Mahaweli Project, Sri Lanka* (Sørensen, 1996) are not covered by the definition, for displacement often occurs for a combination of reasons – not only armed conflicts. The definition should not be open-ended and categories of displacement such as the homeless and rural–urban drifters should be excluded. The issue of when an IDP ceases to be an IDP requires clarification and further study.

The United Nations High Commission for Refugees' operational definition in the *State of the World's Refugees 1997–98: A Humanitarian Agenda* (UNHCR, 1997) is narrower and defines IDPs as those who, if they had crossed an international border or if they had left their country, would be recognized as refugees and excludes displacement caused by natural disasters or development-induced displacement. Given the push within the UN for a more comprehensive approach to providing humanitarian relief and protection combined with the reality in the field, where there are mixed populations of refugees and IDPs often with the same needs, it can be argued that the distinction between categories is becoming less relevant for operational purposes. This is in line with the approach taken by the International Committee of the Red Cross (ICRC), which makes no distinction between non-displaced war-affected people and IDPs. A wide range of NGOs surveyed in *Response Systems of NGOs to Assistance and Protection Needs of the Internally Displaced Persons* (Lambrecht, 1996) also provide assistance based on the needs of the people in danger.

Responsibility

International agreement on a definition for IDPs will facilitate the systematic gathering of data. This will ensure that informed policy decisions regarding appropriate operational responses are made, although primary responsibility for the protection of and assistance to IDPs under international law lies with the territorial state based on the principle of sovereignty and non-intervention. In his article 'State Responsibility for the Prevention and Resolution of Forced Population Displacements in International Law', Chaloka Benyani (1996) stresses that states should be held responsible for causing displacement. By maintaining 'supervisory interest over the domestic jurisdiction of other states', states collectively guard over the protection and promotion of human rights. Unfortunately, states are primarily guided by political concerns and self-interest in these matters, espe-

cially as the international legal enforcement mechanisms are not strong enough to stimulate state responsibility as stipulated in the UN Charter. Preventive approaches based on state responsibility require further development of the rules of state responsibility – see *The State of the World's Refugees: The Challenge of Protection* (UNHCR, 1993).

As states, then, are often unwilling or unable to provide the necessary protection and assistance, external intervention is required. The current institutional arrangements are discussed in *Improving Institutional Arrangements for the Internally Displaced Persons* (Cohen and Cuenod, 1995). As no single humanitarian agency has been assigned statutory responsibility for providing protection and assistance to the internally displaced people, an analysis of the various actors – such as UNHCR and the Department of Humanitarian Affairs (DHA) – is provided as well as recommendations on how to improve the system (due to be restructured following the UN reforms proposed in 1997). Dr Francis M Deng, appointed as the Special Representative of the UN Secretary-General on IDPs in 1992, has played a catalytic role in raising the plight of IDPs. His mandate is to discuss issues of internal displacement at senior government levels, to clarify the legal apparatus applicable to IDPs and to highlight the needs of IDPs. His work to date includes 12 in-depth country reports, the *Compilation and Analysis of Legal Norms* and the formulation of Guiding Principles for the protection and assistance of IDPs.

Some commentators have suggested that UNHCR expand its mandate, which is to protect and seek durable solutions for refugees, to include IDPs. The UN High Commissioner of Refugees, however, conceded that this task exceeds the capacity of a single agency and that a comprehensive joint effort of the UN together with other humanitarian agencies is required. UNHCR's operational responses and involvement with IDPs are discussed in *UNHCR's Operational Experience with Internally Displaced* (UNHCR, 1995).

Some fear that UNHCR's traditional role of securing acceptable conditions of asylum for refugees would be undermined by its involvement in providing protection to potential refugees or IDPs in countries of origin as highlighted in *The Reinforcement of Non-Admission Policies and the Subversion of UNHCR: Displacement and Internal Assistance in Bosnia-Herzegovina 1992–94* (Bartutciski, 1995).

Non-UN bodies include the International Organization for Migration (IOM), whose mandate explicitly includes both internal and international migrants – see *Internally Displaced Persons: IOM Policy and Programmes* (IOM, 1996). International and local NGOs, whose mandates generally do not explicitly include IDPs, provide a wide range of assistance to populations in need. The International Committee of the Red Cross (ICRC) has the clearest mandate to protect and assist in situations where IDPs are civilian victims of armed conflict – see *Refugees and Internally Displaced: International Humanitarian Law and the Role of the ICRC* (Lavoyer, 1995). The organizational strengths of the ICRC are that it works on both sides of the conflict and is perceived as being neutral and impartial in contrast to the UN agencies. Human rights organizations, which are generally not operational, have contributed to raising the profile of IDPs – see *Failing the Internally Displaced: UNDP Displaced Persons Program in Kenya* (Human Rights Watch, 1997).

Up to now the international response to the growing problem of internal displacement has been *ad hoc*, limited and unsatisfactory, a situation exacerbated by the current trend to provide assistance in lieu of the protection.

Protection

The words of the UN High Commissioner for Refugees, 'Humanitarian assistance is much more than relief and logistics. It is essentially and above all about protection – protection of victims of human rights violations and humanitarian law violations', ring true, but hollow. The massacre of thousands in the Kibeho IDP camp in Rwanda testifies to the deficiencies in the current system of international protection for IDPs, which are examined from a legal, operational and institutional standpoint in *The Protection Gap in the International Protection of Internally Displaced Persons: The Case of Rwanda* (Kleine-Ahlbrandt, 1997).

The fallacy that the mere presence of international organizations can protect IDPs has been clearly exposed in Erin Mooney's *Presence, ergo Protection? UNPROFOR, UNHCR and the ICRC in Croatia and Bosnia and Herzegovina* (1995). In an article called 'The Establishment of Safety Zones for Persons Displaced within their Country of Origin', Yves Sandoz (1995) argues that protected zones established by the ICRC within the framework of international humanitarian law and with the consent of all parties might offer a more effective form of protection than UN safety areas, which are imposed on the parties and not backed by the political will to use force. The ICRC then can play an important role in protection given their overall statutory responsibility for the application of international humanitarian law in international and interstate conflicts – see *The Protection of Displaced Persons in Non-International Armed Conflicts* (Plattner, 1992).

Given the reluctance of the international community to undertake any action in former Zaire, the failures in former Yugoslavia (see *A Safe Area: Srebrenica: Europe's Worst Massacre since the Second World War* by Rohde, 1997) and the United States still smarting from Somalia, the creation of UN safe havens does not seem a viable protection option for IDPs.

Unlike refugees, who are protected under refugee law, there is no legal instrument for IDPs. In the *Compilation and Analysis of Legal*

Norms, Deng (1995) identified 17 areas where insufficient protection is extended to IDPs due to inexplicit articulation and a further eight areas where there are considerable gaps in existing international law. At the time, Francis Deng concluded that a new legal instrument for IDPs was required to eliminate these protection gaps and ensure that the special needs of IDPs were recognized. Other legal experts opposed the creation of such an instrument (see Lavoyer, 1995) because they felt that the main problem lay in the non-respect of human rights and humanitarian law. In an article, 'New Standards for the Protection of Internally Displaced Persons: A Proposal for a Comprehensive Approach', David Petrasek (1995) argues that a legal instrument specifically for IDPs is too narrow an approach to the issue of displacement, which involves internal and external displacement and might detract from existing norms, especially established asylum norms. Therefore, a more holistic instrument covering both internal and external displacement and addressing their root causes would correspond more closely to the needs in the field.

Francis Deng conceded in a recent interview in the *Human Rights Tribune* (Wiseberg, 1997) that a convention on IDPs is not palatable to the international community and has therefore compiled Guiding Principles and the report *The Right Not To Be Arbitrarily Displaced*. The Guiding Principles cover legal norms relevant in all three phases of displacement (prevention, actual displacement and solutions) and will hopefully have moral force and may evolve over time into customary law.

The right not to be displaced is gaining support and in *The Right Not To Be Displaced*, Maria Stravropoulou (1996) argues that this right should be recognized as an independent and freestanding right under international law. This right is currently only recognized in soft-law instruments such as the Turk/Abo Declaration of Minimum Humanitarian Standards and the International Law Association's *Draft Declaration of Principles of International Law on Internally Displaced Persons* (International Law Association, 1996).

As the humanitarian duty to intervene (*le droit d'ingérence*) has gained recognition, the notion of sovereignty is increasingly being called into question. Violations of human rights, repression of minorities, indiscriminate violence and persecution are no longer considered as internal matters. Recent interventions without the consent of the host state in Iraq, Somalia and Rwanda attest to this duty. Richard Plender concludes in *The Legal Basis of International Jurisdiction to Act with Regards to the Internally Displaced* (Plender, 1995) that the UN can act in situations where a state arbitrarily refuses to allow relief, which could be considered as an *abus de droit*.

The growing problem of IDPs should be addressed by strengthening the domestic capacity of states to protect human rights and promoting economic well-being in accordance with the UN Charter. The scope of international law is limited in that only political solutions will resolve today's conflicts.

Note:
All references cited in this chapter appear in full in the bibliography at the end of the book.

Part 2
Regional Profiles

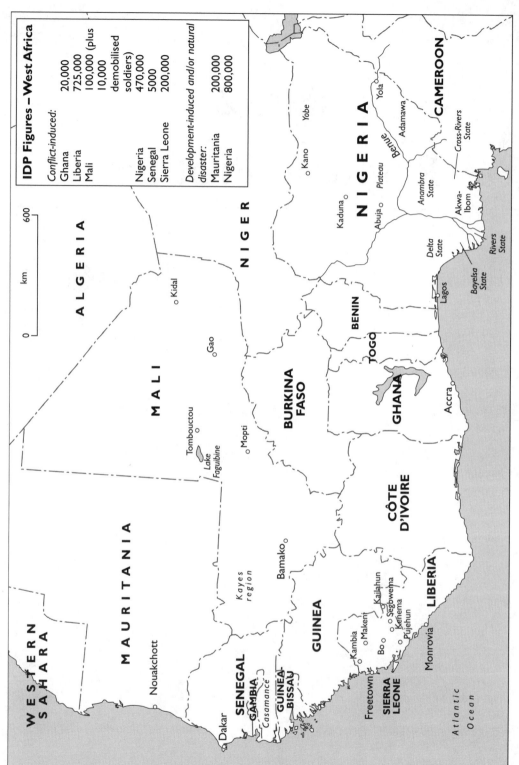

IDP Figures – West Africa

Conflict-induced:
Ghana	20,000
Liberia	725,000
Mali	100,000 (plus
	10,000
	demobilised
	soldiers)
Nigeria	470,000
Senegal	5000
Sierra Leone	200,000

Development-induced and/or natural disaster:
Mauritania	200,000
Nigeria	800,000

Map 1: West Africa

West Africa

Overview
Laura J Marks

West Africa is a complex region ranging from the desert to the tropical rain forest. Its countries include a diversity of languages, ethnic groups, religions and political systems. However, in recent years none has been spared the effects of political upheaval, which in turn has led to population movements as people flee fighting and persecution. The region currently hosts more than three million internally displaced persons. Oppression and violence by governments is a common cause of displacement, but other factors include guerrilla movements, land disputes and climate change. In Nigeria, people have been internally displaced for 30 years, and continue to be forced from their homes because of ethnic conflict. The pollution caused by oil production has also forced people to search for safer places to live. Civil wars in Liberia and Sierra Leone caused vast displacement; however, there is hope that Liberians will begin to move home in the coming months.

People tend to move to regions where they will have access to income as well as safety. In many cases, this means moving to large towns and cities. Often these areas cannot absorb the numbers coming in: there are inadequate sanitation facilities, few jobs, and little land to farm. However, IDPs choose to stay rather than return home for as long as they consider the conditions to be better than those they would find at home.

Determining exact numbers of IDPs in West Africa is difficult. States may not want to disclose that internal disputes have led to displacement. In many cases, IDPs are difficult to count because they are absorbed into their new areas of settlement, living with family or friends. Unlike refugee communities, IDPs rarely have organized committees. This means that little attention is paid to their concerns and few special services are made available to them. There is no regional body to deal with the problem of internal displacement in West Africa. The Economic Community of West African States (ECOWAS) provides troops for peacekeeping, but not for humanitarian assistance. In some cases, development projects provide some relief to IDPs, but few focus on their needs specifically.

At the end of 1997, the problem of displacement in West Africa was relatively stable. In Ghana and Mauritania, the numbers internally displaced are on the downswing. However, in Senegal, numbers are increasing as people flee conflict in the Casamance region. The numbers are small, and should not exceed the number of returnees. Given the unstable political climate and the environmental changes occurring in many West African countries, we are likely to see continued movement internally and across international borders.

Ghana
Iain Beattie

Although Ghana has a sizeable population of internally displaced people, they are essentially those who remain of a considerably larger population displaced by conflict in the northern region of Ghana in 1994. Assuming that there is no recurrence of this conflict, the number displaced is likely to dwindle further.

In February 1994, a land rights dispute

between the Nanumbas and the Dagombas of the northern region of Ghana erupted into ethnic conflict, leading to 2000 deaths and the internal displacement of 150,000 persons. Many villages and large areas of cropland were destroyed before a state of emergency was declared and government troops were sent into the area. The state of emergency lasted until August of that year, and was followed by the signing of a peace agreement in December and a period of relative calm. Many of the displaced had returned home by this time, despite the fact that the issue of land ownership, which had sparked the conflict, had not been resolved.

In mid-March 1995, ethnic tensions once again erupted in northeastern Ghana. Near the town of Bimbila, fighting between Konkomba and Nanumba groups resulted in 150 deaths. Over 15,000 people fled the area, all but a few of them Nanumbas. It has been estimated that the combined population displaced by the 1994 and 1995 violence, was in the region of 192,000 people. Humanitarian assistance was provided by the government of Ghana, the United Nations agencies and an inter-NGO consortium. During 1996, reconciliation efforts by both civil and government groups were successful in reducing the violence. This enabled the vast majority of the IDPs to return to their places of origin, where numerous aid agencies assisted in their return to normal life. By December 1996, it is estimated that only 20,000 remained displaced.

Since the presidential elections of December 1996 there have been no new instances of internal displacement. If this secure situation continues, the issue of IDPs in Ghana could conceivably disappear in the near future.

Liberia

Binaifer Nowrojee

Since the start of the Liberian civil war in 1990, much of the population was forced to flee their homes. Many fled to neighbouring countries; many others did not cross the border. While an accurate count of internally displaced people is not possible, UNHCR estimated that in March 1998 there were 750,000 IDPs, more than a third of whom live in Monterrado, Bong, Margibi and Grand Bassa counties.

On 19 July 1997, the seven-year civil war came to an end through an internationlly supervised election that swept former faction leader Charles Taylor, and his party, into power with 75 per cent of the vote. The new government began the challenging process of establishing its authority. Over the past seven years, tens of thousands of Liberians had been killed. Almost half the population was displaced (total population in 1995 was 2,380,000), and the country's infrastructure had been virtually destroyed. While the end of the war brought much needed peace and security to the country, serious human rights issues remained. After a decade of repressive rule under the previous government, followed by seven years of civil war, Liberia's state institutions and economy have been destroyed, and a culture of ethnic tension, violence and impunity has taken root. One of the major challenges facing the new government is the reintegration of the internally displaced driven from their homes by the violence and insecurity of the past seven years.

Most internally displaced people have been living in squalid and destitute conditions for a number of years, some displaced several times during the course of the war. Yet, there appeared to be little or no preparation at the national or international level to plan for the return of this huge population to their homes. Even information on the numbers and location of the internally displaced was much more scarce than on refugees, because no national or international body has had the exclusive task of addressing the needs of the internally displaced. As a

LIBERIA: IDPs have fled to Monrovia, greatly swelling the city's population (PHOTO: L Taylor/UNHCR).

result, conditions for the internally displaced remained much worse than those of Liberian refugees in neighbouring countries.

In July 1997, the Liberia Refugee, Repatriation and Resettlement Commission (LRRRC) estimated that over half of all the internally displaced people were living in some 30 sites in the Monrovia area. In some cases, displaced people were living in abandoned buildings, such as the shell of the Ministry of Health building, under construction when war broke out, where some 3000 have lived for years in makeshift overcrowded rooms. There were six toilets and one water pump for these residents. At Samukai camp, some 9000 internally dislaced Liberians and Sierra Leonean refugees lived side by side. There were only seven toilets and a few water pumps in working order. Because these camps grew gradually, without international humanitarian assistance, they were not well laid out in terms of services. As a result, latrines or water pumps were placed at uneven distances in the camp or were in short supply.

Many of the camps for the internally disabled were serviced by a variety of humanitarian organizations and the UN. These provided regular food rations, but gave a bare minimum of food to those registered. Where other displaced relatives had joined a family, the food ration was shared with a larger number of people than it was intended for. In one camp, supplementary feeding for children under five was started, as 15–20 per cent of them were malnourished. Since many of the camps where the internally displaced live also contained Sierra Leonean refugees, UNHCR did provide some services that were also offered to the internally displaced Liberians. For instance, in a number of displaced persons' camps, Liberian children at the elementary school level were able to attend the schooling provided by UNHCR. At the high school level, however, only Sierra Leonean refugees received scholarships from UNHCR. In other cases, children were

attending elementary schools set up by humanitarian organizations in the area. However, little or no educational opportunities were available for displaced children of high school age. In some camps, children were not at school at all. In Kakata, one teacher noted that their makeshift schools were full, even though many children were not in school. However, even when children attended school, teachers found it difficult to get them to concentrate, often because they were hungry.

According to a medical assistant at one of the displaced people's camps, the internally displaced were suffering most commonly from malaria, respiratory tract infections (made worse by the rainy season), diarrhoea, and skin diseases. Outside the Monrovia area, the internally displaced people barely received any medical assistance.

Most internally displaced people want to return to their homes, but were unable to because of the lack of material and financial assistance. The repeated refrain was 'we want to go home, but our homes have been destroyed and we have nothing. How will survive if we return? We have nothing to rebuild our homes with or to replant our farms.' For most of them, transport was not the main issue, as much as the question of how they would support themselves once they returned. When they were asked what they needed to return, the items they most commonly cited were agricultural tools, roofing sheets, cooking utensils, nails and food. It would not take much to help these people and communities return on their own.

In some cases, displaced people returned to find what remained of their homes occupied. In particular, returnees of Mandingo origin returned to find their houses occupied. The long-standing discrimination in Liberia against Mandingos as 'aliens' or 'foreigners' has contributed to the sentiment that

Mandingo-owned property could be appropriated.

The one group of internally displaced people that openly expressed an unwillingness to return were those from Grand Cape Mount County. Some of these people expressed the fear that the recent outbreak of fighting in neighbouring Sierra Leone would spill over into Liberia and engulf their home areas.

The Liberian government body responsible for returning the refugees and IDPs, the LRRRC, remained underfunded and virtually non-functional. This body needs to be revitalized and given more qualified staff, training and financial assistance. As of July 1997, the role of the LRRRC was indeterminate. International agencies were not clear how best to coordinate their efforts with the LRRRC, and questioned whether it was a national policy-making body or an implementing agency that would work in the field. The government needs to clarify the direction and vision of the LRRRC, particularly since the commission will be one of the most important government agencies in the coming year.

At the international level, planning for the reintegration of the internally displaced has commenced. The World Food Programme and its implementing partners have begun a detailed assessment of the numbers of internally displaced in Monrovia. The UNDP has begun to put forward a programme plan to assist in the reintegration of the internally displaced. After seven years of war and massive human rights abuses in Liberia, UNDP will need to stretch its traditional capacity to address the operational challenges posed by the situation. UNDP has a broadly defined mandate to promote sustainable development, and has not interpreted its role as formally including human rights work, either in a monitoring and reporting capacity or as part of the design of its programmes. However, successful reintegration in Liberia will require consideration, not only of the effects of past human rights abuses, but also of the need to ensure that the internally displaced are voluntarily returned in conditions of safety and dignity.

Mali
Shyla Vohra

Internal displacement in the Republic of Mali is concentrated in the northern part of the country, comprising the regions of Tombouctou, Kidai and Gao. These regions form two-thirds of the country's territory and are home to approximately 10 per cent of Mali's total population of 10 million inhabitants. Some displacement also occurs from the Kayes region in the southwest of the country.

Internal conflict has been the principal cause of population displacements in northern Mali. Ethnic unrest emerged in mid-1990 when an ethnic group, the Tuaregs, clashed with the central government, claiming marginalization. Hostilities continued through 1991, displacing thousands within the region, while thousands more Tuaregs and ethnic Moors fled to the neighbouring countries of Algeria, Niger, Mauritania and Burkina Faso. A national pact signed by rebel leaders and the government in 1992 temporarily curtailed the violence, but sporadic fighting continued. An intensification of hostilities during the first half of 1994 resulted in the deaths of several hundred people, including many civilians. At this stage, the conflict diversified to include interfactional clashes among different rebel organizations. Despite this resurgence, however, the government and the rebel movements maintained dialogue, and in 1995, the national pact and its provisions were re-established, effectively stabilizing the situation. During 1997, the ethnic situation in the north of Mali has remained stable, and to all appearances the area remains at peace.

MALI: Returnees in Tombouctou region (PHOTO: C Shirley/UNHCR).

During the years of conflict, 150,000 refugees fled Mali for neighbouring countries. Since 1995, most have returned home; as of March 1998, there were 15,000 Malian refugees still in Niger and Algeria.

In addition to the conflict, lack of rain has exacerbated internal displacement in the northern region. As the area becomes more arid and non-arable, survival in traditional areas of habitation is increasingly difficult. This has also hampered the return of those displaced during the conflict.

Internal displacement in northern Mali is difficult to quantify or qualify as its inhabitants are traditionally nomadic. Although the line between nomadic variations and internal displacement can be difficult to draw, the nomads have a traditional settlement or base, to which they return each year and which is regarded as their land. Normally, the elderly, women and children remain in these settlements all year round, while the men move the cattle for seasonal grazing. It is known that the war disrupted the cycle of nomadic movements, and in many cases, forced entire groups to abandon their traditional base.

In this way, pockets of displaced people have been created in most of the settlements in the north; namely, Lere, Gargandou, Farach, Ras El Mas, Ber, Lernep, and the lake Faguibine region, in the region of Tombouctou; Tessalit, Bouressa, Tinz'Awaten, Anefis, Abeibara, and Aguelock in the region of Kidal; and Djebock, Tarkint, Menaka, Bourem, Almoustarat, and Temera in the region of Gao. In addition, IDPs from the Tombouctou region have moved toward Mopti, which is the most developed region in the centre of Mali. Mopti is an important trading point, being accessible by both river and road. This means that it attracts a number of different ethnic groups, which makes identifying the numbers of IDPs exceedingly difficult. One estimate puts the figure for displaced persons from the north in Mopti at between 15,000 and 20,000. The Bamako office of the International Organization for Migration (IOM) places the total figure for IDPs in the north of Mali, as described above, at around 100,000 persons.

The IDPs only settle where their survival is ensured, and to a large extent, their life-styles in their new settlement areas do not vary considerably from before. Nevertheless, these people have been forced away from their traditional lands and wish to return, for historic and ancestral reasons. However, in cases where whole groups were forced to abandon their base, water holes were left untended and have dried up. Coupled with the increasing desertification of the region, this means that the potential for their regeneration is reduced. The effect is that return to the village is usually not possible.

Institutional responses

There are no programmes, either at local, national or international levels, that specifi-cally target IDPs in Mali and offer assistance. However, various agencies have programmes in the region which are likely to benefit IDPs. For example, CARE Mali has a rural develop-ment programme in Tombouctou that aims to increase the living standards of 3000 persons in the region, as well as an emergency rehabilitation project that repairs schools and wells that suffer from a lack of maintenance. Periodic emergency food distribution is also undertaken by CARE to provide relief to dis-advantaged persons, including returning refugees. Other agencies, including the ICRC and World Vision have also undertaken the rehabilitation of wells.

Since the end of the conflict, UNHCR has helped reintegrate some 100,000 Malian refugees who had settled in border camps in neighbouring countries. Its reintegration

programmes – which involve the drilling of wells, ensuring access to water – education and health projects are deliberately targeted to assist IDPs and local communities as well as the returning refugees. UNDP has a number of programmes in northern Mali, which target agricultural development and the environment and aim to assist the people of the north to find sustainable livelihoods. In addition, the International Organization for Migration (IOM) classifies as IDPs demobilized combatants who wish to return to their place of origin and reintegrate into civil society. Together with UNDP and the government of Mali, IOM has reintegrated 9800 former combatants and their dependents into their communities, supporting their new lives by financing self-employment projects such as cattle raising, trading and agriculture.

To a large extent, many of the projects being implemented in the north of Mali depend on factors such as adequate rainfall, temperature and the level of the River Niger. As these factors are beyond human control, the projects' success cannot be guaranteed.

Future considerations

The traditionally nomadic lifestyle of the internally displaced population in Mali calls for special considerations when addressing the problem. Though many Tuaregs, both displaced within Mali and returning from neighboring countries, would like to continue their nomadic lifestyle, increasing desertification makes this difficult. Further considerations such as education for their children mean that some are turning to agriculture and a sedentary existence for a living. For most, the problem of displacement could be addressed through a strong policy of opening and maintaining water holes and supplying cattle. One way to achieve self-sufficiency may be through creating associations to allow the purchase or rental of water-pumps and the encouragement of direct liaison with the technical departments of regional government structures and the provision of technical assistance.

Southern Mali

Displacement has also occurred from the Kayes region in southwestern Mali. Kayes is traditionally a source of emigration both to Europe and to other African countries. The main reason for emigration is the severe underdevelopment of the region. Particularly unfavourable meteorological conditions, resulting in the advance of the desert, are constantly reducing the availability of arable land. The combination of factors such as severe desertification, periodic droughts, a lack of services, infrastructure and development in the region has forced many Kayesians to search for opportunities elsewhere. As well as leaving the country, people from Kayes head south, away from the desert, to the cities of Bamako and Sikasso. Such movements are not large scale, but occur steadily, increasing in times of drought and during the annual dry season from November to March. Very little information is available on the situation of those persons from Kayes who move to Bamako and Sikasso, and their living conditions have never been monitored. In addition, no programmes are being implemented to provide for their assistance or protection needs. However, it can be supposed that, as with most movements from the region, the displacements are temporary, intended only for the time it is needed to earn enough to return home with improved means for self-reliance.

The Mali government is currently undertaking a comprehensive initiative to enhance development in the region. In January 1997, a Round Table of Sustainable Development of the Kayes Region set out a strategy for the government to improve economic growth and living conditions in Kayes.

Mauritania
Iain Beattie

Population displacement in Mauritania has, in the past few years, predominantly occurred as a result of government policies and not as a result of flight from conflict. Due to the nature of these policies, the displacement has resulted in refugees rather than IDPs. Internal displacement has occurred, however, due to a natural disaster in the form of a severe drought.

Historically, in Mauritania there has been an ongoing ethnic conflict between those of Negro-Mauritanian descent and those of Moorish descent. Due to this persistent conflict, and to deterioration in relations between Mauritania and Senegal, the predominantly Moorish government of Mauritania, in 1989, expelled 75,000 black Mauritanians from the country. This population was forced into Senegal. The number of forcibly displaced people rose to a total of 90,000 when the government refused the return of some 15,000 nomads in Mali whom it considered ethnically undesirable. While the government alleged that those expelled were not Mauritanian citizens, it is generally accepted that the action was a form of ethnic cleansing.

Since the expulsion, approximately 30,000 refugees have been allowed to return to Mauritania, with 15,000 of these arriving after relations improved between Senegal and Mauritania in 1996. Those remaining in Senegal seek assurances from the Mauritanian government before they consent to return. The UNHCR has been allowed to assist with the returnees.

In October 1996, multiparty elections resulted in the Democratic Republican Party winning 72 of the 79 available seats in the legislative assembly, with the black opposition party winning only one seat.

The drought, which started in 1996, was exacerbated by lack of rain in 1997 and has resulted in loss of livestock, marked decreases in agricultural production and desertification. According to Church World Services, which supports drought relief efforts in Mauritania, the drought has 'forced the nomadic population into settlements as well as causing a profound rural exodus'. Though it is difficult to determine the exact numbers of people forced to relocate to settlements, the World Food Programme puts the figure affected by the drought at 200,000, between 30 and 40 per cent of the region's population.

Internal displacement in Mauritania is primarily the result of this natural disaster, which is expected to deteriorate further as details of crop losses come to light.

Nigeria
Okechukwu Ibeanu

Although internal displacement has continued to be a significant problem in Nigeria in recent years, the Nigerian government tends to conceal it. Displacement dates from as far back as the Nigerian–Biafran war (1967–70) in which an estimated two million people died and another ten million were displaced. More recently, the main causes of displacement include conflicts in oil-producing areas; conflicts over communal land; ethno-religious conflicts; and conflicts linked to democratization. Currently, an estimated 1.2 million Nigerians are displaced within their country.

With so few empirical studies of IDPs in Nigeria, there is a high level of inaccuracy in the figures. Even in the widely publicized case of displaced people in the Bakassi peninsula, the oil-rich area contested by Nigeria and the Cameroons, few studies have provided accurate head counts. What exist, therefore, are

estimates, and their dependability as a basis for policy and planning is doubtful. Most sources – government, affected communities, relief agencies and the press – tend to be either highly politicized or too sensationalist.

In addition, the fleeting character of the contexts of population displacement makes exact numbers a moving target. For instance, many of the people displaced in the conflict between the Ijaw and Itsekiri in the Warri area have since returned to the towns following the return of normality, even if temporarily, to the area.

Conflicts in oil-producing areas
These conflicts date to the very beginnings of oil exploration in Nigeria. Most of them, however, date to the past ten years and still remain unresolved. Several oil-producing communities, especially in the Rivers, Delta and Cross-River states, have had to cope with continuing military and police 'occupation' and systematic state repression, sometimes taking the form of extra-judicial killings enacted in summary executions. The disputes usually arise over environmental pollution and material deprivation in these communities. Villages like Umuechem, Obagi, Brass, Nembe Creek and Rumuobiokani, as well as dozens in Ogoniland, all in Rivers state, have experienced extensive population displacement resulting from environmental pollution caused by crude oil mining and refining, as well as from material deprivation and state violence. The relationship between the multinational oil company Shell, the Nigerian state and the Ogoni people, which culminated in the mock trial and execution of Ken Saro-Wiwa, is well-documented.

Communal conflicts over resources
Intercommunal conflicts have also been a major source of internal population displacement in Nigeria. The strategy of rural transformation adopted by successive Nigerian governments, which emphasizes

large-scale, mechanized agriculture, has led to land hunger among peasants and driven up the price of land. As a result, not only has land become scarce, but its sale has also become a source of income. Often, such sales are private transactions involving individually appropriated land. They take place with no respect for the traditions which, in most parts of Nigeria, provide for communal ownership of land and prohibit its commercialization. The flouting of traditions is in itself a source of conflict. More importantly, however, with the stakes in land raised very high by speculation and sale, disputes over land have increased tremendously and have also become highly charged. This has been particularly so in the southeastern states of Anambra, Imo, Cross-River and Akwa-Ibom, where population densities are very high. However, in the northern states of Plateau, Benue, Adamawa and Yobe, serious conflicts of this type leading to the displacement of thousands of agriculturalists, pastoralists and agro-pastoralists have also been reported.

Ethno-religious conflicts

This type of displacement-generating conflict occurs mainly in the north of the country between Muslims and Christians. Since the north is predominantly Muslim, their Christian adversaries tend to belong to other ethnic groups, usually from the south of the country. The result is that these conflicts, though primarily religious, also take on an ethnic character. In recent times, there have been major religious conflicts in Kano, Bauchi, Yola, Kaduna and other cities in the north. Sometimes, radical Muslim sects like the Maitatsine group initiate these conflicts, targeting both Christians and more liberal Muslim sects. There is little doubt that the worsening social security situation in Nigeria is leading more and more people into revivalist and millennarian sects in both the Muslim and Christian religions. They are not only ultra conservative in approach but accept holy wars as divinely

ordained. The future points to even more population displacement as a result of ethno-religious conflicts.

Conflicts linked to democratization

The long domination of Nigerian society and politics by the military and the growing demands for democratization have created an important context for conflict and internal displacement. The situation is exacerbated by the manipulation of ethnicity by successive military regimes. Through resource allocation, the creation of new administrative areas and the location of their capitals, and through the demarcation of electoral constituencies and the allocation of political offices, military governments have sought to reward those ethnic and sub-ethnic groups, as well as clans and communities they perceive as their supporters, to the detriment and neglect of other groups.

At the individual level, thousands of Nigerians have had to relocate, both within and outside the country, as the military regime increasingly targets pro-democracy activists. Hundreds of others have been incarcerated without trial.

Generally, Nigeria has an underdeveloped social security system. The poor, unemployed and disabled are rarely statutorily provided for by the state. Most of the burden falls on the extended family system, which itself has been over-stretched. Over the years a number of nongovernmental agencies have come on the scene, but still, resources are generally inadequate. Internally displaced people are in an even more difficult situation. Although there is a Nigerian relief organization working together with external humanitarian agencies and other NGOs, the humanitarian needs of internally displaced people remain widely uncatered for. Lack of funds and statistics are the major obstacles that are cited. But the absence of a clear-cut government humanitarian policy is a major hindrance to providing the needs of internally displaced

Contexts and estimates of internally displaced people in Nigeria

Cause of displacement	Most affected states	Number of IDPs	Receiving formal assistance
Oil production	Bayelsa, Delta, Rivers	50,000	10,000
Transition to democracy	Bayelsa, Delta, Ondo, Osun	700,000	7,000
Land and resource conflicts	Abia, Anambra, Benue, Cross River, Plateau, Taraba	400,000	nil
Ethno-religious conflicts	Adamawa, Bauchi, Kaduna, Kano	20,000	nil
Environmental degradation (natural and man-made, such as soil erosion)	Abia, Anambra, Bayelsa, Imo	50,000	nil
International conflict	Akwa-Ibom, Cross River (Bakassi Peninsula)	50,000	10,000
Total		1,270,000	27,000

people. In addition, the special needs of women and children are not considered and the fact that these are essentially patriarchal societies in which men dominate, and therefore tend to monopolize relief materials, is completely overlooked.

Given this state of affairs, philanthropic individuals, family and other social networks continue to provide the bulk of humanitarian assistance to internally displaced people in Nigeria. Spontaneous resettlement of displaced people, assisted by friends, family, churches and co-ethnics, is a common occurrence. This explains why, for instance, there are virtually no camps or formal settlements of internally displaced people anywhere in Nigeria. In the oil producing communities of the Niger Delta area, oil companies have also been prominent in providing relief materials to people displaced by communal feuds and the environmental effects of oil exploration in recent times. For instance, in the conflict between the communities of Bassambiri and Ogbolomabiri in Bayelsa state over the location of the headquarters of the newly created Nembe Local Government Area, the Shell Petroleum Development Corporation provided relief materials worth one million naira.

The major burden of meeting the needs of displaced people falls on the extended family and communal networks. A strong sense of reciprocal obligation, which family and clan members owe one another, provides the impetus for this resettlement process. In many cases, people facing internal displacement simply relocate to other towns and communities to join other family and clan members. Where displacement occurs in the rural areas, people relocate to neighbouring communities, especially where they have existing ties, for example marriage or blood relations. Others relocate to the urban areas to join relations. Where displacement occurs in urban areas, especially where the displaced are mainly members of 'outsider' ethnic groups, the trend is for the displaced to return to their 'home' villages, where they either resettle permanently or remain until things normalize in their place of abode.

Quite often, displaced people are victims of the physical violence of the state. This is especially the case where displacement occurs as a result of conflicts among groups. The partisanship of the state ensures that some of the displaced will become the targets of state violence. Apart from physical violence, displaced people are often denied social, economic and cultural rights, or placed in a structural position in which they cannot enjoy those rights. For one, being non-indigenes of their new location, they are excluded from a wide range of economic resources and opportunities, including employment. For another, the operation of a two-track legal system in Nigeria (civil and customary or sharia law) ensures that when displaced people come from different cultures, which could vary from one town to another, they are denied many social and cultural rights. Above all, the fear in which many displaced people live creates a psychological state in which they deny their identity in order to survive.

Conclusion

The extent of displacement in recent years has been largely concealed or ignored. The reasons include the following:

- the Nigerian government's preference for playing down the magnitude of population displacement generally, and internal displacement in particular, for political reasons. Where it reluctantly accepts that displacement has occurred, it tends to announce low figures and quickly claims that the problem has been solved;
- lack of organization, activism and advocacy by displaced groups, all of which are necessary to get their plight on the political agenda; and
- the existence of effective family, communal and other social networks to absorb the internally displaced.

In spite of its concealment, the problem of internal population displacement remains very serious and has in fact continued to worsen in Nigeria. Conflicts constitute the most important impetus to displacement in Nigeria. Social insecurity, mediated by state violence and state partisanship, gives rise to group conflicts in Nigeria. These conflicts, in turn, generate internal population displacement. The deepening crisis of internal population displacement has gone hand in hand with a growing tendency to conceal this population. The concealment of internally displaced populations has made their situation even more desperate. There is a need for more serious tracking of groups at risk in order to get timely assistance and protection to them, especially in the face of political despotism and state aggressiveness towards such groups. Apart from constant tracking of groups at risk, a more lasting solution to the problem of internal population displacement in Nigeria would involve the restructuring of the Nigerian state in the direction of democracy and popular participation, a progressive humanitarian policy for Nigeria, social welfare reforms, a more neutral and equity-based system of conflict management, especially in conflicts involving ethnic groups, increased international attention to displaced people within Nigeria, and greater freedom for NGOs to intervene on behalf of the internally displaced.

Senegal
Iain Beattie

Civil conflict in Senegal has largely been confined to the southern region of the country and the resulting population displacement has consisted primarily of refugees in the last few years. At the same time, Senegal has hosted more refugees than its internal conflict has created. At the end of 1996, Senegal hosted some 51,000 refugees (mainly from Mauritania), while only 17,000 Senegalese refugees were present in Gambia and Guinea-Bissau. Nevertheless, internally displaced persons are a factor in the Senegalese conflict. Up until October 1997, reports continued of IDPs fleeing their homes due to conflict in the region.

The people living in the southern region of Senegal, Casamance, have had a long-standing dispute with the government of Senegal about its economic policies, which, they feel, have been prejudicial to the region. Casamance produces much of Senegal's rice production, a situation which adds fuel to claims for greater state attention to the region, and has resulted in separatist tendencies. The separatist conflict came to a head in the early 1990s and, by 1993, 40,000 people had been displaced by the violence. In 1993, there was a cease-fire between government forces and the Mouvement des forces démocratiques de Casamance (MFDC) separatists, and according to a regional delegate for ICRC, in 1994 there were fewer armed clashes and violent incidents than had occurred in the region in previous years. In 1995, despite the cease-fire, the ICRC reported assisting 2800 displaced persons, fleeing fighting between the army and MFDC rebels. Tensions eased in December 1995, after an appeal for peace by the MFDC secretary-general, but talks scheduled for April 1996 did not materialize. Instead, many suspected MFDC sympathizers were taken into custody by the government during this period. Held without trial, these prisoners were often tortured. Likewise, the MFDC was also responsible for human rights abuses. Violence in Casamance also affected the local population by preventing its access to agricultural areas, so vital to the region's viability. Sporadic incidences of violence continued to be reported in the region through September 1997.

Although the crisis in Senegal remains largely confined to Casamance, there has been some degree of population movement within and from this area. Persecution and torture of civilians suspected of collaboration has been perpetrated by both the government forces and the MFDC. Both the UN Committee against Torture and Amnesty International are closely monitoring the alleged human rights abuses. Such violations have, nonetheless, resulted in around 15,000 refugees fleeing to Guinea-Bissau, and 2000 to Gambia. A total figure of IDPs has been hard to determine, although it was reported that 5000 people near the border with Guinea-Bissau fled to Ziguinchor. This figure is unlikely to account for the entire population of IDPs, however; as is often the case with such conflicts, the total is highly fluid and subject to daily revision.

While the problem of internally displaced persons in Senegal is not as serious as in some West African states, the conflict is persistent and is likely to result in more displacement before it is resolved.

Sierra Leone
Iain Beattie

The conflict in Sierra Leone began in 1991 when rebels from the Revolutionary United Front (RUF) crossed the border from Liberia, allegedly with the support of the leader of the National Patriotic Front of Liberia, Charles Taylor. During the first two years of the ensuing rebellion, the government of Sierra Leone was successful in confining the conflict to the southern and eastern areas of the country, yet the harshness with which it dealt with alleged rebel supporters resulted in an increase in support for the rebels. In April 1992, a military coup overthrew the one-party system of Joseph Momoh and his All People's Congress. The fight against the rebels was taken over by Momoh's successor, Captain Valentine Strasser, whose vigorous methods almost eradicated the RUF. The RUF, however, resorted to guerrilla tactics and was able to survive the government's onslaught. By 1994, it was operating throughout Sierra Leone, and by early 1995 it seemed poised to enter Freetown and overcome the government. The rebel force had overextended itself, however, and with the help of foreign mercenaries the government managed to repel it.

In August 1995, a national consultative conference held in Freetown recommended that elections, originally due to be held in December 1995, should be postponed until February 1996. Despite the overthrow of Strasser by his deputy, Brigadier Maada Bio, voting occurred on 26 February 1996, with Ahmad Tejan Kabbah of the Sierra Leone People's Party (SLPP) emerging victorious. Days after the election, the RUF entered into a two-month cease-fire, which, despite numerous violations, endured until November 1996, when a final peace agreement was signed. Despite the cease-fire and peace agreement, fighting continued between government forces, foreign mercenaries, traditional militias or Kamajors and RUF fighters in the districts of Kenema, Kailahun and Pujehun. March and April ushered in further unrest in the Northern province. The conflict culminated on 25 May 1997, when President Kabbah was overthrown in a coup by the Armed Forces Revolutionary Council (AFRC) led by Major Johnny Paul Koroma. A coalition was then formed between the AFRC and the RUF, which collapsed in early 1998 when the AFRC was ousted. Since May 1997, hundreds of people have died in fighting between the various factions in Sierra Leone.

The conflict in Sierra Leone has caused massive human suffering in the rural provinces and cities. Pillaging of villages, extrajudicial killings, torture and flagrant abuses of human rights have characterized this suffering and prompted large-scale migration. According to statistics given in the executive summary of the government of Sierra Leone's National Resettlement, Rehabilitation and Reconstruction Programme, which were collected before the May 1997 coup, the war has been responsible for over 10,000 deaths, the disfigurement and maiming of thousands

more, and the displacement of 2.1 million people, 375,000 of whom are refugees. Finding shelter with family or friends in the major towns or in displaced people's camps, they have faced severe hardships, food shortages and disease. Often, people have been displaced more than once, being forced to move from camp to camp as violence spread. Displacement probably affects more than 40 per cent of the Sierra Leone population, but figures are currently unknown.

At the end of 1995, after five years of conflict, more than one million internally displaced people inhabited camps in Freetown, Bo, Kenema, Segbwema and Daru. The lull in fighting in 1996 caused some of these people to return to their homes. However, the numbers of displaced people rose again when fighting in Liberia forced Sierra Leone refugees to return to their country. In spite of the 1996 cease-fire, the situation remained dire. The major population displacements had hampered agricultural production, resulting in malnutrition and the frequent looting of food supplies. Sporadic fighting was still occurring, and civilians living near the troubled areas continued to live in a situation of neither war nor peace. The security climate improved marginally with the signing of the Abidjan Peace Accord, and the government, UN agencies and the NGO community were able to return hundreds of thousands of IDPs to their areas of origin, primarily in the southern and eastern provinces. By March 1997 many of the 1.6 million people displaced at the height of the war had been returned to their homes.

The violence that occurred during the coup in May 1997 once again sparked a movement of tens of thousands of the population. The ICRC reported movements out of Freetown towards Kambia, Makeni and Bo, and from Kenema to Segbwema and Zimmi. Still others fled to Liberia and to Guinea.

Children have borne the brunt of the conflict in Sierra Leone. They comprise half the estimated 10,000 deaths and 700,000 of the nation's displaced population of 1.8 million at the height of the conflict, among them 9500 unaccompanied minors. The RUF sexually exploited displaced women and used torture and maiming as scare tactics throughout the conflict, without regard for human rights.

Given the characteristics of the conflict, the international development agencies have shifted their interventions from development assistance to support for humanitarian activities. The range of their programmes, from food and health assistance, to camp construction, to social support, has largely prevented a total collapse within Sierra Leone.

The figure for IDPs in Sierra Leone is subject to daily revision given the ongoing conflict in the country. In September 1997, people were arriving in displaced persons' camps in Kissy, seven kilometres from Freetown, as a result of clashes between pro-Kabbah Kamajors and the People's Army. As long as the various factions continue their struggle for control of the country, there seems little hope of the situation improving for IDPs in the near future. The AFRC coup has been ousted and more refugees are moving into Liberia. In March 1998, 200 orphaned children were discovered living alone in the forest, having fled fighting around their orphanage. Before this recent fighting there were estimated to be about 160,000 IDPs in the country. By March 1998, this had increased to an estimated 200,000 internally displaced people who require humanitarian assistance.

SUDAN

KENYA

Arua Gulu Kitgum

Kisangani

UGANDA
Kampala

Rift Valley
Province

Beni Kasese
Lubero

Western
Province

Ruhungeri

Nairobi

RWANDA Kigali

Bukavu

Bubanza
Province Butembo

Kayanza
Province

BURUNDI

Kindu

Karuzi
Province

DEMOCRATIC

Muramvya
Province

REPUBLIC

Kalemi

OF CONGO

TANZANIA

Shaba
Province

ZAMBIA

IDP Figures – Central Africa

Conflict-induced:
Kenya   100,000
Uganda   328,000
Rwanda   180,500
Burundi   470,000
Democratic
Republic of Congo   1,000,000
Congo-Brazzaville   240,000

Map 2: Central Africa

Central and East Africa

Overview
Margaret Okole

During 1997, the crisis in central Africa continued. Significant numbers of people have become or remain internally displaced in the following countries of central and East Africa: Burundi, the Democratic Republic of Congo (formerly Zaire), Kenya, Rwanda and Uganda. In Kenya, this process is independent of events in neighbouring countries. The state-sponsored ethnic violence, which has been a recurrent feature of the Kenyan political scene, was again significant in the election year of 1997. Ethnic groups perceived as supporting the opposition were targeted in the Coast province, and more than 120,000 people were displaced, adding to the numbers similarly displaced in the early 1990s.

The activities of separatist groups in northern and western Uganda, and government action against them, have led to more than 300,000 people being reported as displaced in March 1998. The Sudanese government is alleged to be supporting the separatists in the north; this relates to its own internal troubles in southern Sudan. All groups of separatists in Uganda attack the government on the grounds that it is undemocratic and dominated by Tutsis, a reference to Yoweri Kaguta Museveni's own tribal origins and his support for the Rwandan Tutsis. The distinction between Tutsi refugees from Rwanda, and related ethnic groups who have been resident in Uganda for generations, is lost in this propaganda.

In Rwanda itself, large numbers of internally displaced Hutus, who returned to the country after initially fleeing the (Tutsi) Rwandan Patriotic Front (RPF), were seen by the RPF government as a threat. In 1995 the government moved to close down IDP camps, leading to much loss of life. Since then IDPs have endeavoured to conceal their status, but doubtless many have been unable to return to their homes.

Conflict between Tutsis and Hutus has likewise caused dislocation in Burundi, where between 400,000 and 600,000 people out of a population of 6 million are currently estimated to be displaced, some for years. The situation remains highly volatile, making relief work difficult and in some areas impossible.

The change of government in May 1997, which transformed Zaire into the Democratic Republic of Congo, was accompanied by population displacement estimated at 1–1.5 million, mainly in the east. This has now dropped considerably as people return home. As in Uganda, a significant proportion of the population of eastern Zaire was of Rwandan origin. Pre-existing ethnic tensions were exacerbated by the flood of refugees from Rwanda in 1994, leading to complex and shifting patterns of hostility. The present government is seen as linked to the Congolese Tutsis and to the Rwandan government. Although by the end of 1997 most IDPs had returned to their homes, their situation remains precarious.

Fighting in Brazzaville, the capital of the Republic of Congo in October 1997 caused the immediate displacement of half a million people, half of whom had returned home by March 1998.

Burundi
Patrick Mullen

About 10 per cent of Burundi's population of six million are internally displaced, their displacement related to tensions between the minority Tutsi and majority Hutu ethnic groups. Since its independence from Belgium in 1962, Burundi has suffered from large scale ethnic violence in 1965, 1972, 1988 and 1993, causing the deaths of tens of thousands of people.

BURUNDI: IDPs in Muyinga
(PHOTO: A Hollman/UNHCR).

The proportions of the ethnic groups in Burundi are 85 per cent Hutu, 14 per cent Tutsi and 1 per cent Twa. The Tutsi presently dominate the army, government and the modern economic sector, while most Hutu people are peasant farmers. The Twa are marginalized as landless artisans. Whether or not there are real differences between the groups, a large proportion of Burundians perceive a difference, which fuels the conflict.

In June 1992, President Pierre Buyoya called the country's first democratic elections, losing to Melchior Ndadaye, a Hutu from the Front démocratic du Burundi (FRODEBU) opposition party. In October, Ndadaye was killed in an attempted coup. This led to months of violent retaliation and marked the start of an armed rebellion, as the Tutsi-dominated army confronted Hutu rebel groups. An estimated 200,000 Burundians have been killed since October 1993. Although the FRODEBU government survived, politics became increasingly ethnically polarized. In July 1996, Buyoya returned to power in a coup, and has pursued the war while participating in negotiations with the rebels. In reaction to the coup, neighbouring countries imposed sanctions on Burundi.

Population displacement has been continuous in Burundi since the end of 1993. About 200,000 of those displaced by the violence in 1993 and 1994 remain in camps, mostly in the northern provinces. Those more recently displaced by the ongoing conflict can be estimated at over 100,000, mostly in the insecure northwestern and southwestern parts of the country. Displaced camps are often established in and around public buildings, churches and market centres, usually near a military position. In addition, tens of thousands of people have fled their homes to live with other families, or hide in the bush or marshes. Although many have been displaced for years, some of these groups stay away from their homes for short periods, returning when security improves.

Starting in Karuzi province in the beginning of 1996, and followed by Kayanza and Muramvya provinces at the beginning of 1997, government authorities instructed large numbers of rural people in areas of persistent conflict to live together in camps. More recently, many people have been 'regrouped', in Bubanza province, following an upsurge in fighting there. By the beginning of 1998, most of these camps in Karuzi, Kayanza and Muramvya had closed, leaving the total 'regrouped' population at approximately 150,000.

In total, 551,000 people are estimated to be presently displaced in Burundi.

Humanitarian needs and responses

In a country where the average annual income is among the lowest in the world, neither individual families nor community and government structures have the resources to cope with displacement. The civil conflict, now four years old, has worn down government infrastructures, from the health system to agricultural extension services and reduced the non-military proportion of government budgets, while the ethnic division has affected perceptions of the needs of the different displaced groups. Finally, the price inflation, shortages and general economic effect of the regional embargo on Burundi, in place since August 1996, have affected the country's ability to address the needs of IDPs. International assistance has been provided, although many of these same factors have influenced it.

A particular problem has been presented by the creation of 'regroupment' camps by government authorities. As more camps were created during 1997, donors and humanitarian agencies expressed reluctance to provide humanitarian assistance, which could be seen as support for this policy. Reflecting this concern, UN policy, expressed by the Humanitarian Coordinator in March 1997, was to provide emergency assistance on the basis of needs assessments and to avoid the creation of any type of permanent structures in the 'regroupment' camps.

Insecurity is also a major constraint. Conflict in many parts of the country during 1996 caused reductions in the operations of humanitarian agencies and limited their geographic scope, especially following the deaths of three international ICRC delegates in 1996. Although security has improved in some areas during 1997, much of the northwest and southwest of the country remain off limits to relief workers.

In a primarily agricultural country, distancing people from their land has an immediate and serious effect on their livelihoods. WFP has been the main provider of emergency food assistance to IDPs. From a peak of 500,000 beneficiaries at the end of 1994, levels of assistance were reduced during 1995 and 1996 as many IDPs returned home or developed coping mechanisms to attain self-sufficiency. Since mid-1995, regular food distributions have been replaced with punctual emergency distributions to the most vulnerable groups or to those recently displaced by the continuing conflict. During 1997, nutritional surveys and needs assessments revealed serious food security problems in many 'regroupment' camps, and WFP increased food distribution in affected provinces. At the same time, increased conflict in many areas has recently caused new population displacements. Although there has been no nationwide statistical nutritional survey of IDPs, recent local surveys reveal a high level of malnutrition in several areas. Particularly dramatic is the condition of severely malnourished children and adults who emerge from months of hiding in highly insecure areas. Numbers of beneficiaries in the nutritional programmes supported by UNICEF and WFP have risen from 18,000 in the third quarter of 1997 to 34,000 in the fourth quarter, and are projected to rise further in 1998. Although these figures include nondisplaced people, beneficiary increases are in the provinces most affected by conflict and displacement.

In 1997 the living conditions in IDP camps were overcrowded with inadequate sanitation and limited access to potable water: at the beginning of the year, many IDPs in Cibitoke province had to rely on untreated river water. Over half of the 70 IDP sites did not have adequate latrines or drainage, and 30 per cent had poor access to potable water. A typhus outbreak soon after the formation of large 'regroupment' camps in several provinces at the end of 1996 may have been related to poor water and sanitation conditions. UNICEF and international NGOs are active in water supply, water source renovation and latrine building.

In the most affected areas of the country, humanitarian agencies have gradually taken over much of the supply and functioning of the national health system and nutritional centres, while the Catholic Church (Caritas) and other churches also provide health and nutritional services. Services to IDPs are no different from those for the local population, although many IDPs live in camps far from a functioning health centre. In fact, only 70 per cent of health services remain functional nationwide, and they are non-existent in the most insecure parts of the country. In February 1997, UNICEF found that 20 per cent of the IDPs surveyed did not have access to health centres. In some areas, NGOs, such as MSF-Belgium in Karuzi province, have set up temporary health and nutrition posts in larger IDP camps to provide initial treatments and to facilitate transfers. A February 1997 survey of IDP sites found that 28 per cent had low immunization rates. Indeed, immunization rates among the general population have declined since 1993 from 81 to 51 per cent coverage.

Most Burundian IDPs need basic items such as plastic sheeting, cooking sets, soap, blankets and clothing. Until its withdrawal from Burundi in mid-1996, ICRC was the main distributor of non-food items to IDPs. Since then, different agencies, including UNHCR, IFRC, MSF and CRS, have partly filled the gap with punctual distributions, but ICRC's absence continues to be felt in this area. Bean seeds and hoes are distributed under FAO coordination; more than 600,000 IDPs were beneficiaries before the second growing season of 1997.

A survey in 1997 found that 13 out of 70 IDP sites did not have access to primary schools. In general, primary school enrolment has fallen below 35 per cent, while only two-thirds of the country's primary schools are presently functional. Since 1993, 20,500 children have been registered as having been separated from their families, 60 per cent of whom were orphaned. UNICEF, churches and NGOs assist unaccompanied children through family reunification, orphanages and street children programmes. In February 1997, UNICEF found that almost 6000 children were unaccompanied in 48 of the 70 IDP sites surveyed.

Protection

WFP is presently attempting to disagregate its beneficiary statistics by gender but information is difficult to obtain, especially for recently displaced groups. There are few women among the leaders in IDP camps, though in several places associations of women, often widows, have formed to work together on reconstruction or income-generation projects.

The UN Commission on Human Rights has an observer mission in Burundi which monitors the situation of IDPs. ICRC had an active presence in the field until their withdrawal in 1996. UNHCR exercises its mandate with regard to the protection of returnees. The human rights situation of IDPs is considered in the context of the general situation in the country, for the violation of their rights causes them to flee their homes and often prevents them from returning. At the end of 1996, amid reports of killings and disappearances, the conditions faced by returnees from eastern Zaire were a matter of concern, as many were returning to highly insecure areas such as Cibitoke and Bubanza provinces. In general, IDP sites are often the targets of violent attacks. Of particular concern recently was the formation of 'regroupment' camps in various parts of the country, as questions were raised about the forcible displacement of these groups. An Amnesty International report denounced extrajudicial executions during the 'regroupment' process and life-threatening conditions in the camps.

Continuous population displacements since the end of 1993 have taken place while similar movements of people return to their original homes. For example, over half the people displaced by the crisis in 1993 and early 1994 have returned to their homes, often benefiting from distributions of 'return packages' of food and non-food items, or from house reconstruction projects.

Of the 1993/4 displaced, approximately 551,000 remain in sites, unwilling and afraid to return to their original homes. During 1997, the Burundi government made resettlement a priority, providing funding for those who wished to rebuild their original homes and implementing housing construction projects on resettlement sites. These often simply improve the shelter at existing IDP sites. Some donors and humanitarian agencies decline to provide assistance, concerned that these projects will result in the creation of ethnically homogenous villages, perpetuating divisions in the countryside. During the ongoing conflict since 1994, other groups displaced by insecurity have returned home once it was safe to do so.

During the second half of 1997, government authorities in Muramvya, Kayanza and Karuzi provinces started disbanding the 'regroupment' camps, which had been created at the beginning of the year. By the beginning of 1998, almost 200,000 people had returned to their homes. At the same time, in Bubanza province mounting insecurity has led to an increase in the population of 'regroupment' camps. The needs of the approximately 150,000 people remaining in such camps, along with the tens of thousands recently displaced by the ongoing conflict, continue to present a challenge to humanitarian agencies.

The security situation has stabilized around Bujumbura making it possible for the majority of the people who fled following attacks in January 1998 to return to their home towns. About 10,000 people remain in regroupment sites in the district of Bujumbura, while 6000 are still registered in Buhonga and 600 displaced families remain in the Isale commune.

The dismantling of regroupment camps began, unofficially in June 1997 when 16,000 people returned from Kayanza province to their homes. Since then, approximately 250,000 people from the three main provinces affected by regroupment have returned to their homes with the assistance of humanitarian agencies. In March 1998 the largest displaced population was 100,000 people in both Bubanza and Cibitoke, caused by clashes between the National Council for Democracy (CNDD) and the Palipehutu, a Hutu rebel group.

Conclusion

As the conflict in Burundi continues so will population displacement. As ethnic emnity and distrust continue, many groups, notably those displaced in 1993/4, will not return to their homes. At the same time, continuing military conflict has led both to new IDPs fleeing violence and to the 'regroupment' of the inhabitants of entire areas. As areas become peaceful again, so IDPs return to their homes. These continuous population movements provide a challenge to humanitarian agencies in that they must quickly adapt their programmes to rapidly changing circumstances.

Humanitarian assistance is clearly affected by the political and security context of the country. Not only have humanitarian workers been targeted by violence, but the uses to which assistance is applied can be a subject of controversy, as illustrated by the concerns over 'regroupment' and the resettlement of displaced groups in new villages. The nutritional status, health, living conditions and human rights situation of IDPs cannot be considered separately from that of the population as a whole, which has also deteriorated during four years of civil conflict. In short, the humanitarian needs of Burundian IDPs, and the possi-bilities for addressing them, are not at all clear and straightforward, which in some measure prevents the establishment of systematic and comprehensive assistance.

Congo

Bamanyirwe Aimé Sangara

In October 1996, a military offensive by the Alliance des Forces démocratiques pour la Liberation (AFDL) dispersed and displaced thousands of refugees from the camps in the eastern Democratic Republic of Congo (DRC). These displacements posed unprecedented challenges to the international humanitarian assistance system.

Despite the change of government that finally took place in May 1997, there are still serious humanitarian problems, especially in the eastern part of the country. Most of these problems can be attributed to the inability of Rwandan refugees and internally displaced people to return to their homes because of continuous tensions between various ethnic groups and violent armed clashes between government troops and armed factions.

Only recently have IDPs become an important aspect of forced migration in the Congo. The ethnic persecution and expulsion of Kasaians from the Shaba province in 1992, the continuous ethnic tension between the Banyarwanda community and the indigenous population of north Kivu since 1993 and the seven-month-long military offensive by the AFDL, have led to the displacement of thousands of IDPs in eastern Congo, including three different categories: the already

displaced people from the north Kivu who fled the conflict in the Masisi area; Congolese people who fled from Rwanda after the 1994 crisis and were living in temporary shelter; and those displaced by the war in 1997. Continued insecurity in both places of origin and destination has resulted in successive waves of movements, which make it difficult to ascertain exact numbers involved.

Difficult relationships with the UN

Much to the disadvantage of refugees and IDPs, relationships between the new government in Kinshasa and the UN remained tense for most of 1997 over the question of the alleged massacres of Hutu refugees by some sections of the AFDL troops. Differences between the UN and President Kabila concerning the scope and mandate of investigations resulted in the government suspending UNHCR activities in Kivu province in October 1997.

The UN investigation team was recalled to New York for consultation and was sent back to Kinshasa in November 1997, following negotiation by the United States ambassador to the UN. An agreement was finally reached and the investigation was allowed to start in early December 1997. Humanitarian agencies were denied permission to travel outside towns in November 1997 and access remains difficult due to dense forests, impassable dirt roads and poor security.

Estimating the number of IDPs

Continued insecurity in eastern Congo, suc-cessive population displacement and the world's relative lack of attention to the plight of IDPs means that accurate estimates of the numbers cannot be made. Considerable discrepancies exist between estimates by local and international organizations.

By December 1996, two months after war broke out, between 250,000 and 500,000 Congolese people were displaced. These included the estimated 150,000 to 300,000 people who had already been displaced from the Masisi area in north Kivu by violence and human rights abuse before the armed conflict erupted in October 1996.

The table below provides estimates of IDPs (total 504,000) at various locations as reported by various organizations. The figures in the table represent only those IDPs whom the organizations reached and should therefore not be read as a country total that is likely to exceed one million.

Internally displaced people in the DRC (estimated by various organizations)

Location	Number	Dates of estimates
Masisi area	250,000	November 1996
Kongolo	1,000	March 1997
Kalima	25,000	March 1997
Kisangani	35,000	April 1997
Kivu	40,000	April 1997
Kalemie and Kindu	35,000	Crossed Lake Tanganyika, mainly from Uvira and Fizi areas, April 1997
Fizi	5,000	October 1997
Kaseka	10,000	October 1997
Butembo, Lubero and Beni	4,000	Towns between Goma and Kisangani, November 1997
Bukavu	3,400	November 1997
North Kivu	75,0002	March 1998
South Kivu	3,000	

North Kivu

Ethnic rivalry and hatred in north Kivu have mainly been fuelled by disputes over land rights and tributes to local chiefs dating from the early twentieth century. Under colonial rule, organized population transfers from Rwanda to the Congo took place on such large scales that sometimes the indigenous people became a minority. In Masisi, for example, Hunde customary chiefs hold administrative power despite the Banyarwanda constituting over 70 per cent of the population and holding more economic power. Three main categories of migrants from Rwanda have been living in the Congo: those who migrated in the precolonial era, those who were transplanted under the colonial administration, and successive movements of refugees since independence, from around 1959. The unresolved question of the status of the Banyarwanda, political grudges and the general state of anarchy in this densely populated region since the late 1980s have also played a part.

In 1994 the arrival of around two million Rwandan refugees in the region further exacerbated conflict in an area already ravaged by sporadic violence. The situation was similar in south Kivu.

This long-standing power struggle between populations of Rwandan origin – the Banyarwanda – and the indigenous people has given rise to a highly complicated and multilayered conflict often characterized by changing alliances between the various parties involved. For instance, before 1994, the indigenous Hunde, Nyanga and Nande were fighting against the local Hutu and Tutsi. However, with the arrival of thousands of armed Hutu refugees, a Hunde–Nyanga–Nande–Hutu alliance was formed against the Tutsi, many of whom were forced to flee to Rwanda. This was to be reversed shortly after that when the indigenous people turned against the Hutu, whom they suspected of attempting to carve out a Hutuland from the Congolese territory. After the AFDL took power in Kinshasa, new alliances were formed between Hutu, Nyanga, Nande and Hunde against the local Tutsi population, many of whom have fled to Goma and Rwanda.

In 1996, the US Committee for Refugees identified nine layers of conflict in the region involving the Zairian indigenous tribes (Hunde, Nande, Tembo, Nyanga), their militia (Mai Mai and Bangilima), Rwandan Hutu refugees and their militia (*Interahamwe*), former Rwandan military, Congolese soldiers, Congolese civilian officials, the Congolese Tutsi community, and at times the Congolese and Rwandan governments.

Eastern Congo

The political turnaround – begun with the installation of a new government led by Laurent Kabila in May 1997 – was perceived to have given political ascendancy to the Banyamulenge Tutsi, much to the dislike of the indigenous people. This is believed to be one of the overriding causes of recent conflicts and armed clashes in the region.

In September, violence broke out again in the Masisi area in the north Kivu and in the Ruzizi plateau in south Kivu. A new alliance of local militia (Mai Mai and Bangilima), members of the ex-Zairian army (FAZ), members of the ex-Rwandan army and of the *Interahamwe* militia fought the government troops.

In south Kivu, the local Bembe and Vira formed an alliance with ex-Rwandan and Burundian Hutu soldiers against government forces and the Banyamulenge. This renewed factional fighting displaced more people. Around 3000 people fled to and around the town of Goma in October 1997 following fighting between the Mai Mai and government troops.

Shaba province

By the end of 1992, the eruption of ethnic violence between the Luba and Kasaians in the Shaba province had displaced between 600,000 and 1,000,000 people. Most of them, members of the Luba ethnic group, fled north into Kasai region where they had ancestral ties. Extensive NGO intervention and changes in local government authorities resulted in the return of many by 1996, though some decided to settle elsewhere. Unresolved problems, however, remain over their properties and the compensation they were promised by the government.

During the 1997 military campaign, very little displacement took place in the mineral rich Shaba province, which holds a long-standing opposition to the Mobutu regime and is also home to President Kabila.

Protection and assistance

The plight of IDPs in the Congo has been dramatically overlooked and overshadowed by the refugee crisis. Only after relief organizations realized that they could not proceed with the repatriation and relief operation for Hutu refugees in Kisangani unless something was done for the thousands displaced from Goma and Bukavu, have IDPs moved up the agenda of humanitarian assistance.

In the chaos that followed the AFDL October 1996 offensive, the UNHCR and NGOs complained that they had 'lost their refugees'. For months, most of these refugees depended on the hospitality of local people in the dense tropical forest already unable to satisfy their own needs. Insecurity and unrest, a very poor infrastructure and the scale and pattern of displacement created major problems in the provision of assistance and protection. Where it was possible to reach them, transport was provided for the return of IDPs. Many organizations also distributed 'reintegration packages' or 'resettlement kits' consisting of items such as blankets, jerrycans, tarpaulins, cooking pots, soap, hoes, seeds, biscuits, maize, beans, oil, as well as medical assistance through increased support to available health structures. Since October 1997, the focus has been on the improvement of drinking water and medical care provision.

In April 1997 the ICRC, WFP, UNHCR

and other organizations set up an air bridge between Kisangani, Goma and Bukavu to airlift IDPs stranded hundreds of kilometres from home without resources. By the end of May 1997, thousands had been returned to Goma, including many unaccompanied children. Later in September 1997, the government organized the return to Kisangani by river boat for those who had been displaced to Kinshasa during the war.

By December 1997 many IDPs had managed to return to their war ravaged towns and villages, but they continue to live in precarious conditions with no access to basic necessities. By the end of 1997 there were still pockets of refugees and IDPs scattered beyond the reach of relief organizations.

Creating lasting peace and security

The complexity, scale and pattern of the conflict in eastern DRC and the resulting repetitive population displacements make any attempts to estimate the exact number of IDPs impossible. The shocking levels of human suffering experienced by both refugees and IDPs continues to pose serious challenges to the international community.

Despite the relative stability enjoyed elsewhere in the country since Kabila took power, eastern Congo remains unstable with continued armed clashes between government troops and local militias. With an economy on the verge of collapse, a run-down infra-structure and a dysfunctional administrative machinery inherited from the Mobutu regime, the government still does not seem to have the means to achieve lasting peace in the region.

Unless the international community provides the necessary support to the government's effort to revive the country's economy and to restore peace and security, the plight of IDPs will continue and further displacement can be expected. Concentrating efforts on refugees or IDPs alone will neither create the stable socioeconomic context necessary to reduce ethnic tension nor provide the government with the capacity to manage future refugee crises should they arise. The response of the humanitarian assistance system to the complexities, dilemmas and tragedies of displacement must be viewed within a broader framework encompassing the various socioeconomic issues faced by the country.

Kenya
Binaifer Nowrojee

In August 1997, a series of ethnically-driven attacks in the Coast province killed 40 people and displaced more than 120,000, adding to the hundreds of thousands already displaced in similar violence in the early 1990s. The Kenyan government did not provide adequate security or protection to these people, nor did it take any steps to assist them to return to their homes. Armed gangs from coastal ethnic groups razed businesses and homes belonging to people from inland tribes. Several people were killed by machetes. Leaflets were distributed in some areas attacking certain groups. They stated: 'The time has come for us original inhabitants of the coast to claim what is rightly ours. We must remove these invaders from our land.' The warnings and the attacks were strikingly similar to the 'ethnic' violence that had occurred prior to the 1992 elections in the Rift Valley, and targeted some of the same ethnic groups. In those attacks, there was evidence that the Kenyan government had supported the attacks against those ethnic groups it perceived supported the political opposition. Since the violence followed shortly after voter registration ended, some Kenyan human rights activists surmised that the attacks at the coast had been instigated by the government, after voter registration data had indicated that it would lose the Coast province. The government maintained that the violence was the work of local criminals taking advantage of the volatile political climate in an election year. Some 300 arrests were made by the police, including several members of the ruling party – Kenya African National Union (KANU) – and strong statements condemning the violence were made by the government. However, by November 1997 it was still unclear who was behind the violence, although the gangs had reportedly been organized and trained some months prior to the attacks.

Meanwhile, the Kenyan government continued to consolidate the political gains of state-sponsored 'ethnic' violence from the early 1990s. At that time, some 300,000 people from ethnic groups perceived to support the opposition were driven from their land in large-scale attacks. The government instigated the violence after it was forced to concede to demands for a multiparty system, in order to punish and disenfranchise ethnic groups associated with the opposition, while rewarding its supporters with illegally obtained land. President Daniel Arap Moi and his inner circle adopted a calculated policy against ethnic groups associated with the political opposition. Despite Moi's pronouncements, the violence was not a spontaneous reaction to the reintroduction of multiparty politics. The government unleashed terror, provoked displacement and expelled certain ethnic groups *en masse* from their long-time homes and communities in the Nyanza, Western and Rift Valley provinces for political and economic gain. This was particularly true for the Rift Valley province, which hosts the largest number of parliamentary seats and some of the most fertile land in the country. The government capitalized on unaddressed and competing land ownership issues between pastoral groups, such as the Kalenjin and Maasai, who had been ousted from land by colonial British

settlers and the agricultural labourers who settled on the land after independence. Many of these farms were at the centre of the ethnic clashes. During the years that followed this violence, local government officials have continued to countenance fraudulent land transfers and land sales under duress in the Rift Valley province, thus further entrenching the gains.

By 1993, Human Rights Watch/Africa estimated that 1500 people had died in the clashes, and that some 300,000 were internally displaced, of whom an estimated 75 per cent were children. The clashes pitted members of President Moi's small Kalenjin group and the Maasai, against the larger Kikuyu, Luhya and Luo ethnic groups. Kikuyu, Luhya and Luo-owned farms were attacked by organized groups of Kalenjin or Maasai 'warriors' armed with traditional weapons such as bows and arrows. It was subsequently found that ruling party officials had paid some attackers a fee for each house burned and person killed, and that government vehicles had been used to transport the attackers. Security forces often stood by during an attack, and appeals for protection went unheeded. By contrast, counterattacks against the Kalenjin or Maasai were usually more disorganized in character, and less effective in driving people off their land. The great majority of those displaced were members of the Kikuyu Luhya and Luo ethnic groups from the Rift Valley, Western and Nyanza provinces. Following a 1992 election win by President Moi and KANU, the frequency of the attacks diminished, but periodic incidents continued. Meanwhile, those displaced by the attacks fled to nearby churches, market centres or abandoned buildings. Largely ignored by the government, they congregated in squalid conditions, receiving assistance largely from the churches and local NGOs.

In 1993, the UNDP took the initiative to create a reconciliation and reintegration programme, implemented jointly with the government, for those people displaced by the 'ethnic' clashes. The general consensus among local and international NGOs, diplomats and even some UNDP employees who worked on the UNDP's displaced persons' programme in Kenya is that its tremendous potential was never fulfilled. Ultimately, the greatest attention was placed on relief – the easiest and least politically controversial part of the programme to administer. Protection, human rights and long-term needs, which would have required UNDP to adopt a more critical advocacy role in relation to the Kenyan government were neglected. By 1995, the UNDP was immobilized. Because it lacked political will, the UNDP neither used its expertise to address the long-term developmental issues for reintegration nor channelled sufficient pressure on the government. As a result, thousands of people remained displaced when the programme ended in 1995, and the key issues underlying the displacement remained unaddressed.

By the time the UNDP programme began in 1993, levels of violence had diminished significantly, and reintegration had begun to occur in some areas, particularly in Nyanza and Western province. However, at the same time, the government steadily undermined reintegration through active obstruction of reintegration efforts on some fronts and inaction on others. There has never been any government commitment or action to reverse the damage, nor restore the displaced people to their lost land and livelihood without regard for their ethnicity, nor a search for lasting solutions for reconciliation. Although the government did take steps to increase security and protection in some clash areas, there was never any concerted directive to re-establish security in all areas or to create an environment that would have enabled all those displaced people to return to their land.

Even though emergency food and material assistance needs were met in 1993 and 1994, and some reintegration occurred, a climate of mistrust and insecurity persisted in many parts of the Rift Valley. Numerous difficulties remained, largely due to government resistance to full reintegration and a lack of political will by the government to restore security and to address land reform. Kenyan government officials – army, local government, police and politicians – continued to harass and intimidate the displaced people after they were driven from their land.

The government brought charges against those who criticized its policies towards the displaced people, but allowed the instigators and perpetrators of the violence to enjoy complete immunity. Where the displaced people were congregated in groups that could attract negative attention, they were dispersed with threats or force by local government officials, often without regard for their safety and with no alternative accommodation. Those assisting the displaced people or journalists attempting to report on their plight were sometimes denied access to certain areas, arrested or harassed. When reintegration occurred, it was usually due to the efforts of the communities themselves or because a local government official quietly acted on personal initiative. In the more contentious areas, where Kalenjin and Maasai residents had vowed not to permit the displaced to return, or where local or national government leaders obstructed reintegration, no steps were taken by the government to restore the rule of law.

Most importantly, the government took no action to work with UNDP to seek long-term solutions for redress and prevention, particularly with regard to the issue of land registration and tenure. Throughout the programme, the government was able to evade its responsibility to reintegrate by forcibly dispersing identifiable groups of displaced people. Since the UNDP neither prioritized data collection nor conducted a census, it was unable to remedy the situation. NGOs working with displaced people accused it of inflating the estimates of reintegrated people in order to improve the image of its programme.

Due to the lack of data, it is difficult to assess the number of people who remain displaced. However, according to local NGOs that continue to assist displaced people, the number is well over 100,000. To date, the Kenyan government has condoned the illegal occupation of land by its political supporters and the continued displacement of citizens from ethnic groups who are perceived to support the political opposition. The government continues to countenance land transactions that prevent reintegration of displaced people. Land continues to be fraudulently transferred, illegally occupied, and sold or exchanged unfairly, further disempowering the internally displaced people and contributing to the removal of certain ethnic groups from the Rift Valley province. The government has taken the minimum steps necessary to allay public criticism of its policies of ethnic persecution and discrimination. Although some of its actions have promoted reintegration, the Kenyan government has never sought to redress fully the destruction and loss it instigated, nor has it addressed the political grievances that created the conditions for such violence. As a result, many people are still not back on their land, and may never be. In some areas, the effect has been to reduce the numbers of Kikuyu, Luhya and Luo residents, in keeping with the calls by some high-ranking government officials for the expulsion of these ethnic groups from certain areas. More importantly, as the 1997 violence at the Coast province indicates, the grievances that allowed for the manipulation and explosion of ethnic tension can as easily be fanned today as they were in the early 1990s.

Rwanda
Stephanie Kleine-Ahlbrandt

The case of Rwanda raises several key issues concerning internal displacement, particularly those of providing protection within IDP camps, protection against forcible return, the screening of criminal suspects and people alleged to have committed war crimes, and the coordination of international efforts in humanitarian and protection needs. Rwanda also offers insight in the development of effective responses to internal displacement in the wake of complex humanitarian emergencies.

The international community was unable to protect thousands of displaced people, mostly women and children, who were killed in a military operation to close IDP camps in southwest Rwanda in April 1995. Returning refugees who have not yet reached their homes within Rwanda are not considered IDPs for this study. The roots of the tragedy lie in a complex array of historical, institutional and political factors anchored in the international community's unwillingness to face the immense social, human and political consequences of genocide.

During the Rwandan genocide of April to July 1994, the UN withdrew most of its peacekeeping troops (UNAMIR), allowing the extremist Hutu party to carry out its genocidal campaign unopposed until the intervention of the Rwandan Patriotic Front (RPF). The result was the slaughter of between 500,000 and 1 million Tutsis and some Hutus. Massive displacement was caused by the widespread massacres, fear of RPF reprisals as it rapidly took control of the country, and the interim government's orders for Hutus to leave Rwanda. Approximately 500,000 refugees fled into Tanzania and at least a million into Zaire. Combined with the flight of refugees into Burundi and Uganda, approximately two million Rwandans sought exile in neighbouring countries.

By 4 July 1994, the French government created *Opération turquoise* – a 'safe humanitarian zone' in Rwanda's southwest corner, equivalent to about one-fifth of the national territory. At the RPF's proclamation of a new government on 19 July, roughly 1.2 to 1.5 million IDPs had fled to this zone, most of whom had escaped the advance of the Rwandan Patriotic Army (RPA) in June and July. Many of these people susequently fled to Zaire and Burundi, while some returned to their homes or dispersed elsewhere in the country. As the deadline for French withdrawal drew near, a collaborative effort between political, military and international humanitarian organizations successfully encouraged a significant number of the displaced persons in the southwest to remain in Rwanda, rather than continue their flight abroad. When *Opération turquoise* ended on 21 August, some 390,000 IDPs remained in 33 camps.

Government perception of IDPs

The new Rwandan government believed that the IDP camps gave sanctuary to persons implicated in the genocide and were being used for the formation of an anti-government militia. This fear was justified since neither the UN mandate for *Opération turquoise* nor the objectives of the French government included the disarming or arrest of soldiers. Thus, criminal elements intent on destabilizing Rwanda and sabotaging voluntary IDP return, were able to consolidate in the camps. In addition, refugees surrounding Rwanda, both those responsible for the genocide and innocent civilians under their authority, were rearming and launching cross-border incursions. Unable to defuse this threat while the terms of a UN arms embargo appeared to be blatantly flouted and international aid

continued to flow to refugees and IDPs, the government increasingly viewed the IDPs as a threat to its territorial integrity.

Institutional responses

Attempting to fill the void created by the absence of a clear international mandate for IDPs, the UN Department of Humanitarian Affairs established the Integrated Operations Centre (IOC), an interagency coordination body based in the Rwandan Ministry of Rehabilitation in Kigali. The IOC, consisting of representatives of UN agencies, NGOs, major donors and the Rwandan government, attempted to foster dialogue and compromise to solve the IDP problem and served as a focal point for return operations.

Responding to the government's impatience with the continued existence of the IDP camps at the end of 1994, the IOC launched *Opération retour* to facilitate voluntary return. While an estimated 40,000 IDPs returned to their communes of origin during the first six weeks, the number fell significantly at the end of February 1995. Meanwhile, camp populations swelled due to reports of returnee arrests, increasingly overcrowded prison conditions, the illegal occupation of homes as well as a general lack of confidence in public authorities. In the Kibeho camp, for example, the population grew from 70,000 to 115,000 in just a fortnight. Criminal elements manipulated security warnings as tools for propaganda, exerting pressure and intimidation on camp populations to remain. By late March, some 220,000 IDPs still remained in the camps.

The IOC therefore developed a strategy designed to reconcile the government's preoccupation with national security with the international community's concern for 'voluntary return in dignity'. Although the use of force was to be avoided, the strict meaning of 'voluntary return' was compromised: the camps were to be closed in a series by ending food and relief distribution and transferring

RWANDA: IDPs at a way-station in Butare Prefecture receive assistance packages
(PHOTO: A Hollmann/UNHCR).

IDPs to home communes.

Massacre at Kibeho

Prior to the implementation of this strategy, the RPA had already moved on 18 April 1995 to close Kibeho – the largest of the camps – by surrounding it and cutting off its food and water supply. Within the period of a few days there was increasing violence as RPA soldiers attempted to contain crowds and opened fire on stone throwers. The death toll, a subject of acute contention, was probably between the government's estimate of 338 and the UN's figure of 2000. The total population of Kibeho camp was 150,000 according to the camp leader and the UN, and 110,000 according to ICRC and MSF. Several hundred UNAMIR troops were present during the massacre but failed to take action according to their mandate to 'contribute to the security and protection of displaced persons' (Security Council Resolution 918 of 17 May 1994).

Displacement since Kibeho

Within three weeks of the forced closure, the IDP camps in southwest Rwanda were completely evacuated. While many people returned to their home communes, several thousand crossed into Uvira, Zaire. Many returning people avoided registration with local authorities or refused to continue to their homes.

Some IDPs eventually mingled with refugees in camps in Rwanda. For example, a group of approximately 150 Rwandans living among Burundian refugees in Kigeme refugee camp in Gikongoro prefecture were identified by the government and transported back to their homes in Kigali South prefecture in February and May of 1996. To identify remaining IDPs in the country, an identity card system obligated Rwandan citizens to register with authorities in their places of origin.

Lessons learned

The Rwandan IDP crisis was avoidable. There had been several warning signs of the impending disaster. The first involved the differing priorities and perspectives of the Rwandan government and international agencies regarding IDPs. The IOC failed to appreciate the urgent concerns of the Rwandan government and thus heightened RPA suspicions about the international community's intentions. Furthermore, it lacked the flexibility and resources to implement projects with a view to encouraging voluntary IDP return or to devise an effective camp closure strategy within a time frame that would have responded to the government's security concerns.

Moreover, the Rwandan government's participation in the IOC task force was sporadic and non-representative, especially that of the key ministries of defence and of the interior. Clearer recognition that the Rwandan government had in fact rejected the IOC and its principles might have led it to consider a more effective strategy. But the IOC structure diffused responsibility for IDPs. While the IOC's approach may have prevented any single agency from bearing the brunt of criticism, in effect it prevented the development of a realistic, timely and coherent strategy.

Lack of political will

The divergence between the international community and the Rwandan government concerning internal displacement reflected a lack of political will on the part of the international community to develop a coherent approach to the post-genocide situation in Rwanda and in the central African region. Despite its pledges to respect human rights and refrain from reprisal killings, the Rwandan government was starved of necessary resources to rebuild its devastated infrastructure, especially the paralysed judicial system. At the same time, however, donors provided substantial resources for humanitarian assistance to refugee camps in neighbouring countries that harboured forces of the former regime, without supporting efforts to separate those who should have been excluded from refugee status. The slowness in establishing an international criminal tribunal to prosecute individuals for participation in the genocide, further demonstrated a weak commitment to the reconciliation process in Rwanda. Consequently, a peaceful solution to the IDP problem became more difficult.

The inability of the IOC to reconcile humanitarian with political and strategic interests, and its reluctance to recognize the fragility of the consensus between the parties involved, allowed the Kibeho tragedy to occur despite the IOC's commitment to the well-being of innocent civilians in the camp. The failure of the international community to respond to the traumatic consequences of the 1994 conflict on Rwandan society, made the violent camp closure, while tragic, somehow foreseeable. The Rwanda experience indicates that solutions to the problems of internal displacement can neither ignore regional dynamics nor be based on the substitution of humanitarian action for military, political or diplomatic solutions. An opportunity for reconciliation of the positions of the government of Rwanda and the international community could have occurred had the latter been more responsive to the human dimensions and regional implications of the genocide and the massive displacement it caused.

New patterns of internal displacement have occurred in Rwanda in 1997 totalling 180,000 IDPs. Significant displacement occurred at the end of the year in the northwest regions of Gisenyi and Ruhengeri, due to the intensifications of armed conflict between members of armed groups comprised of certain members of the Rwandese armed forces (ex-FAR) and the *Interahamwe* militia, and counterinsurgency operations by the Rwandan Patriotic Army (RPA). The local people have been caught in the middle of the conflict since both armies seek the support of the local population, making it difficult for civilians to remain neutral. While some attacks are indiscriminate, armed groups have targeted returnees, genocide survivors, local civilian authorities and persons considered to be collaborating with the RPA. These attacks are often followed by RPA counterinsurgency operations resulting in high numbers of civilian casualties. Much of the population is therefore disillusioned with the possibility of being protected by the RPA. Thousands of people have left rural areas and outlying sectors to seek safety closer to communal offices and urban locations. By the end of 1997, attacks by armed groups, were not only increasing in number, but also taking place nearer to urban areas.

Following the Kibeho incident, the government of Rwanda remain opposed to the establishment of camps or concentrations of IDPs. While forced return has not reportedly been a problem, people are often encouraged by local officials to return to their home sectors. Many IDPs live 'on the move', sleeping in different locations and rarely returning to their homes.

This situation highlights the problems inherent in providing protection and assistance to IDPs in situations of armed conflict in which humanitarian and UN agencies have limited access to the affected people. Following fatal attacks on several expatriates in northwest Rwanda in early 1997, the majority of international non-governmental organizations withdrew their personnel and suspended activities in the region. The UN Human Rights Field Operation, which recalled its staff from the region in early 1997, undertakes trips to these regions for one to several days at a time, but still does not have access to certain areas. Efforts by WFP to provide food to displaced people in the northwest have been severely frustrated by the precarious security situation, including attacks on its convoys in October–November 1997. This difficult access for humanitarian organizations and UN agencies to the northwest regions of Rwanda makes accurate numbers of IDPs difficult to obtain.

Uganda
Geofrey Mugumya and Erin Mooney

Though internal displacement in Uganda has been a long-standing problem, it was exacerbated throughout 1997 with new displacements of tens of thousands of people having to leave their homes, particularly in the southwest of the country. Armed conflict is the primary cause of displacement: clashes involving three separate insurgencies occurred over half of the country. In the northern districts of Gulu and Kitgum, the Lord's Resistance Army (LRA), comprising mostly of ethnic Acholi and allegedly supported by the government of Sudan, has been active since 1986. Among the insurgent groups, it is widely considered to be the most serious human rights offender, systematically committing attacks on the civilian population, including the mass abduction and forcible recruitment of children. In the northwestern districts of Arua, Moyo and Nebbi, the West Nile Bank Front (WNBF), comprising predominantly ethnic Kakwa and Alinga, has pursued its aim of creating an independent Islamic West Nile state by carrying out insurgent activities, including from bases in Sudan and the Democratic Republic of Congo (DRC), since 1995. In the southwestern districts of Kasese, Kabarole and Bundibugyo, armed clashes between government troops and the more recently formed Allied Democratic Forces (ADF), composed mainly of Muslims of the Salaf sect, have intensified since June 1997 and resulted in massive civilian displacement.

Aside from these various insurgencies, cattle raiding also has caused significant internal displacement over the last decade, especially in the Kitgum, Gulu, Lira, Kabarole and Bushenyi districts. Another category of displaced people within Uganda are the refugees who have returned spontaneously from Sudan and the Democratic Republic of the Congo because of attacks on their camps. They have been unable to return to their home areas due to the lack of security.

Although there is no precise figure for the total population of IDPs in Uganda, it is commonly estimated to be over 400,000 and growing. At least half of the internally displaced population is located in the northern districts of Gulu and Kitgum.

IDPs from areas where LRA attacks against the civilian population are particularly intense have either fled spontaneously to seek refuge in local trading centres or have been relocated by the government to 'protected villages' near army posts. In other areas, 'nocturnal displacement' allows people to work on their farms during the day but requires them to flee insecurity at night, hiding in churches, caves and in the bush.

National response
The government recognizes its responsibility for addressing the plight of IDPs and has requested international assistance in this regard, particularly in the areas of food, health and sanitation. Even so, certain needs of displaced people, especially protection, require greater attention. In the north, the government relocated civilians to 'protected villages' for their own safety. The location of these settlements near military detachments, however, is problematic, for it exposes the uprooted people to the dangers of crossfire. On the other hand, distancing the villages from military detachments would make it more difficult for the military to respond quickly in the event of an insurgent attack. Insofar as such attacks target the civilian

population more often than military detachments, the present arrangement appears the
better of the two options. It is one that could
be enhanced, however, especially since
logistical and communications problems
reportedly impair the capacity of the army to
provide effective protection to IDPs in the
'protected villages'.

At the national level, the Ministry of
Labour and Social Welfare is responsible for
meeting the needs of IDPs. The government
also has established in each affected district a
disaster management committee (DMC)
responsible for the distribution and
management of relief. While such institutional
mechanisms provide a framework for
addressing the needs of IDPs, national and
local capacities need strengthening.
Accordingly, UNDP has been assisting the
government in formulating a disaster
management and preparedness policy and,
together with UNICEF, has been
strengthening the capacity of the DMC for
more effective management of relief support
for IDPs.

International response

A number of international humanitarian and
development agencies, most notably WFP,
UNICEF, ICRC and UNDP, as well as NGOs
including the NRC, undertake activities on
behalf of IDPs. UNHCR limits its benefits to
Sudanese refugees in northern Uganda despite
a request in 1996 from the government to
extend its activities to the internally displaced
population in the same area. It is noteworthy
in this regard that UNHCR previously had
been involved with IDPs in Uganda from 1979
to 1981.

With a view to coordinating the
humanitarian response, UN agencies have
formed the UN Disaster Management Team
(UNDMT) and a Humanitarian Assistance
Coordination Unit (HACU), the latter of
which is specifically mandated to coordinate
assistance to IDPs but does not include

protection in its terms of reference.

Gaps in protection and assistance

Notwithstanding national efforts, most
notably in the creation of the 'protected
villages', the government lacks sufficient
capacity to provide effective protection to
IDPs. Technical and logistical assistance is
required to strengthen national capacities to
assist IDP returns, particularly in the area of
clearing landmines, which is essential for
people's safety during their search for
firewood. Technical assistance could also help
remove the logistical and communications
bottlenecks that reportedly impair the
government's capacity to provide protection.

Most reported threats to personal security
are attributable to insurgent forces, which
raises the question of whether significant
protection is possible while conflict persists.
The ICRC meanwhile makes efforts to
familiarize government troops and insurgent
forces alike with the standards of international
humanitarian law.

Local sources report incidences of discrimination against IDPs by host communities, lack of documentation for IDPs, round-
ups of IDPs in Gulu municipality on the suspicion that they are sympathizers or collaborators with the opposing forces, and forcible
return to areas still considered unsafe. IDPs
returning briefly to their fields and gardens do
so at considerable risk. Continued insecurity
in several areas to which IDPs return,
temporarily or otherwise, underlines the need
for monitoring the safety of returnees as well
as of areas of potential return.

There are reports of women being raped
in and around IDP settlements. The local
press also have reported incidents of women
being attacked, often by other women, at
water points on the suspicion that they are
collaborators with rebel forces. To address
these and other protection concerns of
internally displaced women, attention needs
to be paid to practical preventive measures

such as adequate lighting near latrines and escorts for women when they fetch water or firewood. Such measures as set forth in detail in UNHCR's *Guidelines on the Protection of Refugee Women* provide a useful reference for the government, UN and NGOs involved in the management of the IDP camps. There are also reports of women having to exchange sexual favours to obtain food rations and supplies. In order to avoid such problems, WFP has wisely taken the decision to distribute food only through women. This practice should be adopted by other relief efforts and extended to non-food items as well.

Children, boys and girls alike, are at severe risk of forcible conscription by insurgent forces, especially the LRA, which relies on this practice to furnish at least 50 per cent of its troop strength. While hundreds of children have managed to escape, their home communities may be reluctant to accept them, for fear of reprisals from the LRA. Moreover, the psychological trauma suffered by abducted children makes their reintegration difficult. In several areas of the country, UNICEF and several NGOs provide much-needed reintegration and psychosocial support to those children who manage to escape. Among returning girls, the problem of sexually transmitted diseases is widespread. The World Health Organization (WHO) is assisting the Ministry of Health in ensuring the availability

of medication for those affected, but these efforts are hampered by a lack of health workers. That many health workers themselves have fled from conflict areas suggests that serious problems remain in the areas to which the abducted children are returning. Although some positive preventive work has been done, abductions persist in some areas. Human rights monitoring and advocacy, such as the work of Amnesty International and UNICEF, could be expanded.

Where displacement continues and safe return is not possible, income-generating activities for IDPs become particularly important. The UNDMT has identified carpentry, masonry and tailoring as some of the areas in which skills training among IDPs would be useful, especially for women.

Conclusion

Displacement in Uganda has traditionally related to refugees, both in terms of exodus and influx. In recent years, however, internal displacement has grown enormously, and IDPs are currently double the number of refugees in the country. The latest available figure for internally displaced people was estimated at 400,000 in March 1998. Recent events indicate that the number of IDPs in Uganda may continue to rise as hostilities escalate.

IDP Figures – Horn of Africa

Conflict-induced:

Sudan	2,600,000
Ethiopia	15,000
Eritrea	unknown
Somalia	250–350,000

0   km   600

SAUDI ARABIA

Port Sudan

Red Sea Province

Red Sea

SUDAN

Gash Barka Province

Asmara

ERITREA

YEMEN

Khartoum

Om Hagar

White Nile Province

Tigray Province

Makale

Gulf of Aden

Kost

Nuba Mountains

Damazin

DJIBOUTI

Somaliland

Addis Ababa

ETHIOPIA

Jonglie Province

Bor

Bahr-el-Ghazal Province

Juba

Equatoria Province

SOMALIA

Yei

Torit

Mogadishu

UGANDA

KENYA

Indian Ocean

Kismayo

Map 3: Horn of Africa

Horn of Africa

Overview
Ana Maria Harkins

The political upheavals in the Horn of Africa over the last ten years have provided a chilling precedent for those concerned with complex emergencies. Population displacement emerged as a strategy, rather than simply a by-product, of the civil wars in Ethiopia and Sudan. The connection between refugees and the fuelling of cross-border insurgency in Sudan, Ethiopia, Uganda and Somalia is well documented. Aid agencies in the 1980s faced the stark reality that famine itself had become a weapon of war. In Sudan, Somalia and Ethiopia, not only have IDPs fled their villages, but established camps have been attacked. Food aid is not always neutral; it often brings the international humanitarian community into the war strategies of the various fighting factions.

The UN's access to conflict areas in the Horn of Africa was severely restricted in the 1980s. The situation changed dramatically in 1989 when Operation Lifeline Sudan (OLS) established the principle of 'humanitarian access' in wartime, made possible by negotiating parity of distribution to both sides of the conflict. Soon after, the hugely expensive, and ultimately flawed, interventions in Somalia became synonymous with 'failed aid' and the withdrawal of military humanitarianism. Throughout this period, internally displaced people adapted and responded by moving from outlying areas to be closer to the aid distribution points. Traditional coping mechanisms such as nomadic migrations and the storing of foodstuffs had been disrupted. In Sudan, convoys of food destined for the south are frequently impounded by the government, which shows little concern for the civilians caught on the 'wrong' side of a seemingly endless war. Beyond the reach of aid organizations, there is essentially no protection for these IDPs.

Almost a million people have returned to Ethiopia since the fall of communism in 1991. Many have not returned to their original homes but have found a durable subsistence living elsewhere. Drought is the main cause of the displacement of 15,000 people today. Sudan, by contrast, has 2–4 million internally displaced people, including an estimated 2.5 million around the capital, Khartoum. The almost total destruction of pastoralism for most southerners will result in increasing urbanization. In Somalia, the highly factionalized population will find it increasingly difficult to sustain an economy given the anarchy that grips the country. In the absence of a central government, the Somalia Aid Coordinating Body was created to establish aid policies and to serve IDPs. Assistance needs to be geared toward promoting local capacities and self-reliance. In southern Sudan, attempts are being made to foster rehabilitation.

In Eritrea, the efficiency of the government may have offset some of the worst problems inherited from the 1980s, but some conflict-induced displacement continues, particularly in the Red Sea Hills. Villagization has led to involuntary displacement; the tensions between traditional semi-nomadic lifestyles and the demands of environmental control and central economic planning are likely to persist.

Eritrea

Art Hansen and Mark Davidheiser

Three decades of warfare from the early 1960s to the early 1990s, as well as intermittent droughts and famines from the 1970s into the 1990s, caused many Eritreans to become displaced both externally and internally. The southwestern lowland region of Eritrea was known as Lower Barka during colonial times, and was renamed Gash-Setit when Eritrea became independent in 1991, and more recently was subsumed into Gash-Barka province. This frontier region (bordering both Sudan to the west and Ethiopia to the south) is especially significant to the future of Eritrea because returning refugees are being encouraged by the Eritrean government to resettle there. Simultaneously, the government has been forcing or encouraging villagization of existing residents.

Eritrea has not been characterized by clearly homogeneous areas in which race, language, religion or livelihood coincided, and the interweaving has been made more complicated by historical migrations and by people changing their religions, livelihoods and identities. The Gash-Setit region is a complex socioeconomic environment with seven different languages (Arabic, Hidareb, Kunama, Nara, Saho, Tigré, and Tigrigna) and a history of high population mobility, ethnic mixing and a rapid transformation of social and economic life. Everyone in the region has been responding for decades to the major stresses of war, drought and hunger.

The following are some important historical dates relating to warfare and drought. In 1961, Ato Hamed Idris Awate announced the start of the armed struggle against Ethiopian rule. A lot of fighting took place in the Gash-Setit region, causing entire villages to move or be abandoned. In 1969, villages in Shandeshna district were burned

and abandoned; in 1976 the town of Om Hager was bombed and abandoned; and in 1980 the town of Guluj was burned and abandoned. During 1984/5 there was a drought, and many people and livestock died or were forced to migrate. Warfare continued until 1988 and, when the Ethiopian army was defeated, they retreated through the region *en route* to asylum in Sudan. Between 1989 and 1991 most areas experienced drought, and there was a major locust infestation in 1993. Villagers either fled from the warfare and drought as refugees to Sudan or Ethiopia, or were displaced within Eritrea. Many migrated into the Gash-Setit region fleeing war and drought. Widespread displacement caused by warfare occurred in waves that were triggered by discrete incidents that motivated one or more specific villages to flee.

Higger district shows how a peacetime advantage can become a wartime disadvantage. Location on or near a main road is helpful during peacetime, and roadside villages are usually more developed than the villages that are more isolated and harder to reach by vehicle. During wartime, the roadside location can be deadly, as both sides struggle to control the roads.

During the 1960s most of the villagers living near a road sought refuge in Sudan, where many still remain. The rest scattered into the bush or mountains to live in other nearby villages, or moved to start new village sites. Now that the war is over, the roadside villages are slowly being repopulated. None of the inhabitants of villages further away from the road became refugees or internally displaced, though they would flee into the mountains or bush for several days at a time if soldiers or fighting came too close.

Grenfit district village experiences during the war varied with ethnic identity and length of residence in the district. As with other districts of mixed (Kunama-Tigré) ethnicity, the Kunama were resident before most of the Tigré arrived. Tigré villagers had immigrated into the district because of the 1984/5 drought and were 'looking for better grazing'. Two of the Tigré villages were related and had a complex migration history. They had moved into the district long ago but fled back to Barka in 1967 after Ethiopian bombings; at that time many of their relatives from another village fled as refugees. Another Tigré village split into four because people were afraid of air raids if they remained as a large village.

Fanco subdistrict contains mixed villages with different ethnic groups having different wartime experiences. One village was burned by Ethiopian soldiers who took the villagers to the town of Tesseney; the villagers later returned and rebuilt their homes (similar stories were heard in many of the Guluj district villages). The inhabitants of sections of two other villages also migrated because Ethiopians had burned down their homes.

Guluj district's violent history has generated many IDPs and refugees. People in four of the six villages surveyed were forcibly relocated in the town of Guluj by the Ethiopians after the villages were burned. In one case, 55 villagers were killed. Guluj itself was then burned by the Ethiopians in 1980, which caused the flight of many more people. Only one village was not moved because of the war, but those people did not immigrate into the district until forced by the 1984 drought.

Om Hager district (bordering Ethiopia and Sudan) also has a violent history that generated many refugees. The town of Om Hager was attacked by the Ethiopians and was abandoned for years. A village was also abandoned. Both have been partly repopulated by returning refugees and people who were internally displaced by war or drought.

Development-induced displacement

In 1994 the government was implementing a villagization programme, one type of forced internal displacement. Villagization means relocating villages much closer to each other and may also include their social or political incorporation into larger village units. The development-oriented rationale is that the government will be able to provide facilities such as schools and clinics more easily and economically to larger villages than to many small villages. The extent of planned villagization in the region varies among districts.

Many villagers were outspoken in their opposition to being moved. One of the biggest problems about villagization is that it moves people away from their farmlands and water sources. Most villages are currently sited close to the farmlands and grazing. The new central village sites are often located a great distance away from people's farmlands, which means that, to be able to keep farming, they would have to walk long distances with their tools. Although the government promised to provide a school, clinic and potable water at each new central village site, few such facilities have been provided, which is one reason why a number of villages are rejecting villagization. Villagers are reluctant to move to sites where the water may be inadequate when they are leaving behind established and adequate supplies of drinking water. Several villages also face major economic losses by relocation because they are currently living close to sources of drinking water they can exploit by raising livestock.

Another issue was that new villages may be relocated on other villages' farmlands, converting farmland into residential land. The host village, which loses valuable farmland, will resent the newcomers, who recognize they have no traditional right to be there. This attacks the existence and enforcement of the traditional (and still current at the village level) system of land tenure and law in which the elders of each village can adjudicate.

There were some villages where people felt comfortable with the change and even welcomed the relocation. In these cases, the displacement is not forced.

Nutritional needs

In early 1994, there was a widespread need for short-term food relief throughout the region because almost all the villagers in the province were experiencing a severe shortage of staple foods (sorghum and pearl millet). Instead of being able to rely on their own stored supply of the major staple food (sorghum), villagers were searching daily for work to buy sorghum for that day. With this hand-to-mouth existence, everything that people earned went immediately into food to eat.

Long-term food security is another key issue. Agencies should focus on existing agricultural and ecological systems and should learn how to increase sustainable production and develop the local physical (water-management projects, roads) and institutional (farmers' groups, extension-farmer relationships) infrastructure. Food and income crops, livestock, and indigenous plants are all important, for people use them in their search for sustainable survival strategies. Non-domesticated indigenous plant species become especially important during years when domesticated crops fail, and many of the woodland trees and plants are important in construction and income-generation. Off-farm employment is also important for many people during the dry season and especially during years of drought or locusts.

War, drought and famine have been factors in generating waves of IDPs and refugees, and a current programme of villagization is forcing more displacement. Internal displacement has varied from villagers fleeing for only a few days at a time into nearby mountains to the destruction and abandonment of entire villages and towns. This border region is the home of many IDPs and is also a key destination for many repatriating refugees. Therefore, this region has critical immediate needs for assistance and

is important in the future development of Eritrea. The government and international organizations need to focus on short- and long-term food security, the settlement of repatriating refugees, and the peaceful integration of IDPs, residents and repatriating refugees.

The worst regional floods in over 30 years affected parts of southern and eastern Eritrea at the end of 1997. The Eritrean Red Cross assisted 400 families with shelter materials while the government provided food assistance.

Ethiopia
Steve Redding and Art Hansen

In 1991, Ethiopia emerged from a period of authoritarian socialism, severe food shortage and chronic civil conflict under President Mengistu Haile Miriam, into a constitutionally based federal republic making a transition from relief to development. The Ethiopian government's policy of recognition of ethnic groups and ethnic areas has quelled a number of civil conflicts and brought the majority of the previously conflictive partners to the table in a government of national unity.

Ethiopians forced to flee their homes due to civil conflict in the 1970s and 1980s continued to return home. An estimated one million have returned since 1991. Many have not returned to their original homes, preferring to remain either in special camps (where recent repatriates continue to receive UNHCR assistance) or integrate into local communities.

The past seasons of good rain have stabilized the country's food production and wiped out the food deficit, which was so devastating in the mid-1980s. GDP has grown by 7 per cent in the last year and inflation has been brought down to below 2 per cent per annum. Most of this development has been restricted to the areas in and around Addis Ababa, the capital, leaving a base of extreme poverty in the rural areas that still exist on subsistence agriculture. This leaves them vulnerable to environmental changes and droughts, especially as their per capita income remains around US$ 120 per year. It is this fragility that could lead to increased displacement. At the beginning of 1997 there were less than 15,000 IDPs in the whole country. The displacement is largely seasonal and based on crop failure in small areas, and in pastoral areas due to cross border cattle raids from Kenya, Somalia and Sudan. However, severe flooding at the end of 1997 caused thousands to be displaced particularly in the Somali regional state in Ethiopia. The International Federation of the Red Cross claimed that 65,000 people were displaced by floods, though access is severely hampered by conditions on the ground.

In February 1997 the ICRC assisted 2000 displaced families in the Dolo area of Ethiopia, near the point where the borders of Ethiopia, Somali and Kenya converge. The families had fled the tense situation on the Ethiopia/Somali border. Around 10,000 people of the Merehan and Rahanwein tribes were receiving no assistance from either the authorities or international organizations. These people also included about 3000 Rahanwein who had fled fighting in Baidoa in Somalia. In the absence of any formal recognition of refugee status – and the fact that these tribes traverse an indistinctive border – their status as 'displaced' is appropriate.

Systems to monitor the climatic changes and crop yields in the country have been linked to emergency response mechanisms within the government to ensure effective targeting and rapid response to food short-ages. Agricultural early warning systems and a strategic grain reserve should prevent nutri-tion crises that would lead to population movement toward food sources. Therefore, the country's internal coping mechanisms and those of the international community work well to treat any displacement emergencies.

Somalia
Steve Redding and Art Hansen

The British and Italian protectorates of Somaliland and Somalia joined in 1960 to form the independent Somali Republic. The united Somalia experienced difficulties in its first decades under a succession of leaders, culminating finally in the accession to power of Siyad Barre in 1969. Barre's highly centralized and authoritarian regime promised reforms under the heading of scientific socialism, and did much to quell internal dissent while the Cold War superpowers provided tacit and material support for the regime.

In the early 1980s, rebel movements began to spread as Barre's authority began to wane. In 1988, the fighting escalated in the northwest and led to a civil war throughout the country. The rebel groups formed an alliance in 1990 and drove the battle closer to Mogadishu. They forced Barre and his troops out of the capital and into exile in early 1991. This marked a new phase of the Somali conflict. The informal alliance of rebel forces broke up along clan lines and engaged the entire country in an anarchic civil war of which Mogadishu was the centre. In the same year, the rebel faction Somali National Movement (SNM) in northwest Somalia declared an independent state of Somaliland and appointed a breakaway government. Meanwhile, in southern Somalia, the United Somali Congress (USC) forces, under Farah Aideed battled in the streets of Mogadishu with the forces of Ali Mahdi.

In 1992, the United Nations Operations in Somali (UNOSOM) sent its first 500 soldiers

SOMALIA: Returnees and IDPs in Gedo Region receiving assistance from a UNHCR-funded 'Quick Impact Project' (QIP) (PHOTO: B Press/UNHCR).

to Somalia to protect relief supplies. Although further UN troops were subsequently brought in, the force proved ineffective and, in December 1992, UN Resolution 794 authorized 40,000 troops (three-quarters of them from the USA) to be sent under the United Nations Task Force (UNITAF). It was an unprecedented fiasco, now much cited in the annals of aid history. By March 1995 almost all troops had withdrawn, leaving Somalia in perhaps an even worse state of anarchy. To date, no authority has been established at Mogadishu, with armed clans still in shifting control of areas in the south. Fighting has erupted again in south Mogadishu as a result of personal disputes among clans controlling different areas. Tension is still high in the Jowhar/central regions, and in Kismayo and the southern regions sporadic looting has continued as rival clans vie for power. Northeastern Somalia has

been quiet recently, but is still subject to random acts of violence.

The north has followed its own path. After the declaration of the independent state of Somaliland, the government of President Igal has brought the clans together and formed a relatively peaceful climate in which economic and social rehabilitation is taking place.

Events causing displacement

The character of Somalia's displaced people is complicated by several factors. Since the civil war, virtually everyone has either had to leave the country or has been permanently displaced following fighting. A large part of the population is nomadic, and so has no fixed residence. The war has taught Somalis how to be resourceful and, therefore, they can easily 'displace' themselves if there is an opportunity to gain something by it through relief channels. These factors make it almost impossible to put a fixed number on IDPs within Somalia at any one time.

The United States Agency for International Development (USAID) estimated at the end of 1995 that there was a total of 350,000 displaced people in all areas of the country. Through the vagaries of war, this number has increased and decreased over time. In 1996, it had fallen to an estimated 250,000 internally displaced people and increased again throughout 1997. These fluctuations can only be monitored by the increase in new admissions in feeding programmes in different parts of the country.

Recently, in south Mogadishu, feeding programmes reported increases in new admissions for both supplementary and therapeutic feeding. In north Mogadishu, therapeutic feeding numbers have been decreasing, while supplementary feeding numbers are on the rise. The IDP cases seem to be coming from villages to the urban centres, suggesting that the prevailing drought conditions might have as much to do with the movements as the endemic insecurity.

The needs of the IDPs are driven by their access to food: in the rural areas, far from city markets, access is more limited than in the urban centres. Security is a major concern for everyone in Somalia, although the nomadic population has largely learned to live with a pervasive level of insecurity. The insecurity and weak economic structure in the country have made the displaced people more susceptible to drought and chronic food shortages.

Health services for IDPs are much needed. The civil war and the absence of a central government have wiped out the government health service. Health care is provided by NGOs and through market channels at a cost. IDPs are outside the system of health coverage and are constantly on the move, so cannot access health cards, or undergo any long-term treatments. There are too few clinics to provide for the settled population, let alone the IDPs who come and go.

There is a constant problem of providing education to families in flight. Schools should be tailored to the needs of nomadic youth, and practical skills should be taught, beside the normal regime of literacy and numeracy.

As in other chronic emergency situations, women and children are the most vulnerable. Many female-headed families, whose men are either serving with the clan militias or dead, have gravitated toward the urban centres in search of food and health services for their malnourished children. The special health needs of women of childbearing age are also important. Emergency services are needed in the south of the country, whereas in the north rehabilitation after periods of displacement is needed most.

There are far fewer vulnerable people in the northwest than in the south. In an expanded (though still quite limited) economy, the northwest is busy rebuilding houses to accommodate the new arrivals expected from refugee camps in Ethiopia.

Somalia's relief network is governed by an overseeing aid body of donors and NGOs known as the Somalia Aid Coordinating Body (SACB). This group has established humanitarian ground rules for engagement in Somalia and, in the absence of a functioning government, works as a clearing house for aid policy. Most of the relief work is shared out to local and international NGOs in an informal framework. This minimizes duplication or conflicting action among the member organizations. Aid is also coordinated through the growing village council movement, which acts as a grass roots administration. Village councils represent a potential for institutionalization of care for IDPs. Several NGOs are working with village councils to build their capacity for self-help.

In the past, great emphasis was put on revitalizing Somalia's market economy through the monetization of food for relief. In fact, USAID's programme for Somalia was based on this principle, which replaced much of the market infrastructure that existed before in areas where security could be guaranteed. An expanded market base would provide more opportunities to absorb IDPs into a productive economy.

IDPs tend to group around larger towns and relief programmes where they will have the chance to get resources. Informal local protection has developed along the lines of clan and subclan affiliation and alliance in some areas. In the northwest the government has followed a policy of giving land to IDPs for agriculture to re-establish them. In other areas of the country IDPs are outside the mainstream of Somali society.

Somali IDPs are not effectively monitored and there is a lack of information on numbers and conditions within the country. A good place to start would be to define, in the Somali context, who is an IDP, and the level of needs these people have. Currently aid is indiscriminate with little follow-up, even for those in receipt of assistance.

There is fundamental work to be done with the village councils to make them better stewards of IDPs in their areas. This would include sensitivity training in the special needs and conditions of IDPs, resources to provide basic needs to them, and monitoring and evaluation tools to help track their conditions. Capacity building is already underway in a number of the villages by a host of NGOs: a specific component dealing with IDPs could be included.

In the northwest, where there is a more stable environment for work with IDPs, the gaps are in the provision of fertile land, health infrastructure and primary and secondary education. Economic recovery projects include micro-enterprise and agriculture training projects, but resources for such projects are limited.

Some 13 UN agencies continue to provide emergency humanitarian assistance to Somalia in collaboration with 50 international and 10 national NGOs. In December 1996, a UN consolidated appeal requested US$ 46.5 million from the international community (plus US$ 54 million for the various UN agencies' own programmes). By August 1997 about half of this had been received.

The UN estimated in December 1997 that there are approximately 1,170,000 internally displaced Somalis. But there may actually be a confusion with the number of people requiring emergency assistance, those on food for work projects, returnees and IDPs.

Sudan
Laurel Fain, Art Hansen, Steve Redding and Patty Swahn

Sudan has been ravaged by civil conflict for 30 of the last 40 years, the most recent outbreak of which began in 1983. Government forces and the National Islamic Front (the northern Sudanese fundamentalist Islamic party) have been fighting a range of opposition organizations. Although some organizations are based in northern Sudan and are Islamic, the conflict is often summarized as a civil war between the Islamic north and the Christian or animist south. In April 1997 a peace accord was signed between the government and four of the rebel factions: the United Democratic Salvation Front, the Sudanese People's Liberation Movement, the South Sudan Independence Group, and the Equatoria Defence Forces. The main rebel faction, the Sudan People's Liberation Army (SPLA), refused to enter the peace process. It has made large gains in Bahr el Ghazal and Western Equatoria, and threatens the southern capital and government garrison of Juba in Eastern Equatoria.

Combatant forces have repeatedly targeted civilian populations by burning and bombing villages and abducting civilians. Sudanese attempting to return to their homes or to establish themselves in a new area are commonly forced to flee once more when their village is seized by a new faction. At times, access to populations in need has been denied to relief workers, and established camps for refugees and displaced persons have been attacked.

Four million Sudanese can currently be labelled IDPs. Of these, 90,000 are reported to be in Juba. Approximately 170,000 displaced people live in official camps in the south, and hundreds of thousands have settled themselves in rural southern areas without any official aid. There are also smaller pockets of displaced persons throughout Sudan, such as the Red Sea province, which had about 8000 IDPs as of December 1996, and the Kordofan states (14,270). In December 1997, IDPs in greater Khartoum numbered 2.6 million, with 80,000 in four official camps and the rest in squatter and settlement areas. The government has reportedly been conducting a 'campaign of genocide' against the Nuba peoples of south Kordofan state. According to Africa Rights Watch, parts of the Nuba mountains lie under the control of opposition factions and the population has been targeted for destruction by government forces. Many Nuba have fled destruction from shelling and landmines, though there are no reliable estimates for IDP figures. The Sudanese government states that military manoeuvres in the Nuba mountains do not represent the campaign of genocide and gross violations of human rights reported by Africa Rights Watch, but are merely a military response to the latest SPLA offensive. However, in 1996 the UN Security Council voted to impose diplomatic sanctions and flight restrictions on Sudan because of the government's support of international terrorist activities and reported human rights violations.

In January 1997, what was described by the government as an attack by Ethiopians and Eritreans in the south Blue Nile area displaced between 27,000 and 50,000 people. Of the displaced, about 10,000 fled into the city of Damazin, where many were taken in by relatives. Approximately 12,000 others were forced to move to official displaced camps around Damazin, while the rest of the displaced were hosted by families in rural areas between their own destroyed villages and the city.

While the entire country has been transformed by 14 years of war, most of the fighting has taken place in southern Sudan, where more than one million have been killed and around 650,000, or 80 per cent of the current estimated population of southern Sudan (Bahr el Ghazal, Upper Nile and Equatoria), have had to flee their homes. The bulk of those displaced belong to the Dinka and Nuer ethnic groups, who are primarily pastoralists, though many have shifted to settled agriculture over the years. Almost all displacement has been from rural areas to other rural areas or to small towns.

In official displaced camps, the displaced have no claim to the land on which they live, but have better access to services and receive more relief aid from both government agencies and NGOs than other areas. In squatter areas, IDPs have no legal rights to the land on which they build homes, which may belong to other individuals or the government, and typically have extremely limited access to services. In official settlement areas (often called peace villages), IDPs are allotted a plot of land and are entitled to buy the leasehold title to it from the government, though individual rights in these areas remain unclear.

The main reason for displacement is lack of security. In the wet season roads become impassable and IDPs largely stay put. The dry season is the traditional period for offensives by the opposing combatants, and the consequent movement of populations. Secondary to security, economic hardship also impels movement. In the northern regions of the south (Bahr el Ghazal and Jonglei/Upper Nile), sparse rainfall allows only bare subsistence agriculture. The Equatorias' relatively wetter climates provide more of an agricultural base, and frequently produce surpluses. These, however, tend to rot on the ground as impassable roads in the rainy season and insecurity of movement in the dry season make access to markets extremely difficult.

Health infrastructure in southern Sudan is non-existent. Guinea worm infection, on the decline in all other parts of Africa, is still prevalent. Sleeping sickness has recently developed into epidemic proportions in Western Equatoria. For IDPs, simple nutrition is paramount. The malnutrition rate among children stands at 34 per cent (moderate and severely underweight) throughout the region, while adult nutrition is not much better. Currently, the WFP relief effort is only able to provide between 3 and 5 per cent of the area's total nutritional needs. Poor nutritional status renders children and women of childbearing age especially vulnerable to tropical diseases, which waste them further. Reproductive health services for women of childbearing age are needed, as well as health and immunization programmes targeted at the young.

In areas that are relatively secure, self-reliance programmes are needed to promote rehabilitation. These would include micro-enterprise projects, skills development projects and small agricultural schemes.

Southern Sudan's major aid effort is coordinated by Operation Lifeline Sudan (OLS), a UNICEF-sponsored umbrella. In conjunction with WFP, OLS aims to deliver material and food to southern Sudan by a daily air bridge. Reduced international funding of OLS has undermined its effectiveness almost as much as the Sudanese government's obstructive attitude in refusing flight clearances. Donors have limited their pledges

in an effort to push the UN into reforming OLS's operations, making them more cost effective through restructuring and cost recovery.

IDPs in southern Sudan are virtually unprotected. Geography and politics keep them outside the country's legal framework. Where they are able, they drift to IDP camps in search of the meagre food and services provided, and come under the informal protection of the NGOs running the camps. This is a protection negotiated with the effective administration of the area, and can easily be lost when control of the area changes.

Factors other than the civil war also displaced Sudanese people in 1996. The government forcibly relocated approximately 3000 IDP families in the Khartoum area, many to areas with no or inadequate services. Severe droughts in western Sudan forced many to migrate to camps and settlement areas in Khartoum for survival. From July to September, heavy rains in the Khartoum area affected tens of thousands of families by destroying houses, threatening livelihoods and creating environmental and health hazards.

The displaced people of Khartoum live in squalid lodgings made of mud or poles and scraps of plastic, with limited access to water, health care and food, and few opportunities for employment. Major causes of morbidity and mortality include malaria, diarrhoeal diseases and acute respiratory infections, increasing dramatically during the rainy season due to poor sanitation and drainage. In 1997, the government announced its housing plan, which was to include the clearing of squatter areas, the dismantling of displaced camps and the relocation of residents to peace villages on the extreme fringes of greater Khartoum. Thousands of homes in Karton Kassala and Khartoum North have been destroyed, while the residents are supposed to move to Hai Barraka, an empty site 10 kilometres east in the desert, without even the most basic services.

The IDP camps in the town of Kosti in White Nile province are populated by displaced agriculturalists who are unable to farm due to prohibitive demands and restrictions placed on land use by local landlords. The only sources of income for them are scarce opportunities for casual labour, which require frequent travel. In Red Sea province, displaced farmers have adopted alternative sources of income including the production of charcoal and firewood, but resources are very scarce.

The availability of information about the displaced in Sudan is strictly limited by government restrictions. It is extremely difficult for any organization to conduct surveys or gather other forms of data in the camps and settlement areas. The lack of data and coordination, along with restrictions imposed by the government, are among the greatest challenges faced by NGOs working in the Khartoum area.

Cabinda

DEMOCRATIC REPUBLIC OF CONGO

IDP Figures – Southern Africa

Conflict-induced:
Angola   1,200,000
Mozambique   30–50,000
South Africa   20,000+

Luanda

Malanje

Lobito
Benguela

ANGOLA   Luena

Cubal   Jamba   *Moxico
Province*

Menongue

ZAMBIA

ZIMBABWE   Beira

MOZAMBIQUE

NAMIBIA

BOTSWANA

Johannesburg   Maputo

SWAZILAND

KwaZulu-Natal

LESOTHO   Pietermaritzburg

*Atlantic
Ocean*

**SOUTH
AFRICA**

*Indian
Ocean*

Cape Town

0   km   600

Map 4: Southern Africa

Southern Africa

Overview
Bronwen Manby

The end of the conflict in Mozambique in October 1992 and the installation of a democratically elected government in South Africa have led to a great reduction in the numbers of IDPs in southern Africa. An estimated three million people were displaced in Mozambique and almost all have now returned to their homes, or to where they intend to settle. In South Africa, more than 3.5 million people were displaced by National Party government 'bantustan' policies of forced removal, and more than half a million by political violence leading up to the 1994 elections. Forced removals have ceased, and the new government has begun programmes of land redistribution and resettlement to alleviate some of the legacy of the past. However, little has been done to assist those displaced by political violence, and in Kwazulu–Natal, the most volatile province, fresh conflict is still causing new displacements.

Angola remains the main source of IDPs in the southern African region, as its 30-year civil war continues, despite a range of peace accords. UN bodies estimate that approximately 1.2 million Angolans are internally displaced, with another 300,000 refugees outside the country. Regional assistance efforts for IDPs are concentrated in Angola. Fighting during 1997 displaced several thousand more people – many of them no doubt displaced several times before. The number of IDPs in the southern African region is between 1.5 and 2 million.

Migration to South Africa to escape war or persecution or in search of better economic opportunities has increased dramatically since 1994. While formal recruitment of mineworkers has dropped, an estimated 300,000 Mozambicans who fled to South Africa during the 1980s have remained in the country (their compatriots in other countries having mainly returned to Mozambique). They have been joined by hundreds of thousands of other Africans, leading to a rise in xenophobia in South Africa against 'unchecked' immigration and demands for the borders to be closed. A government Green Paper has resisted these calls, and recommends a more 'rights-based' immigration policy, with favourable treatment for citizens of the Southern African Development Community (SADC). In the meantime, deportations under existing legislation continue, although the South African government has introduced an *ad hoc* procedure for dealing with refugees, using the wider definition set out in the OAU refugee convention. South Africa has, however, resisted calls for free movement of labour within SADC, and, with the entry of the Democratic Republic of Congo to the organization, will no doubt continue to do so.

Angola
Alex Vines

Angola has known little peace in the past 30 years. It has experienced three wars, the independence war (1963–74), the post independence war (1974–92) and the post-multiparty election war (October 1992–November 1994) when UNITA (National Union for the Total Independence of Angola) rebels rejected electoral defeat and returned to conflict. This recent war was the most devastating: the UN estimates that more than

300,000 died, 3 per cent of the population. At its peak in 1993, as many as 1000 people were dying daily from conflict, starvation, and disease – more than in any other conflict in the world at that time. By September 1994, the UN Secretary-General reported that there were nearly 3.7 million Angolans, mostly internally displaced and conflict-affected, in need of emergency supplies, including essential medicines, vaccines and food aid.

The third war was notable for widespread systematic violations of human rights by both the government and the UNITA rebels. In particular, indiscriminate shelling of starving, besieged cities by UNITA resulted in massive destruction of property and the loss of untold numbers of civilian lives. Indiscriminate bombing by the government also took a high civilian toll. The US deputy assistant secretary for African affairs noted at the time that: 'This type of warfare bears mainly, cruelly and disproportionately on the populace, which is caught between the warring parties.' If the human cost is staggering, so is the lack of international attention. Angola earned the title 'the forgotten war'.

Following the signing on 20 November 1994 of the Lusaka ceasefire protocol between the Angolan government, led by the Movement for the Popular Liberation of Angola (MPLA), and the UNITA rebels, Angola has been on a tortuous path to re-establish peace and security. Although a new Government of Unity and National Reconciliation (GURN) was inaugurated on 11 April 1997, sporadic fighting continues, including the laying of landmines by both sides. Widespread human rights abuses by the government and UNITA continue, including conscription of child soldiers and the intimidation and detention of journalists. Movement around the country is difficult. By September 1997, as confidence in the peace process deteriorated, old checkpoints had been reactivated and new ones set up in both government and UNITA areas. Acts of

banditry have also escalated. The government in 1997 continued to acquire new arms in contravention of the Lusaka Protocol, the 1991 Bicesse Accords and UN Security Council resolutions.

The civil war in neighbouring Zaire was a significant factor in the power struggle in Angola during 1997. UNITA had been supporting President Sese Seko Mobutu of Zaire in return for supply lines for arms and a marketing route for diamonds. In February and March the MPLA sent two battalions of Katangese Angolans (originally from Shaba province in Zaire) to help Laurent Kabila, the leader of the rebel forces in Zaire. In June 1997, Kinshasa fell to the rebel forces and Zaire became the Democratic Republic of Congo. The immediate impact on Angola was that UNITA became more vulnerable as the Kinshasa government shifted its alliance to Luanda. In May and June, Angolan government forces invaded 10 per cent of UNITA-held diamond areas in Lunda Norte in order to reduce UNITA's power base in the northeast and to expand the diamond-producing areas held by the government.

This fighting created a new wave of IDPs: the UN estimated that more than 10,000 people in the Lunda Norte and Lunda Sul provinces had been forced to flee. Some 2000 of these passed through Nzaji in Lunda Norte in May 1997, fleeing from the fighting further south. Few of these have returned to their homes. UNITA is also reported to be maintaining camps of IDPs who are used for forced labour, portering and diamond production.

Fighting in the oil rich enclave of Cabinda resumed during 1997. The Angolan government had restarted negotiations with the separatist Front for the Liberation of the Cabinda Enclave, but these negotiations broke down and there was an increase of military activity, including incidents of new landmine warfare and indiscriminate shelling of villages. Dom Paulino Madeca, the Catholic

ANGOLA: IDPs and refugees, Moxico Province (PHOTO: C Sattlberger/UNHCR).

bishop of Cabinda, accused government troops of massacring civilians in the Maiombe forest. This resulted in large numbers of people being displaced from the northern districts of the enclave, many of them moving south to Cabinda city.

Counting the displaced

The UN estimates that there are currently 1.3 million IDPs in Angola, with an additional 300,000 Angolan refugees in neighbouring countries. A number of factors make an accurate determination of IDP numbers extremely difficult. More than 30 years of war have displaced large numbers of people over a broad geographic region, many of them several times. Those uprooted many years ago may no longer consider their areas of origin to be home. Even people uprooted more recently, especially those who have moved to the coast, may feel settled where they are, and have no intention of returning home.

IDPs can be subdivided into two categories: those in government-controlled areas, often in the country's major cities, and those in UNITA-dominated areas. The number of IDPs in UNITA areas is more difficult to assess, but must be several hundred thousand. Displaced people can be found in significant numbers in Bailundo, UNITA's headquarters and in Jamba, its former headquarters in the south. Many of these have been forcibly moved to the locations in which they now reside.

Some 40,000 people remain trapped against their will by UNITA in Jamba, where conditions are very bad. Although UNITA has claimed it has invited the international community to evacuate these people, in effect UNITA has refused to allow civilians to move out of UNITA zones. During 1997 there was also increasing evidence that UNITA was using Jamba for military training and that illegal flights carrying weapons and other supplies were landing there. The Namibian authorities exacerbated the situation by keeping the border near Jamba closed, fearful that an open border would permit a mass exodus of Jamba residents onto Namibian soil.

Most of the IDPs live in the large government-controlled coastal towns of Luanda, Lobito and Benguela, and the interior cities of Malanje, Luena and Menongue. In the inland cities many live in abandoned buildings or with friends or relatives. Many of the displaced on the coast live in shanties thrown up on the outskirts of towns, or in camps set up away from the cities themselves.

Cubal in Benguela province first received large numbers of IDPs in the late 1970s. They remained there until 1992, when most went home after the Bicesse Accords were signed. However, in 1994, when fighting resumed, more than 100,000 displaced people again moved to the town. Many in Cubal have made short visits home to assess the security situation, but are not confident of leaving the security of the town for good.

In the capital of Moxico province, Luena, a town of 150,000, some 60,000 people are estimated to be internally displaced from other areas of Angola. They have taken over several municipal buildings, including the old seminary, cinema, museum and railway station. The World Food Programme distributes some food and health care. The living conditions of the people are miserable, their motivation to return home poor; they remain socially isolated in ghettoized buildings in the town centre.

Assistance

Since the Lusaka Protocol, general food dis-tribution and the provision of special assis-tance to vulnerable groups has contained the humanitarian crisis. During 1997, over 70 per cent of relief aid was distributed by land and an increasing number of people became accessible to relief efforts. The general policy of the government and agencies working with displaced people is to try and provide assistance to communities, rather than to individual families. This includes rehabilitation of schools and clinics and the provision of seeds, tools and 'seed-protection' food until the first harvest can be reaped. The nutritional condition of the general population is improving and some displaced people have started to move back to their places of origin spontaneously as soon as they consider it safe to do so. Safety requires not only an end to active hostilities but also security from taxation of crops and from arbitrary harassment by local commanders and politicians.

During 1995, more than 12,000 IDPs in Benguela province returned to their homes, travelling for more than 100 kilometres without assistance with transport. The Catholic Relief Services had provided seeds and seed-protection food and some agricultural advice, but external assistance was minimal. After one planting season most families had rebuilt their homes and regained food self-sufficiency. But the majority of IDPs have not come back, for landmines and insecurity impede their return.

Migration to the towns

At independence in 1974, the urban population consisted of just 15 per cent of the total. As well as reflecting colonial control, this figure gives an indication of the healthy agricultural sector before independence. After 30 years of intermittent warfare, 55 per cent of the population is urban. The basic infrastructure of Luanda was designed to provide services for 30,000 people. In 1988 Luanda's population was 1.1 million and by 1996 it had risen to 3 million.

Despite peace, urbanization is increasing. As more rural areas become relatively peaceful and there is a relaxation of military restrictions on land travel, and civilian transport increases, the rural population leave their villages for the towns. This is because of continued sporadic fighting in sensitive areas; a lack of sense of lasting peace; an increase of rural banditry, based on stealing of crops, setting up of road blocks and taking produce from passing trucks; and an almost complete lack of trading support that would enable farmers to move surplus crops to market or buy seeds, tools and fertilisers.

The national Humanitarian Coordination Group (HCG) is chaired by the Ministry of Social Assistance (MINARS) and is the main coordination and policy body for humanitarian issues in the country. With the assistance of UN agencies, IOM and NGOs, MINARS initiated the national programme for the return and resettlement of IDPs in Angola in 1995. MINARS operates at national and provincial levels and has planned a staged return of 780,497 IDPs through to the end of 1998. However, the UN consolidated appeal of January 1998 put the total figure for the country at 1.2 million IDPs, of which 900,000 would be covered by the appeal. The UN estimates that 70 per cent are women and children and that 30 per cent of the households are female-headed.

Most of the return and reintegration of IDPs will continue to take place in the provinces of Benguela, Bie, Huambo, Huila, Luanda, Malange, Moxico, Uige and Zaire, probably until at least 1999. UNHCR has set up six reception centres and a fleet of 60 vehicles to assist with the return, initially in 1998, of some 160,000 people. A further 100,000 people are to receive transport and medical services from IOM. UNICEF, other UN agencies and NGOs are paying particular attention to traumatized children, child soldiers, street children and orphans. WFP is to provide approximately 60 per cent of the estimated 128,000 tonnes of food aid required for returning populations.

At the end of 1997 there were 120 NGOs involved in humanitarian work in Angola. Donor fatigue, however, is evident for two main reasons: first, there is increasing irritation with the Angolan parties, particularly UNITA, who have let the peace process drag out interminably; second, Angola has enormous income from oil and diamonds, but little is shared and hardly any is channelled into social welfare and relief.

Mozambique
Alex Vines

In October 1992, 16 years of civil war between the ruling Mozambique Liberation Front (Frelimo) and Mozambique National Resistance (Renamo) rebels ended in the Rome General Peace Accord. At the signing of the peace agreement it was estimated that in addition to nearly two million refugees in neighbouring countries, more than three million people were displaced within Mozambique. Of these, about one million were living in squatter camps, seeking protection in small, overcrowded islands of safety, such as Maputo, the Mozambican capital, which quadrupled in size to more than two million people during the civil war.

Large numbers of people converged on the country's major east–west rail lines, including the heavily guarded railway line between the port city of Beira and the Zimbabwe border, known as the 'Beira corridor'. The result was a 150-mile-long serpentine collection of settlements less than ten miles wide providing shelter for half a million displaced people. Other communities were displaced within Renamo territory, cut off from all contact with the outside world. The figures for displaced people in Renamo areas were never accurately assessed.

In addition to those displaced by violence, in 1977 the government embarked on a forced villagization programme, which involved removing people to new settlements without their permission. By 1981, 1.8 million people had been moved into 1266 communal villages. As Renamo's insurgency

spread, these villages became the main targets for attack.

As the war progressed, both the government and Renamo rebels used relocation as a military strategy, practising 'scorched earth' methods and military force to move hundreds of thousands of civilians into their respective areas of control. The villagization programme, originally designed to spearhead socialist development of the countryside, also took on a counterinsurgency role. Although the number of accusations of forced resettlement carried out by government forces declined sharply in 1991, it only stopped after the war ended in 1992.

Resettlement after the war

At least one million IDPs headed home soon after the October 1992 peace accord; by mid-1993 another million had returned. By the time the multiparty elections were held in October 1994, most IDPs had returned to their homes or to the areas in which they wanted to settle, although the legacy of tens of thousands of landmines posed a threat to resettlement and there was an increase in landmine victims. In some remote rural districts of Mozambique, such as in the municipalities of Muembe and Mavago in Niassa province, Renamo has continued to dissuade people it abducted during the war from leaving. However, each year the number of such reports declines, indicating a steady improvement. It is virtually impossible to estimate the number of people who wish to return to their homes, and tens of thousands of people possibly remain displaced.

Land ownership has been one of the most sensitive issues in post-conflict Mozambique. The desire to reclaim land was one of the prime reasons why IDPs moved back to occupy their ruined homes after the General Peace Accord. Although many of these people claim their present residence as their area of origin, many had been displaced several times over the last 16 years and such claims are

MOZAMBIQUE: IDPs and returnees receive relief supplies in Tete Province
(PHOTO: C Sattlberger/UNHCR).

difficult to assess. However, the number of land disputes has been small, and disputes are usually settled within the local communities by village elders or traditional authorities.

South Africa
Bronwen Manby

More than three and a half million South Africans are estimated to have been forcibly removed from their homes during the period of apartheid. The National Party government policy was to remove all black South Africans from 'white' South Africa and to relocate them in bantustans, nominally self-governing states, where they would form a pool of migrant labour available to white South Africa but without any rights in South Africa. Farm evictions were the single largest category of forced removals, but removals of people from freehold land ('black spots'), and other removals specifically designed to consolidate bantustan areas, together accounted for at least 1.3 million displacements. In all likelihood, most of those today living in former homeland areas were themselves, or are descended from those who were, forcibly removed under the National Party's policies. However, all residents of homeland areas had full citizenship rights restored to them by the new constitution in 1994 and are not counted as displaced in this survey.

From 1985, forced removals in support of apartheid policies reduced (though did not cease), and political violence within black communities became the most important cause of internal displacement in South Africa, escalating during the lead up to the

1994 all-race elections. Between 1990 and 1994, it was estimated that more than 14,000 people died in political violence in the Kwazulu homeland and elsewhere, largely in conflict between the Zulu-dominated Inkatha Freedom Party (IFP) led by Chief Mangosuthu Gatsha Buthelezi and the African National Congress (ANC). The extent to which such violence was orchestrated and planned by the National Party government, using the IFP as its tool, has been confirmed by recent criminal trials and the investigations of the Truth and Reconciliation Commission.

It is estimated that up to one million people were internally displaced by political conflict in South Africa during the decade to 1994, mostly in Kwazulu and Natal, although all such statistics are unreliable. Those driven from their homes have rarely formed identifiable camps of displaced people, but have moved to shanty towns around the major cities or joined relatives in formal township housing. In many cases, decisions to move were influenced not only by violence but also by the greater economic opportunities available in urban areas; opportunities that became accessible as the government ceased strict enforcement of the hated pass laws and Group Areas Act, even before they were formally repealed in 1991.

Current causes of displacement
Since 1994, forced removals in support of racial separation have ceased. Nevertheless, people desperate for land and housing have on occasion been removed from land on which they have settled that has been designated for other purposes (including, in some cases, low-cost housing). In October 1997, for example, approximately one thousand shacks were demolished that had been illegally built on municipal land in Randfontein, west of Johannesburg, displacing more than one thousand people who had recently settled there. Official efforts have generally been made to find alternative

accommodation for these people, so they are not counted as 'internally displaced' for this survey.

Farm evictions have continued under the new government. White farmers, anticipating legislation to protect the rights of farm workers and in some cases themselves facing financial hardship, have continued or even accelerated evictions of their black farm workers since 1994. Like those displaced by political violence, those thrown off land where they have lived, in many cases for generations, have moved either to homeland areas or to shanty towns around the major cities. Numbers displaced are therefore difficult to calculate, but probably run into the thousands.

Political violence has decreased since 1994. Nevertheless, it remains a significant problem in some areas, notably in rural Kwazulu–Natal where conflict was worst during the apartheid years. As a result of such violence, displaced people in many areas have still not returned, while new displacements have occurred. Within Kwazulu–Natal, conflict still occurs between the ANC and IFP, but new dynamics have also been introduced. During 1996 and 1997, some of the worst violence has taken place in the Natal mid-lands, close to Pietermaritzburg, where many people are still displaced since some of the most serious IFP–ANC violence in the province took place in the area during the 1980s. In April 1997, ANC MP Sfiso Nkabinde was expelled from the party amid (long-standing) allegations that he was a police informer and involved in 'warlord' activities. Since his expulsion, violence between his supporters and those who have remained with the ANC has escalated, while IFP–ANC violence has continued, and several thousand people have left their homes in the Richmond area – some of them already displaced during violence in the 1980s. (Nkabinde has since been charged with 18 murders.)

Serious violence has also occurred over

the last two or three years in the Eastern Cape districts of Qumbu and Tsolo, within the former apartheid homeland of the Transkei. Several hundred people have been killed in conflicts related both to stock theft and to rivalry between trade unions in the Johannesburg area, where many of the men are migrant workers. At various times, houses have been burnt, displacing families who have taken shelter at local court houses or other official buildings. However, no formal encampments of IDPs have formed on a permanent or semi-permanent basis and once again there is no agreed total for the numbers of those unable to return home.

Resettlement

The ANC-led government elected in 1994 has implemented a number of measures to provide redress to those forcibly displaced by the previous government. The Restitution of Land Rights Act of 1994 provided for the establishment of a Commission on the Restitution of Land Rights and a land claims court to consider claims by individuals and communities displaced by apartheid policies or by government action dating back to 1913 (the first Land Act). Applications must be made within three years, and more than 22,000 applications had been filed by late 1997, though indications were that most

would not succeed. Other legislation has given increased security of tenure to farm workers of different categories (though sometimes with perverse effects, as noted above) and allocated state land for resettlement of displaced populations. State housing subsidies have enabled some communities to negotiate private deals for the acquisition of land.

In the townships of Thokoza and Katlehong, east of Johannesburg, several hundred houses gutted in ANC-IFP violence during 1993 were occupied by IFP supporters from nearby hostels and others damaged too badly to be fit for occupation. Since late 1996, illegal occupants have been – largely peacefully – evicted from about 600 of these houses; these houses and others have been refurbished with money from the government's Reconstruction and Development Programme, enabling their original occupants to return. Elsewhere, however, there has been no concerted effort to resettle those displaced by political violence since 1985. Although a resettlement plan for those displaced by violence within Kwazulu–Natal was announced in December 1996 by the Kwazulu–Natal Peace Committee – a government-backed structure – no government action has been taken to implement this plan.

Map 5: Latin America and the Caribbean

Latin America and the Caribbean

Overview
Gordon Hutchison

The displacement of people resulting from internal armed conflict in Colombia and southern Mexico continued in 1997, with peasant and indigenous people most affected.

In Guatemala, Peru and Haiti, programmes with internally displaced people concentrated on returnee and rehabilitation efforts. In the rest of Latin America and the Caribbean massive migration continued to occur for economic reasons both within countries and across borders. The consolidation of neo-liberal economic policies throughout Latin America and the Caribbean is producing large-scale movements of people in search of employment. A major effect of these economic policies is the destruction of local rural economies with the subsequent migration of large numbers of the peasantry to urban centres or abroad. In the first half of 1997, 100,000 Central Americans were deported from Mexico. In Costa Rica in recent years up to 300,000 Nicaraguans (10 per cent of the Costa Rican population) arrived, fleeing the devastated economy of their country. Displacement has also been caused by illegal drug trafficking activities, economic projects such as mining and oil exploration in Bolivia, Ecuador, Colombia and Peru, and peasant unrest and land takeovers in rural Brazil.

In the wake of the peace agreements in Nicaragua, El Salvador and Guatemala, ending over 30 years of civil conflict in Central America, many regional support networks have folded. New initiatives are underway in the post-conflict scenario of Central America – bringing together a variety of government and non-government institutions working on migration, displacement, asylum and refuge. In October 1996, a meeting on human rights for refugees and IDPs took place in Costa Rica organized by the offices of the ombudsmen for the different Central American countries, the International Organization for Migration (IOM) and the Inter-American Institute for Human Rights.

In March 1996 in Puebla, Mexico, the first regional Conference on Migration was held, sponsored by the governments of Canada, Mexico and the United States. A follow-up conference took place in Panama City in January 1997 with the participation of the governments of the Central American countries, IOM and UNHCR. The Conference on Migration is at present the only forum on migration and displacement in the region, incorporating governments, multilateral organizations and NGOs.

The UNHCR–NGO Partnership in Action (PAR in AC) held meetings in Brazil and Costa Rica in 1997 and is also broadening its scope in Latin America to include work with migrants and internally displaced people. In 1997, the Project Counselling Service (PCS) sponsored meetings in Panama and Venezuela attended by NGOs, church groups and UNHCR to discuss the issue of Colombian refugees, migrants and internally displaced people.

Colombia
Project Counselling Service

The violent political situation in Colombia from the 1950s onwards has been accompanied by an increase in the internal displacement of people.

Figures for the numbers of internally displaced people in Colombia vary from around 500,000 to over a million. The internal conflict worsened in 1997 with an estimated 100,000 to 150,000 new IDPs, especially on the Atlantic coast where camps were opened in the Urabá region. The paramilitaries, who are alledgedly supported by the Colombian army, have extended their action in the past year from their Atlantic coast stronghold to virtually all of the country's 33 departments. The Colombian Red Cross estimates that up to one million people in conflict areas are vulnerable to displacement.

The armed conflict between the army and the Revolutionary Armed Forces of Colombia (FARC) and the National Liberation Army (ELN) guerrillas has intensified. Paramilitary groups, who are acknowledged to have the support of the army, have extended their activities and have declared open war on the guerrillas and on anyone they judge to be 'aiding and abetting' the guerrillas. Their 'enemies' are mainly peasants who are not involved in the conflict but are under pressure from both sides, community leaders, non-government and church organizations providing humanitarian aid to conflict victims, and leaders of left-wing organizations and the smaller political parties.

Under the pretext of the armed conflict, people are being expelled from areas where developers have economic interests in agro-industrial projects, exploiting natural resources, or opening roads and waterways. The army and paramilitaries may accuse them of supporting the guerrillas, but rural and indigenous people in many parts of Colombia also threaten certain economic interests. They inhabit key areas of land and oppose the commercial landowners, economic groups and multinational companies.

According to the Consultancy on Human Rights and Displacement (CODHES), between December 1995 and December 1996 some 36,202 households (181,000 Colombians) were forcibly displaced. Four families were displaced every hour because of violence, and since 1985 about 920,000 Colombians have been displaced. Most of the internally displaced people are women and children. Those responsible are paramilitaries (33 per cent), guerrillas (28 per cent), armed forces (14 per cent), urban militias (6 per cent), national police (2 per cent), drug traffickers (1 per cent) and others, including the Venezuelan National Guard, hooded assailants, unknown persons and common criminals (14 per cent). The majority of the IDPs move to the capital Bogotá or neighbouring municipalities in the department of Cundinamarca (27 per cent), while the city of Medellín provides refuge for 20 per cent. Others are scattered around the cities and municipalities.

The crisis in Urabá

One of the regions most seriously affected by the escalation of violence in 1997 is Urabá, situated in the far northwest of the country and incorporating several municipalities in the departments of Chocó and Antioquia. In the north of Chocó department many of the municipalities have been occupied since December 1996 by paramilitaries calling themselves the peasants' self-defence committees of Córdoba and Urabá. They have used selective killings and threats to force people from their homes.

According to information provided by the Catholic diocese of Apartado, over the past year up to 20,000 people (mainly peasants) have fled the armed conflict in Chocó with most arriving in Urabá and others going to the departmental capitals of Quibdo (Chocó) and Medellín, or to Panama.

The displaced people from Chocó have taken refuge in several makeshift camps in different parts of Urabá. Between February and April 1997, some 6500 people arrived in the municipality of Mutatá (department of Antioquia). Another several thousand sought refuge in community centres and *barrios* in the department of Antioquia.

Overcrowding, inadequate water supply and sanitation, and inactivity have been the most difficult problems faced by displaced people in Urabá. The government has distributed food and other basic provisions via the Colombian Red Cross, but belatedly and in a disorganized way. The displaced people in the camps are afraid for their safety, since there is evidence of relations between the army units allocated to guard them and members of the same paramilitary groups who forced them out of their homes.

Despite government promises of aid and several meetings in Urabá in search of solutions, the displaced people have seen no improvements in their living conditions, and there is no prospect of their being resettled or returning to their communities. While the government, through its spokesman Mr Cesar Manuel Garciá Nino, the presidential adviser on displaced people, claims that the security situation in Chocó allows for the return of the displaced people, this is being refuted by the ICRC.

Other serious cases of displacement

During 1997, the paramilitary offensive extended to the northeast; the department of Bolívar; the municipality of Yondó in Antioquia; department of Cesar; the department of Sucre; the oil-rich departments of Casanare and Arauca; and the eastern Llanos region. In some of these places, under the pretext of flushing out 'supporters of the guerrillas', large areas of land have been cleared for agro-industrial economic projects and the exploitation of natural resources. Clashes between armed groups, pressure from the army in the form of aerial bombardment, and pressure from the guerrillas aiming to exacerbate conflict in the regions, have also caused displacement.

Between July and September 1997, two paramilitary operations resulted in the displacement of some 3000 people. After a paramilitary raid in which more than 20 people were tortured and extrajudicially executed in the municipality of Mapiripán (department of Meta), more than 800 people fled to villages in the jungle in the eastern part of the department. In the Atlantic coast department of Sucre, following the massacre of five persons in the municipality of Ovejas, some 2000 displaced people sought refuge in the centre of the town.

As a consequence of the constant activity of armed groups, and in particular of paramilitary groups in the departments of Magdalena and Bolívar, thousands of people have sought refuge in the Atlantic coast cities of Cartagena, Santa Marta and Baranquilla. One single *barrio* of the city of Cartagena, called Nelson Mandela, is home to up to 27,000 displaced people.

Flight to neighbouring countries

In 1997 several groups of displaced peasants fleeing the conflict in Chocó, sought refuge in Panama. In April 1997, 325 Colombians, half of them children, who had taken refuge in Panama, were forcibly repatriated by the Panamanian authorities and temporarily resettled by the Colombian government on a *hacienda* in the department of Chocó. In November 1997, 90 of the 400 people who had taken refuge in the same border villages were forcibly repatriated following an agreement between the Colombian and Panamanian governments. In both these instances of *refoulement,* the Panamanian authorities denied access to the refugees by the UNHCR.

Colombian and Panamanian NGOs and church organizations have protested at the Panamanian government's illegal detention and *refoulement* of Colombian refugees. These were in violation of the 1951 UN Convention, 1967 Protocol on Refugees and the 1984 Cartagena Declaration on Refugees, all of which have been ratified by the government of Panama.

In February and October 1997, the PCS sponsored meetings in Panama and Venezuela attended by NGOs and church groups from Colombia, Costa Rica, Panama, Venezuela, Ecuador and UNHCR to discuss the situation of Colombian refugees and migrants in neighbouring countries. Further meetings are planned.

The government's response

The Colombian government has repeatedly expressed its interest in supporting displaced people and has been willing to respond to the recommendations of international missions such as the visit of Dr Francis Deng, the UN Secretary-General's Representative for Internally Displaced Persons, in June 1994, and the November 1993 and April 1997 fact-finding visits of the Permanent Consultation on Displacement in the Americas.

In August 1997, following congressional approval, President Ernesto Samper approved Law 387 covering the adoption of measures to 'provide attention, protection and socioeconomic consolidation and stabilization to internally displaced people' and to 'prevent forced displacement'. This followed the approval in April 1997 of Decree Law 1165 establishing the Advisory Office of the Presidency for the Integral Attention to the Population Displaced by Violence (Consejeriá Presidencial para la Atención Integral a la Población Desplazada por la Violencia) to coordinate activities of the various ministries and government and non-government organizations working with displaced people.

Law 387 has been the target of criticism from Colombian NGOs and human rights organizations working with displaced people. According to the Colombian Commission of Jurists (CCJ), the law provides neither an integral proposal for attention to displaced people nor a framework for the prevention of displacement. The CCJ considers that it is not enough to speak of preventing displacement, and that reference must be made to 'preventing the causes of displacement'. The draft articles of Law 387 included guaranteeing displaced people's rights to their property but these have been discarded, and there is no clarity over penalties for those responsible for forced displacement.

The international community's response

The international community has begun to take heed of the problem of internally displaced people in Colombia. In 1997, ECHO began supporting emergency programmes for displaced people, implemented by local NGOs and church organizations in collaboration with 11 European NGOs. These programmes include the running of camps, emergency relief, and socioeconomic reconstruction projects in resettlement zones. These international NGOs maintain a dialogue with the Colombian government, church organizations, local NGOs and social organizations, advocating for clear policies for government assistance for displaced people and programmes to prevent further displacements.

In February 1997, the European Commission and the Danish Refugee Council (DRC), through the Bogotá office of PCS, initiated a 'Programme of Social and Economic Reconstruction of the Displaced Populations in Northeast Colombia'. This programme is an EC 'pilot project' with the possibility of increased EC support for IDPs in Colombia.

Protection and security concerns

Displaced people in Colombia live in constant fear for their safety and in general seek anonymity in the large cities where they become the main population of the shanty towns, finding very few viable alternatives for rebuilding their livelihoods.

Assistance programmes to displaced people in Colombia are under constant threat from the parties to the armed conflict. The paramilitary groups have threatened humanitarian relief organizations with retaliation if they persist in their programmes for displaced people. Furthermore, government backing for the establishment throughout the country of rural security cooperatives called *Asocaciones Convivir,* is a serious cause for concern. These organizations are being accused of violations of human rights, including forced displacement.

The task of protecting displaced people and the local NGOs and church organizations who work with them is a priority concern for the ICRC. During 1997, the ICRC played a vital role in accompanying the displaced communities in Urabá, mediating in the delivery of provisions and negotiating the release of those detained by the armed parties. The Peace Brigades International (PBI) are also playing an important role in accompanying and protecting displaced people and the organizations that support them in Bogotá and the Magdalena Medio region.

However, neither the ICRC nor the PBI possess adequate human resources to attend to the emergency conditions existing throughout the country. The sheer magnitude of the internal armed conflict now affecting virtually all of Colombia's 33 departments makes it extremely difficult to extend protection to all displaced people.

The Colombian government has acknowledged the need for international help, not only to deal with displacement but also to help restart the peace talks with the guerrillas, which were suspended in April 1992. To this end, in June 1997 the Colombian foreign minister, María Emma Mejía, requested that UNHCR open an office in Colombia. In response to this request, in November 1997 UNHCR sent a high-level mission to Bogotá to assess the situation and to make proposals for the opening of an office.

Possible solutions

Besides the implementation of clear governmental policies to address social deprivation common to many parts of rural Colombia, and the consolidation of joint programmes with international organizations, forced displacement requires a negotiated settlement to the internal armed conflict and the resolution of the issue of land tenure, which lie at the root of the problem. In 1997, the final year of the administration of President Ernesto Samper, first steps have been taken to renew negotiations with the guerrilla organizations, but a question mark still hangs over the issue of how to confront the paramilitary groups.

Guatemala
Inforpress Centroamericana

Although the signing of a definitive peace accord between the Guatemalan government and the Guatemalan National Revolutionary Unity (URNG) on 29 December 1996 brought to an end a 36-year civil war, 250,000 people have been displaced by the war. One million Guatemalans may have been displaced at least temporarily by the violence – affecting about one-seventh of the total population.

Violence peaked in the early 1980s when the army's counterinsurgency strategy forced the displacement of hundreds of thousands of civilians. Between 1978 and 1984, approximately 100,000 people were killed, 40,000 disappeared, 440 villages were destroyed and 750,000 people were internally displaced, while 250,000 fled the country. The most affected region was the western highlands where 80 per cent of the mainly Mayan indigenous inhabitants left their homes at least temporarily between 1981 and 1982.

The UN Population Fund and the governmental National Commission for Attention to Refugees, Returnees and

GUATEMALA: IDPs in El Quiché (PHOTO: Dag Hoel/NRC).

Displaced People indicates that some 242,400 organized IDPs are the largest sector of the total uprooted population, which amounts to about 324,200. There are no figures for dispersed IDPs. The internally displaced Communities of Population in Resistance (CPR) number 15,850, while returned refugees make up 65,960. About 29,000 refugees still reside in Mexico, but government agencies were optimistic that nearly half this number would have returned by the end of 1997. The rest are accepting the Mexican government's offer of residency.

The western highland department of El Quiché still has the highest number of IDPs, with about half the national total, particularly in the mountainous Ixil triangle and extensive low-lying Ixcán municipality. Apart from the capital and surrounding areas, other major concentrations are in the northern Alta Verapaz department, especially in the regional capital, Cobán, in the neighbouring department of Baja Verapaz, the northern department of El Petén and the south coast Suchitepequez department. Other regions affected by the displacement but not highlighted by the study are the central part of the department of Chimaltengo and the western department of San Marcos.

While refugee statistics are quite accurate, IDP estimates vary widely. There has been no comprehensive IDP survey, but analysts do not believe that this would be possible. Popular organizations may often inflate figures for political reasons, while the use of community records as a source can lead to duplication of figures or contradictory accounts.

The lack of a uniform definition, blurred by the grey area of classifications that combine economic migrants and IDPs, complicates the collection of statistics. Objective estimations are made problematic by the relative invisibility of IDPs who, fearing persecution during the conflict years, preferred anonymity. As a survival strategy, particularly apparent in the capital, IDPs – the majority of whom are indigenous – were forced to integrate quickly and shed ethnic markers of their identity.

An important factor in identifying IDPs is recognizing that the status is temporary. As the original reason for flight has now disappeared with the resolution of the civil war and no new displacement is taking place, IDP numbers appear to be gradually decreasing.

With integration into new communities underway, numbers are expected to continue to fall. More IDPs plan to find land on which to resettle permanently. For example, the CPR in the Ixcán area moved to a new area in 1996 with the Catholic Church providing funds for the purchase of land, after conflicts arose between them and former occupants returning home. In the Ixil triangle, CPR communities are involved in similar disputes with neighbouring displaced groups wanting to return to their former properties. These CPR communities are negotiating with a government commission for land on the south coast.

A record of IDPs by gender or age is unavailable. If, however, their demographic composition is similar to that of Guatemala as a whole, at least half the population is under 15. A Guatemalan government study in the mid-1980s showed that at least 200,000 children had lost either one or both parents in the conflict. This violence was often accompanied by displacement.

Multiple needs

The Accord on the Resettlement of Populations Uprooted by the Armed Conflict, signed on 17 June 1994 by the government and URNG, identifies the needs of displaced people and gives specific guarantees for reintegration. The main necessities it identifies are the official acknowledgement of the uprooted population as civilians; provision of personal documentation; the purchase and/or titling of land; and recognition of informal education and training.

A Technical Commission for the Resettlement Accord (CTEAR), comprised of representatives from the government, the URNG and the uprooted population, was created to design and supervise resettlement projects. In addition, a Consultative Assembly of the Displaced Population (ACPD) was created to channel the needs and opinions of communities to CTEAR: in June 1997, the ACPD represented 104,200 displaced people. In August 1997, the congress approved a temporary documentation law, which will be in operation for three years to issue important personal identification papers such as marriage and birth certificates to uprooted people.

But the resettlement accord fails to target IDPs living in urban areas and places emphasis on rural IDPs, indicating that the resettlement areas are primarily rural.

Among the most important needs are the purchase of land, facilitated by the availability of credit, and the provision of basic infrastructure for permanent relocation in new locations. The ACPD further calls for a compensation programme for IDPs who suffered human rights violations committed during the conflict, while the Guatemalan widows' coordinator (CONAVIGUA) demands the creation of a fund for widows and women.

Rural IDPs' primary concern is land and the resolution of conflicts caused by the return of original occupants, either from Mexico or from other areas within Guatemala. Rural IDPs are also hoping for demilitarization. However, with the reported resurgence of armed groups the government announced in July 1997 that military garrisons are to be reopened in some areas.

The priority of urban IDPs is housing and basic services, employment, cost of living – especially health care – and personal security.

Many IDPs throughout Guatemala have to contend with mental health problems caused by war, displacement and family disintegration. In the capital, this is exacerbated by stress caused by urban living. Given that Guatemala has 23 indigenous language groups, displacement has often meant living with people from outside their language group. It also caused a disruption to Mayan traditional social organization and customs, which are highly localized, as land is not only an economic resource but also central to indigenous identity.

Institutional responses

The UN Mission to Guatemala (MINUGUA) monitors human rights and is present in areas of the IDPs. Apart from one department set up to oversee the implementation of the Resettlement Accord, it does not work specifically with IDPs.

Only a handful of grassroots organizations and local NGOs deal specifically with IDPs and are members of the ACPD. The National Council of Displaced Persons (CONDEG), the CPR and regional representatives of uprooted communities in the major displacement areas represent the organized sector of IDPs. Other groups working with specific sectors of IDPs are the Mutual Support Group for Relatives of the Disappeared (GAM), and CONAVIGUA. Numerous community groups, most of which provide assistance to slum dwellers, operate independently from the major organizations. Having been largely excluded from the few official channels of support, they have

organized self-help networks.

Few international organizations target IDPs. This is partly a legacy from the last decade of conflict when assisting IDPs was politically sensitive and often led to persecution, causing many to adopt a community-based approach in areas with a high number of IDPs, particularly on the south coast and in the capital. Another reason for the lack of projects is the sparcity of information on IDPs, a sector of the uprooted population that is far less visible than refugees and returnees. IDPs tend to be assisted by poverty programmes aimed at a wider population.

Despite its commitments under the Resettlement Accord to prioritize the displaced as needing 'special attention', the government has also failed to target IDPs. Instead, the assistance provided by the Government Plan 1996–2000 targets the poor population as a whole. The government has also formed several new entities responsible for distributing aid and carrying out projects established in the peace accords, such as Fonatierra (the Land Fund) and Fodigua (the Indigenous Fund). The ACPD is critical of the lack of government, particularly CTEAR, action on implementing the accord. With regard to land, the ACPD rejects the government's land survey on locations available for resettlement of displaced people because it only contained information on five of the 21 departments.

Groups of IDPs that over the years have developed a high level of organization, such as the CPR, have achieved more progress in negotiations with the government on their most important needs, compared with more recent affiliates to the ACPD.

ECHO funds several IDP projects implemented by European NGOs. Since 1984, the European Commission has also supported programmes for returnee and IDPs.

With difficulties identifying IDPs and conflicts arising over competing claims to limited resources, the UNHCR has replaced its population-based approach, prior to 1996, with a territorial-based one. Thus, instead of targeting specific groups, it now focuses on the local population as a whole. While reluctant to distinguish between different types of uprooted population, IDPs receive UNHCR support if they are present in the same regions as returnees. The 1996 Strategic Plan for the Reintegration of the Uprooted Population in Priority Areas includes 8000 IDPs.

The UNDP signed an agreement with CTEAR in August 1997 to formulate 37 local development projects, including six for the purchase and/or legalization of land for displaced people.

Gaps in assistance

Despite increased assistance earmarked for financing the implementation of the peace accords, IDPs continue to be a neglected sector of the uprooted population. The initial stumbling block in reaching IDPs continues to be the lack of information, particularly regarding dispersed IDPs on whom there are hardly any data. Neither is any protection or assistance directed at more vulnerable IDPs, such as women, widows and children.

Overall, IDPs remain an unknown quantity, not officially recognized and therefore outside or on the margins of mandates of both national and international organizations. Forced into a silent refuge, IDPs often prefer to remain anonymous, taking on an identity of a poor urban dweller or rural farm worker rather than an internally displaced person.

The signing of peace has shifted international attention away from human rights. The international community has repeatedly praised the current administration of President Alvaro Arzu·in this regard. Further dialogue between the international community and the Guatemalan government must take place on a level in which both sides are fully aware of the reality facing the IDPs. Although the government has been successful

in securing funds for the peace process, these funds have yet to be effectively channelled directly to beneficiaries named in the accords. The international community should continue to monitor the peace accords and their implementation rigorously to ensure that money is not just being redirected to the government's own budget or the creation of bureaucracies.

Given that few NGOs work directly with IDPs now or in the past, institutional strengthening of local organizations such as CONDEG is also an important task.

Haiti
Shyla Vohra

Haiti is the poorest country in the western hemisphere and one of the world's most underdeveloped nations. It was subject to military rule from 1991 to 1994, when the population was terrorized, repressed and international sanctions crippled the economy, rendering the people even more vulnerable. Haiti continues to face overwhelming social problems, including high unemployment, overcrowded urban settings, severe environmental degradation, the lowest school enrolments and literacy rates in the western hemisphere and a population growth rate of 2 per cent per year, net of migration.

It is estimated that more than 300,000 Haitians were internally displaced as a direct result of either persecution or repression by the military regime. Military and paramilitary crackdowns in the slums of Port au Prince forced thousands to flee into the countryside. Repression in rural areas had the reverse effect, sending thousands of farmers and community leaders into Port au Prince, Cap Haitian and other cities. This form of displacement was called *marronage*: the Haitian 'marrons' were fugitive slaves who escaped from the inhumane working conditions on eighteenth-century plantations and fled to the hills. With the return of the constitutional government and the improvement of the security situation throughout the countryside, large movements of people due to human rights violations have abated. Internal displacement in Haiti today is largely due to a rural exodus to urban centres, caused by the diminishing capacity of the agricultural sector, the concentration of economic activities in two or three urban centres – especially Port au Prince – and by centralization of social and educational services. Agricultural production per capita has steadily fallen over the last 20 to 30 years as a result of discriminatory policies and under-investment in people and services.

This rural to urban migration is either temporary, during difficult climatic periods, or longer-term when farmers can no longer sustain a livelihood from agriculture. A severe 10-month drought in 1997 in the northwest region of Haiti resulted in an estimated 8000 people moving temporarily from the countryside to Port-de-Paix and Gonaives. Widespread environmental degradation, deforestation and high population growth have led to an annual reduction of 6000 hectares of land suitable for agricultural or economic use. The impoverished peasants head towards Port au Prince, Cap Haitian, Gonaives and Port-de-Paix and stay in shanty towns on their outskirts.

Since the constitutionally elected government was re-established in October 1994, the human rights situation has dramatically improved, prompting neighbouring countries to encourage Haitians to return home. Mass deportations of Haitians from neighbouring countries have been occurring and these exacerbate the precarious situation of returnees. From January to August 1997, an estimated 20,000 Haitians were deported from the Dominican Republic alone. The weak absorption capacity of Haiti means that repatriation often results in internal displacement.

The majority of recent returnees are destitute, having sold their land and belongings. Upon return to Haiti, they face an uncertain future, and find themselves homeless and impoverished. Urban slums proliferate.

The slums lack basic sanitation and services, with stagnant open sewers and rampant disease. Slums are also crime-ridden, as gangsters fight for control of the areas and a frustrated population moves towards social discontent and violence.

Port au Prince is estimated to receive an average of 125 displaced people daily, including people coming from the Haitian countryside and from neighbouring countries. Of an estimated 800,000 IDPs in Port au Prince, some 600,000 live below the poverty level. In Cap Haitian 100,000 displaced people live in desperate conditions; in Gonaives there are 125,000; in Port-de-Paix up to 50,000; making a total of one million IDPs in Haiti.

The IDPs living in the slums of Haiti's major towns are not fully absorbed into urban life. They remain mobile, moving from one ghetto to another and, as an uprooted people, are unable to integrate into any social structure. They need food, shelter, health care, sanitation, employment and education. Many adults and children survive on temporary work, commercial sex or criminal activities. Although there are still claims by returnees of harassment, their validity cannot be verified. Security in the slum areas remains low, but whether murders and attacks are politically motivated, or linked to the increasing drug trade and gang wars, is uncertain.

Institutional responses

Many international agencies and local organizations are active in Haiti attempting to address the country's poverty and associated problems. Many concentrate on development programmes, addressing environmental degradation, education, job creation and basic necessities such as health care and sanitation. Some development programmes undertaken by international agencies target the carrying capacity of the rural sector, which ultimately should reduce rural to urban displacement. Short-term relief is also provided by the international community, which feeds 1.3 million Haitian people per day. While many international agencies and local organizations exist to help displaced people and returning refugees, they are not coordinated and there is little monitoring of their activities. Haiti's national NGOs are active in rural development projects, cooperative schemes, lobbying for rights, urban neighbourhood improvement and vocational training.

At the government level, the National Office for Migration (NOM) was established in 1995 to assist repatriates and IDPs, and apply a national migration policy. In 1996, the Migration Management Programme was conceived, jointly executed by the NOM and the International Organization for Migration (IOM). This programme provides reception and reintegration assistance to returnees and IDPs in Haiti through customized assistance packages. In addition, it seeks to strengthen the capacity of the NOM to address migration issues including assessment and monitoring of the conditions affecting the returnees and displaced persons, and to reinforce the work of local NGOs and community groups.

International and local agencies have implemented projects to improve living conditions in the slums of IDPs and their host communities. CARE has initiated projects to strengthen public infrastructure. One slum community of IDPs on the outskirts of Gonaives has been organized to carry out urban improvements such as building latrines and improving drainage in return for food. The Haitian Red Cross helps homeless women from rural areas who are living with their children on the streets of Port au Prince. Many of the programmes of the Red Cross have recently had to be reduced due to a severe lack of donor funding. Major donors include ECHO, USAID, the International

Monetary Fund, the Inter-American Development Bank, the United Nations agencies, and the governments of Canada, France, Japan and Germany.

UNHCR has obtained five years of funds for community-based projects in areas most affected by displacement or repatriation. Its office in Haiti was closed in April 1996, but monitoring returnees continues from its Washington office.

Despite the efforts of the international community and local initiatives, however, there is still a weak capacity to oversee population movements in Haiti. In effect, this means that where movements go unmonitored, the needs of the displaced cannot be met, and that programmes targeting IDPs are difficult to devise and implement.

Future considerations

Internal displacement in Haiti remains interlinked with the country's economic and political stability. To spur Haiti's economic recovery, international development banks and donor agencies have pledged to provide more than US$ 2000 million in assistance by 1999. This will address the chronic problems of unemployment, lack of social services, lack of infrastructure and poverty, which continue to lead people to leave their homes. In 1997, the number of people attempting to leave Haiti for other countries increased compared with previous years since 1994, and an increase in slum-dwellers on the outskirts of major towns has been noted. Assistance must continue to be generated towards meeting the basic needs of IDPs as well as towards long-term development and economic growth, to prevent internal displacement from continuing.

Mexico
Project Counselling Service

In Mexico, the problem of internally displaced

people has become a major domestic and international issue in recent years due mainly to political tension in the state of Chiapas. The situation turned increasingly violent after the Zapatista Army of National Liberation (EZLN) uprising in January 1994, remaining so despite a truce between the Zapatistas and the Mexican government. At the height of the fighting in 1994, an estimated 40,000 IDPs were in Chiapas state, reduced to 5000 by mid-1997.

During 1997, internal armed conflicts between EZLN guerrillas and the army in the state of Chiapas and between Popular Revolutionary Army (EPR) guerrillas and the army in the states of Guerrero and Oaxaca continued during the year causing displace-ment of the rural populations. In addition, takeovers of land by peasants, often violently expelled by paramilitaries or state security forces was another cause of displacement in the rural areas.

Army incursions into areas where guerrilla groups operate and land-related conflicts in the states of Oaxaca and Guerrero are also generating displaced people, albeit on a lesser scale than in Chiapas. Economic and political conflicts, often disguised as differences between Catholic and Evangelical church members, led to expulsions of 30,000 people from indigenous communities in the 1970s and 1980s. These IDPs eventually resettled elsewhere.

The situation today

Two phenomena are responsible for the current displacement of people in the states of Chiapas, Guerrero and Oaxaca:

- takeovers of land, especially idle land, by peasants who are subsequently and often violently expelled, either by armed guards hired by landowners, or by the state security forces, or both. Takeovers have become more frequent since 1994; and
- specifically in Chiapas, a state-directed and

financed policy of containment and roll back of EZLN influence and peasant gains, that creates instability through armed violence, as implemented by paramilitary groups.

Paramilitary groups

Paramilitary groups arose in 1995 mostly in the northern zone of Chiapas, but are currently spreading to other areas of the state. The northern zone covers the municipalities of Tilá, Tumbalá, Salto de Agua, Sabanilla and Chilón, with indigenous people comprising between 34 and 81 per cent of the total population, mainly of the Chol ethnic group. The creation of paramilitary groups is said to be part of the 'low intensity warfare' strategy carried out by the government; a military truce currently prevents the use of standing troops for offensive operations, a function now assumed by the paramilitaries. These groups are said to be government sponsored, given their ties to the governing Party of the Institutional Revolution (PRI), the training received from the army, access to sophisti-cated arms and the tolerance shown them by law enforcement agencies. Three main paramilitary groups are currently operating: Paz y Justicia, the main paramilitary group in the northern zone (in Tilá, Salto de Agua, Tumbalá and the Sabanilla area); Los Chinchulines, in Chilón; and San Bartolome de los Llanos in Venustiano Carranza municipality, outside the northern zone.

A new paramilitary group, the Indigenous Revolutionary Antizapatista Movement (MIRA), signals the spread of paramilitary groups from the northern zone into the highland area of Chiapas. There is no information regarding the presence of paramilitary groups in Guerrero or Oaxaca. In these states, however, there is no observed truce between the government and the guerrilla groups known to be operating there. Therefore, the army in Guerrero and Oaxaca, as opposed to Chiapas, can operate freely. All three states are reported to be EPR strongholds.

The pattern of violence

In Chiapas, the paramilitary groups have harassed populations and randomly killed individuals alleged to support the EZLN and/or opposition PRD (Party of the Democratic Revolution). The violence creates terror and, to avoid repression if accused of harbouring sympathies towards the EZLN or PRD, families flee to the surrounding countryside or to other villages. Abandoned homes are often then pillaged and set ablaze. Since peace negotiations began between the EZLN and the Mexican government in February 1994, 1600 indigenous peasants have been murdered in Chiapas, there have been 2300 land invasions and hundreds of operations to remove squatters. Hundreds of indigenous people have been imprisoned on charges mostly related to land takeovers. On 22 December 1997, the massacre in the northern zone village of Actene by paramilitaries of 45 indigenous displaced men, women and children, provoked widespread international protest.

An additional factor that has provoked tension throughout Chiapas is the build-up of army troops, given their covert support for the paramilitary groups. The military is present in half the state's 111 municipalities, with an increase in 'points of presence' of 182 per cent since February 1995. Over half the army's regular troops are stationed in Chiapas, Guerrero and Oaxaca.

In Chiapas the situation is further marred by religious prejudice. The PRI-aligned paramilitary groups tend to be evangelical Protestants, while the other side, linked to the PRD and/or the EZLN, tend to be supporters of the Catholic Church. Members of both churches tend to live in the same rural communities.

As a result of violence from the paramilitary groups, an armed vigilante organization, Abuxú, was formed allegedly by Zapatista supporters. Abuxú has retaliated against the Paz y Justicia group, murdering reputed leaders, which has also generated displaced people.

Estimates and needs assessment

Estimates of numbers of people presently displaced in Chiapas vary widely. No institution, government or non-government department has a mandate to track IDPs systematically. Mexican government sources claim that 5000 people are displaced in Chiapas. The Catholic diocese of San Cristóbal de las Casas estimates that there are 4000 displaced people in the northern zone. Figures are scarce for IDPs in Oaxaca and Guerrero, faced with land-tenure problems, heavy militarization and a pattern of violence similar to that of Chiapas. Based on a comparative study of their respective levels of violence as reported in the national press, an approximate figure of 1000 displaced people can be given. However, the newspaper *Excelsior* reported that 2600 rural inhabitants of the Ahuacoutzingo municipality of Guerrero were preparing to abandon their homes in June 1997 and travel to the state capital, accused by the Mexican army of supporting the EPR.

There is no reliable estimate of how many displaced people have been unable to find shelter in a different community and are therefore living in the open. Integration and acceptance into host communities is said to be difficult, given the existing scarcity of food, water, fuel and building materials.

Aid to IDPs

The Chiapas state government has been giving IDPs some assistance, but there are charges that PRI-linked displaced people receive preferential treatment. Army troops have been participating in 'social outreach' programmes by attending to medical and dental needs, distributing food and clothing, and working on construction projects within communities affected by displaced people.

The Catholic Church, through the Cáritas office in Chiapas, is offering emergency food, medicine and supplies in the northern zone. Church officials state, however, that because paramilitary groups often block roads around rural communities, it is often difficult, at times impossible, for aid to reach victims. The diocese of San Cristóbal de las Casas has indicated a need for basic supplies such as food, potable water, clothing, building materials, medicines and medical supplies, as well as trained personnel, especially doctors.

NGOs in Chiapas are attending to the needs of displaced people as they become aware of particular cases, but there is no overall, coordinated relief plan. Because of the dangerous conditions, NGOs have avoided a systematic presence in the northern zone. In October 1997, several NGOs in San Cristóbal de las Casas held a workshop with peasant organizations, representatives of displaced people and other parties interested in displacement. They shared information about the numbers, places of origin and refuge, and needs of IDPs.

The Mexican Red Cross is attending to other health needs in Chiapas, but offers no permanent attention to displaced people. NGOs in San Cristóbal have reported that the displaced have asked for the presence of the ICRC, human rights organizations and civilian peace camps. By the end of 1997 the ICRC was not attending to the needs of IDPs in Mexico, and had no direct operations in Chiapas. Conditions in the northern zone have impeded a more sustained presence. In 1995/6, the European Community Humanitarian Office (ECHO) funded an emergency project to provide medical and food aid to IDPs in Chiapas. The Irish NGO Trocaire administered the project in conjunction with a local NGO coordinating body, Coordination of Chiapas NGOs for Peace (CONPAZ).

The Estación Norte, a coordinating body of Chiapas-based and international NGOs concerned with the violence in the northern zone, was forced to abandon plans to establish an office in the area when a delegation sponsored to investigate conditions was fired upon in February 1997. The group subsequently disbanded. The Costa Rica-based PCS is supporting IDPs in Chiapas with loans for reconstruction, planting and tools.

While the July 1997 elections saw the weakening of the governing PRI party, with its loss of overall control of the congress, and ushered in a period of democratization – with the hope that an end to armed struggle in Mexico would be in sight – the EZLN and EPR have still to lay down their arms. There is strong hope for a renewed peace dialogue with the EZLN, but this is not likely with the EPR.

The Mexican political system continues to be unstable and a lot now depends on how genuinely democratic the country becomes. The run-up to the presidential elections in 2000 will be a crucial period for Mexico, during which many political battles will be fought. The international community needs to give more attention to Mexico to help it through the historical democratization process. Should the internal armed conflict in the states of Chiapas, Guerrero, Oaxaca and in other parts of the country continue, the international community should be prepared to condemn any further human rights violations and to provide protection and emergency relief to internally displaced people.

Peru
Ana Maria Rebaza

In Peru, while no peace accords were reached between the Peruvian government and guerrilla organizations, the defeat of the armed groups by the Peruvian government in 1992 has nevertheless allowed many displaced peasants to return to their homes in the central highland region. Nevertheless, political violence continues in Peru and 1997 saw renewed armed confrontations between Sendero Luminoso (Shining Path) guerrillas and the army in the department of Huancayo, which caused new displacements.

According to Peruvian government figures, up to the end of 1996, some 300,000 displaced people had returned to their home communities, while the non-governmental National Platform on Displacement estimated 68,574 IDPs. The return programmes supported by international and local NGOs, the European Commission and the governmental Programme to Support Repopulation (PAR) are expected to continue for at least two more years.

Political violence

During the worst period of political violence in Peru, between 1980 and 1992, there were successive waves of internal displacement, basically from rural to urban area zones. The number of displaced people was estimated to be about 600,000. Violent incidents have occurred throughout most of the country, the principal areas being the departments of Ayacucho, Huancavelica, Apurímac, and the highlands of the department of Junín; the central and northeastern jungle region; the jungle areas of the departments of Junín, Huánuco, and San Martín; and in Lima, the national capital.

Armed insurgent groups, in particular Sendero Luminoso and – with less intensity and different characteristics – the Tupac Amaru Revolutionary Movement (MRTA) generated violence and terror directed against civilians, with massacres, selective killings, robbery, rape, bombings, arson and forced recruitment. The armed forces then declared states of emergency, which implied political-military control of the affected zones, and to launch indiscriminate attacks on civilians, with human rights violations such as disappearances, extrajudicial executions, massacres, rape, arson and robbery.

In 1989, the civil defence committees called *rondas* were also responsible for violent actions among the peasant communities, though they gradually came under the control of the community authorities. In 1994, the army registered 4200 of these committees with a total of about 240,000 members. Paramilitary groups were also active during the American Popular Revolutionary Alliance (APRA) government of 1985–89. More recently, commandos belonging to the state intelligence service, aiming to intimidate the opposition, have carried out criminal actions. Finally, drug trafficking has been a constant factor complicating the situation of violence in the central and northeastern jungle regions.

Fundamental to the strategic defeat of Sendero Luminoso were the actions in self-defence of the Andean communities. And, though neither Sendero Luminoso nor the MRTA has threatened to destabilize the country at the levels experienced in 1992, they have nonetheless generated situations of serious violence, and in the case of Sendero Luminoso have continued to carry out armed actions (selective killings, bomb attempts, raids, and the like) in most of the departments of Peru. Between the beginning of 1995 and the first half of 1997, 1456 violent actions occurred, causing 851 deaths. Twenty-five provinces and three districts, involving 1,700,000 persons, continue under states of emergency.

Current problems and needs

Having lost all they owned, suffering from psychosocial effects and living in unfamiliar and sometimes even hostile surroundings, the displaced people have had to cope with the limited support of their relatives, compatriots and a few institutions. They lack personal documentation and penal investigations are unjustly applied: about 9000 people have been interrogated on charges of terrorism.

Women are the central support of the family in these emergency conditions, though female heads of families have not always been able to consolidate their new skills with self-affirmation.

Despite the violence, which still affects large parts of the country, since the military defeat of Sendero Luminoso in 1992 many displaced people have returned spontaneously. This was especially visible between 1993 and 1995, and is now steadily diminishing. The main thrust of the return movement is occurring from the rural centres of refuge, and to a lesser extent from the smaller towns, towards the people's places of origin. The situation in the jungle region is more complex, owing to the extremely unstable conditions of security. Returning communities, such as the Asháninka indigenous people, become the targets of attacks by Sendero Luminso's columns, and the armed forces, far from offering security, demand that civilians organize civil defence committees.

Rehabilitation and reconstruction are taking shape among displaced people in most of the country, although emergency situations still exist as a result of persistent political violence, particularly in the northeastern and central jungle regions. The general needs are:

- recognition of the active social role played by the organizations of displaced people in consensus-building at local, regional and national levels;
- a legal framework offering protection to displaced people to rebuild their local communities destroyed by the conflict;
- guarantees of security in both rural and urban areas;
- attention to the psychosocial consequences affecting everyone who has suffered political violence;
- regularization of the personal documentation of displaced persons;

- resolution of the problem of unjust interrogations by judicial authorities (for example 'judges without faces');
- resolution of problems concerning land ownership;
- technical capacity-building to enable displaced people to undertake more lucrative employment;
- literacy teaching in rural and urban areas;
- access to credit, for rural and urban contexts;
- improvements to housing in precarious condition;
- macro-economic policies, which encourage the development of rural areas and thus encourage IDPs to return home; and
- public health and education services to rural areas.

Organized responses from different social actors

Civil society and the churches organized responses to the emergency in 1986, and were later joined by international NGOs such as Diakonia (Sweden), PCS and Oxfam. In 1992, the International Council of Voluntary Agencies (ICVA) helped in the creation of the National Platform on Displacement in Peru (MNDP), a collective structure of more than 55 institutions working with displaced people all over the country. The MNDP has taken an active part in advocacy directed at the Peruvian state and international institutions and in strengthening the organizations of the displaced population. In April 1996 the National Coordination of Displaced People and Communities in Reconstruction was formed and held its first congress for eight regional organizations.

In 1993, the government decided to address the issue of IDPs by creating a PAR. This body has been growing in strength and acquiring more functions partly as a result of pressure from civil society and partly due to the interest and concern of the international community, especially the UNDP. However, it does not focus on the protection and promotion of human rights, and its attention is centred only on returning displaced people, who are in the minority (68,574 persons according to the MNDP's current figures). Those displaced people who opt to remain in the cities receive no assistance from the state. Moreover, since this is an institution of central government, there is little consideration to local coordination.

Up to December 1996, the PAR supported 23 organized returns involving more than 1282 families. The PAR also supports infrastructural work in affected communities and gives emergency assistance to communities where there have been spontaneous returns. But its effort has not had the impact expected, because of inadequate follow-up. The most widely-publicized returns, and those supported by the PAR, have taken place from Lima, but they do not constitute a quantitatively significant sector. The government's quoted figure of 300,000 returnees is more than four times the figure the MNDP has been able to establish.

In the jungle regions, the number of returns organized has been very small and they have been organized with great difficulty owing to the lack of material resources. The PAR records 17 communities, totalling 870 families, having returned to their native areas. The Asháninka emergency committee recorded in 1997 a further 12 communities, with 406 families, returning to their native areas.

In 1995, Dr Francis Deng, the UN Secretary-General's Special Representative for Internally Displaced Persons, visited Peru and wrote an important report, which has not been widely disseminated.

UNHCR carried out a diagnostic assessment in 1993, but no plan of action was proposed as a result. In the framework of this process, PAR in AC sponsored a forum in 1996 entitled 'legislative initiatives for the protection of the displaced population', which was organized with displaced people's organizations and local government authorities. At this forum a proposal for legislation offering a framework for legal protection was drafted.

ECHO supports a programme of emergency aid for returnees implemented by a number of international and national NGOs. In 1995, the European Commission's refugee and displaced persons budget line (DG1) approved a project in cooperation with the Peruvian government and with the participation of local NGOs. This programme will administer ECU 3 million over three years and in September 1997 began to be implemented.

Over the last year the People's Ombudsman was set up, proposing as one of its objectives the development of actions to protect the rights of various social sectors, including displaced people as a priority. The service's work plan emphasizes legal support, which is provided by the Programme of Protection for Displaced People and Assistance for Affected Communities, based in Ayacucho.

Both the Peruvian government and the international community need to develop an integrated, human rights based approach to social problems such as displacement, which have sprung from political violence in the country. They should not confine their focus to the rural areas as sites of reconstruction. Moreover, these areas are being addressed merely as emergency assistance and are not considered as part of the national development strategy. Local rural areas should be strengthened via policies of decentralization, and concerted action between the state and NGOs.

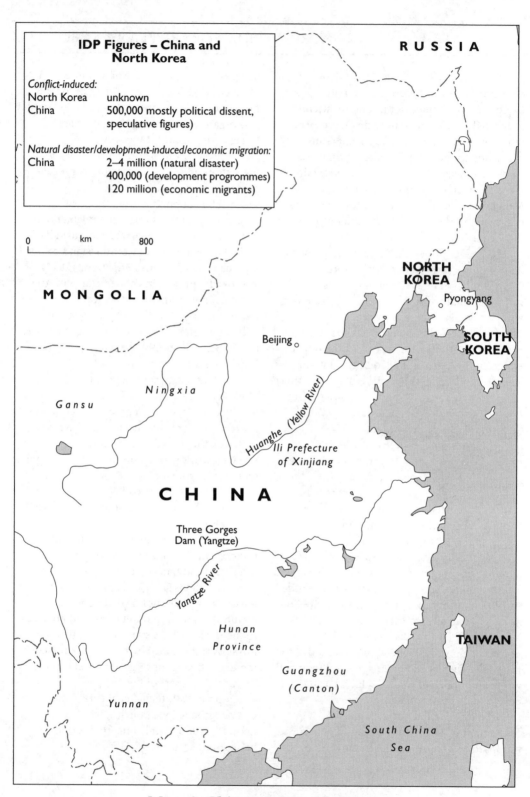

IDP Figures – China and North Korea

Conflict-induced:
North Korea   unknown
China   500,000 mostly political dissent,
   speculative figures)

Natural disaster/development-induced/economic migration:
China   2–4 million (natural disaster)
   400,000 (development progrommes)
   120 million (economic migrants)

0   km   800

RUSSIA

MONGOLIA

NORTH KOREA

Pyongyang

Beijing

SOUTH KOREA

Ningxia

Gansu

Huanghe (Yellow River)

Ili Prefecture
of Xinjiang

CHINA

Three Gorges
Dam (Yangtze)

Yangtze River

Hunan
Province

TAIWAN

Guangzhou
(Canton)

Yunnan

South China
Sea

Map 6: China and North Korea

Northeast Asia

Overview
Jon Bennett

In China the high figures for economic migration, development-induced displacement and natural disasters are matched only by our ignorance of details and the impossibility of obtaining more than broad estimates based on intermittent reports. Political persecution, including the enforced exile of 'undesirable' communities and individuals, makes China one of the most criticized states in the world for its human rights record. In a centralized communist state the term 'forced' migration takes on a particular meaning: it is a tool of population control and enforced political compliance rather than simply a result of conflict. China is also host to the largest dam construction project in the world – the Three Gorges Dam – which continues to displace thousands and to cause widespread impoverishment. Again, the term 'forced' begs the question: how could it have been otherwise in a state where decisions are passed down from a remote leadership backed by powerful state machinery?

The pervasive control over society of the government of the Democratic People's Republic of Korea (North Korea), its global isolation, collectivized agriculture and economic failure bear a close resemblance to the situation that provoked some of the worst famines of the twentieth century in China (1958-62) and the Soviet Union (1931-32). Unlike these earlier disasters, the authorities have recently allowed some access to international agencies and observers. However, state control will ensure that international intervention continues to be tightly controlled and observers are restricted.

Critical gaps in socioeconomic and geographical knowledge of the famine characterize current relief efforts. Up to now, tight control of population movement has largely prevented internal displacement at the expense of the freedom to leave areas of crisis.

In 1995, and to a lesser extent in 1996, severe flooding in North Korea opened doors for an international relief operation. The current relief operation is still defined by these recent natural disasters, although the term 'complex emergency' more accurately describes the new situation. The current famine requires a more strategic humanitarian framework, including assessments of political, gender-related and socio-economic variables. It is not yet clear whether the priorities of the international aid community – targeting vulnerable groups, access to all areas and monitored distribution – match those of the government, and some mutual suspicion remains. What is clear is that relatively small amounts of pledged food aid (for example the EU's contribution of 155,000 tons in May 1997) will be dwarfed by estimates of national food requirements. Furthermore, avoiding the diversion of these supplies to favoured groups of people (including the military) might be impossible to avoid.

China
Martin Stein

Forced displacement in China from 1996 centres on three primary issues. First, there were perhaps 500,000 migrants made homeless by political persecution (including more than 2000 political dissidents in labour camps). Second, as many as 400,000 people have been forced from their homes as a result of imposed development programmes (including 100,000 so far displaced by the Three Gorges Dam). Third, natural disasters account for between two and four million displaced people. Unemployment has also accounted for approximately 120 million migrants within the country.

These are enormous figures, which in total outweigh accepted global IDP figures by a factor of about six to one. Perhaps more than any other country, China begs the question of how we define internal displacement and what constitute the coercive methods the international community should notice. Accurate reporting on this and other facets of China's human rights situation is impossible, since Chinese networks for reporting violaions of rights have nearly all been suppressed. Each year hundreds of thousands of people in China are displaced coercively in ways that fall outside the UN-adopted definition of an IDP. To draw attention to China's problem of internal displacement, the current definition of an IDP would need to be broadened.

The omnipotent state security apparatus in China is capable of suppressing major internal displacement and cross-border refugee flight from regions fraught with dissent. Geographical barriers against exit are also significant deterrents. Those fleeing Tibet must endure a perilous journey exposed to freezing temperatures for one to four months. Xinjiang's borderlands with central Asia are also predominantly impassable, and the border with Pakistan is now being barricaded with barbed wire. *Refoulement* has occurred among small numbers of refugees who have recently entered Pakistan, and CIS governments cooperate with the suppression of dissident groups. State persecution leads to controlled displacement within China's borders, but many instances are probably unreported.

Development-induced displacement

Where displacement is officially benign in

intent – as it is in forced displacement for development – the outcome may also be politically informed. In the first 40 years since the 1949 revolution, China resettled an average of 800,000 people per year for development purposes, some voluntary, many not. In particular, the displacement of 1,200,000 or more people from the Three Gorges Dam area is the largest dam resettlement in history. The government's frequent resort to the Public Security Ministry applies intimidation so that the operations appear outwardly orderly. In the case of voluntary episodes of resettlement, which occur mostly in anti-poverty operations, 'voluntary' has a different meaning in China, where strong state inducements deprive those affected of the option to appeal. Compoundng these critical victimization issues, many findings suggest that resettlement all too frequently implies abandonment of those displaced to conditions of chronic impoverishent. Thus, there are problems occurring on a massive scale as a result of poorly conceived safeguards and a pervasive lack of administrative responsiveness to aggrieved groups. If coercive factors are not noted, administrative forces at work in displacement appear perfectly above board and sincere. There is an enormous capacity for persecution operating *sub rosa* in displacement issues.

Expulsions

Displacement is an ever present risk for anyone who has been detained by the government for any reason. In China, people who have been detained, regardless of whether charges are brought against them, automatically receive a police record, and are thereafter legally forbidden to return to the activities – from religious study to unregistered employment – for which they were detained. If they fail to comply, expulsion or rearrest may follow. This puts enormous numbers of people potentially at risk; for instance, expulsion frequently is employed to 'disperse' groups the state finds undesirable. Often, those detained for undesirable activities have migrated from other areas, and thus leave 'voluntarily' because of the risk of being forcibly displaced.

Expulsion as a tool for persecuting dissident religious activity occurs pervasively in Tibetan and Muslim centres of worship, and appears less frequent against Christian groups. Official reporting on expulsion is irregular and omits all details.

In Tibet, the use of police 'work teams' is ubiquitous in monasteries and nunneries. Those religious institutions not officially sanctioned by the state are demolished and monks and nuns are expelled or arrested. By state law, all monks and nuns under 18 years of age are automatically expelled from the monastery's locale. Tibet Information Network confirms several hundred expulsions each year apart from those of underage monks. Three major waves occurred before the lifting of martial law in April 1990, in 1993, and most recently since 1996.

In the prefecture of Xinjiang alone, the site of the February 1997 uprising in Guljia/Yining, the provincial 'strike hard' campaign 'dispersed' 499 'underground scripture students' in addition to arresting many thousands, purging at least 444 local leaders, demolishing 133 mosques and shutting down 105 schools. Among Christian sects, reports of displacement are few but one official report recently surfaced in Yanling county, Hunan province, where 1000 followers of the Disciple Church sect were 'dispersed' after the arrest of their 'subversive' leadership. Very often, those who are sentenced by the state to forced labour or imprisonment are routinely deprived of jobs and/or the right of return to their homes after release. Because it is extremely difficult to elude the state authorities in China, sentencing dissidents to forced labour in remote areas (*laojiao*) could be considered

displacement. The state authorities treat this punishment, which frequently occurs without trial, separately from imprisonment. The threat of exile to labour camps is used, for example, for religious congregations. Currently, there are officially 230,000 people in forced labour camps around China, but no accurate estimates of how many are politically-motivated cases of internal exile.

Malevolent resettlement

Counterinsurgency campaigns, under the guise of anti-poverty resettlement, represent a malevolent use of resettlement. By and large, anti-poverty resettlement programmes are voluntary and used to depopulate destitute areas. However, forcible resettlement has sometimes been employed after the suppression of a regional rebellion, to shatter the core of political resistance and isolate dissident communities. During the Miao rebellion in the 1970s village communities in Yunnan province were forcibly resettled from the lowlands to highland areas. The same strategy of displacement was probably a covert component of the Gansu and Ningxia anti-poverty resettlement programmes in the 1990s, in areas where Hui Muslims loyal to Sufi sects have rebelled against state authorities.

Uighur activists in Xinjiang have claimed the forced displacement in 1990/1 of 'tens of thousands' of Uighurs and lesser numbers of Mongols residing along the borders with the Commonwealth of Independent States (CIS), following ethnic disturbances in previous years. The borderlands of Xinjiang and Inner Mongolia were then populated by loyal paramilitary militia families (*bingtuan*), formally known as the Xinjiang production and construction corps. Various aggrieved ethnic minorities in China cite the relentless state-sponsored settlement of Han Chinese in autonomous homelands as a significant background pressure leading to displacement.

Rural-urban migrants – in contrast with

displaced industrial workers who are handed the necessary identity papers to find work wherever they are able – are unregistered and face prejudice from the government. The high incidence of criminal charges against unregistered displaced people – between 50 and 80 per cent of arrests in some cities – intensifies these tensions. An estimated 330,000 displaced people arrive each day in Shanghai and 170,000 in Beijing. Expulsions of migrants by the Public Security Bureau are at short notice, arbitrary and relatively frequent. In 1995, the Beijing authorities demolished the well-known Zhejiang village, which had housed 100,000 IDPs. In 1996, at least 60,000 migrants in Guangzhou (Canton) were repatriated involuntarily.

Disaster-induced displacement

The estimated toll from natural disasters in China is between 10,000 and 20,000 deaths per year: possibly 17 to 25 per cent of the country's revenue is lost to disasters. According to official statistics, 5 million people were resettled and 12.6 million were left temporarily homeless in 1996. In addition, every year tens of thousands of IDPs leave areas that local communities could not rebuild.

China's ability to forecast earthquakes has improved slightly, using meterological satellites, but there are no resources available to earthquake-proof buildings. There is still the possibility of a repeat of the 1976 Tangshan earthquake, for which estimates of the numbers killed vary from between 250,000 and 600,000. In February 1996, an earthquake devastated Lijiang in Yunnan province, which, according to China's contradictory statistics, killed 322, destroyed 340,000 homes and left 180,000 homeless. An earthquake in March 1996 in Xinjiang killed 26 and left 10,000 homeless.

The 1996 floods reportedly left 2–4 million people homeless, and 10,000 deaths went unreported in Hunan province after four

dikes burst. Monsoons soak the southeastern provinces in summer, when mud-flows put 20 million people at risk in the Himalayan foothills, and flooding occurs in the far north and west. Ironically, in the flood basins of the Yangtze (380 million people), Yellow River (100 million), and Huai River, China has both too much and too little water: drought plagues many of the same flood-prone areas. Water is sometimes horded in reservoirs in Anhui and elsewhere until the dams have to be opened abruptly, causing disastrous floods.

The Himalayas drain through rivers all the way east across the country. Yet the scale of disaster is to a large degree human made. Chairman Mao's early development strategy of rapid population growth and grain production at all costs had the effect both of displacing sustainable, traditional river industries such as fisheries and reed-weaving, and of draining and over-populating the natural flood reservoirs along the country's plains. More recently, logging around Tibet and Sichuan and an influx of settlers attempting to apply lowland agricultural techniques to the upper mountains have eroded and denuded whole mountains, so that river basins at lower altitudes have silted and outgrown their dikes. Also one-quarter of medium and large reservoirs and two-fifths of small ones are in need of repair.

The flood prevention arguments for building the Three Gorges Dam on the Yangtze and Xiaolangdi on the Yellow River, are not strong. The Three Gorges Dam will be built too far upriver to curb flooding fully in the downriver provinces. Both dams are expected to silt up in 20 years, potentially increasing the flood threat behind them.

The government is ambiguous in its attitude towards flood relief: 1996 was only the second year since 1949 that it appealed for international aid to help victims. There is evidence that the Chinese state media withhold details on the effects of disasters: recent flood coverage may be exaggerated to demonstrate to foreign critics the necessity for the Three Gorges Dam. Yet serious, possibly man-made disasters, such as Hunan province's 1996 death toll of 10,000, are not reported. International assistance is still accepted for the most part in kind rather than in manpower, although humanitarian agencies have an interest in praising flood relief efforts if it means the possibility of opening up space for outside participation.

North Korea
Anuradha Harinarayan

The Democratic People's Republic of Korea (DPRK) is in the depths of a severe economic and food crisis. The present situation has, however, long been in the making. With the collapse of the Soviet Union and the end of the Cold War in the late 1980s, North Korea lost the support of its strongest ally and largest trading partner. This worsened a decline initially set in motion by a centrally-controlled economy based on the ideology of *juche*, or self-sufficiency in food production and economic growth. North Korea's system of collectivized agriculture and controlled industries, the global isolation of trade, and maintenance of the fifth largest military force in the world have all contributed to the erosion of the already weakened economy. A modern industrial state has collapsed: fuel is as scarce as food; factories have closed down and whole cities are now dark at night. The electrified rail network is disabled by frequent power cuts. In its pursuit of food self-sufficiency – an unattainable goal given the country's limited arable land and unforgiving climate – the government has promoted unsustainable agricultural practices. Massive flooding in late 1995 destroyed an estimated 20 per cent of North Korea's farmlands, only to be followed by severe flooding again in

1996, and drought and typhoon in 1997.

Chronic food scarcity has become acute after two years of crop failures, with famine a possibility. According to the UN, the country will face an estimated deficit of one million tons of food in 1998 (after accounting for commercial imports and pledged food assistance carried over from the marketing year 1996/7). In February 1998 the government announced that food stocks would run out by mid-March. Certainly, the small amounts of food aid pledged so far (for example the EU's contribution of 155,000 tons in May 1997) will be dwarfed by estimates of national food requirements.

Food and relief assistance
The situation in North Korea is quite unlike other complex emergencies familiar to the international relief community. Unlike emergencies resulting from civil strife, the government of North Korea maintains strict control over its people, has a strong military capacity and is primarily responsible for coordinating relief efforts.

In 1995, and to a lesser extent in 1996, severe flooding in North Korea opened doors for an international relief operation. The context for the current relief operation is still defined by these recent natural disasters, although the current situation requires a more strategic humanitarian framework, including assessments of political, gender-related and socioeconomic variables. The priorities of the international aid community normally include targeting vulnerable groups, access to all areas and monitoring distribution. The government of North Korea may have other priorities, such as supplying food to favoured groups of people, including the military. Avoiding the diversion of this might be impossible to avoid.

General distributions of food aid in the country are currently provided through the centrally-controlled Public Distribution System (PDS). The PDS is the mechanism for distributing food and non-food items based on work requirements and sex and age groupings. Given the absence of markets, the population has been dependent on the PDS. However, the PDS probably supplies food to less than 20 per cent of the population. The 1997 FAO/WFP Food and Crop Assessment Report estimates that the rations distributed through the PDS over the past two years have declined from 2200 kilocalories per day to fewer than 1250 kilocalories per day, accounting for less than half of normal daily food requirements.

Problems with relief assistance

The system of food aid distribution in North Korea has been the subject of intense debate. Concerns have been expressed that the government supplies food aid, both domestic and relief, only to those people who are politically and economically important, to the detriment of vulnerable people living in marginalized areas. Parts of the mountainous northeast provinces, for example, are believed to have been cut off from all food distributions through the PDS in recent years. By January 1998 they were receiving only 58 grammes of grain per day each – less than 10 per cent of a normal diet. Targeting and monitoring of assistance are controlled by the government, a regime concerned not to assist the most vulnerable but, rather, to protect the most valuable people. Given limited access, it is not possible to ensure that relief food reaches vulnerable people, although UN agencies and NGOs indicate that access has improved in recent months. In 1997, the World Food Programme distributed food to 7.5 million people – a third of the population. The ICRC believes that five million North Koreans are at risk of starvation. One report suggests that 15 per cent of the population may have succumbed to malnutrition and famine related deaths, while others indicate that the situation has vastly improved since the provision of food and relief assistance. To complicate relief efforts further, the quality of information is suspect because of the state's control of the media, unreliable information sources and the general population's pervasive fear of interacting with foreigners. All visits by relief workers are closely monitored. These constraints have severely hampered efforts to gather human rights information.

Internal displacement in a communist regime

Despite regional variations in food availability, there are few indications of mass population movements in North Korea. Some have commented that North Korea is experiencing a 'stay at home famine'. This contrasts with Africa, for example, where similar deficits have resulted in migrations of hungry people in search of food. To understand this dichotomy, it is important to reiterate the pervasive control of government, especially the strict checks on internal and external movements. Unauthorized population movements are precluded by a system of identity cards and armed checkpoints. In addition, people who elect to migrate lose their only support: their family and work unit on whom their allocations from communal production or the PDS depends.

Despite these deterrents, internally displaced people are seen foraging in city streets. There are also movements across the Chinese border from northeastern North Korea, as well as increasing numbers of refugees crossing into South Korea. Some people risk crossing the Tumen River, the border with China, in order to beg, scavenge or barter food to take back to their children. The people on the Chinese side of the river share the same ancestry, history and language as North Koreans. Many are prepared to risk fines for helping intruders by giving or selling them food. Unusually, migration from urban to rural areas has increased as a result of food shortages. The UN believes that more food is available in rural areas: workers on state collective farms often have small plots of land on which to grow their own family's food. Reports indicate that the government has attempted to reduce the numbers of potentially politically volatile urban people. There are reports of people moving into the mountainous regions of the northeast, where military control is believed to have weakened. All these accounts of internal displacement, however, are based solely on anecdotal evidence.

Who are the internally displaced?

Where possible, families have sent their children to live with relatives in areas where food is more readily available. This constitutes the only internally displaced population that is not at heightened risk due to migration. The elderly have reduced their food intake to provide for the young, while other people have tried to find wild foods from the rural and mountainous regions. Given the limited monitoring of food assistance by the international community and the government's policy of preferential allocation of food through the PDS, it follows that the people who are displaced in North Korea are the most vulnerable. These are the people identified by the state to be of little productive use and who have been left to find their own means of survival or to die. There have been uncorroborated reports of government executions related to charges of cannibalism, which heighten concern about the predicament of abandoned and displaced children. The government has refused to acknowledge that displaced people exist, so relief agencies cannot directly broach the topic. Admission would indicate a failure of the policy of *juche*, an intolerable outcome.

While internally displaced people ought to be one of the primary targets of relief intervention, they remain beyond the reach of the relief community. It is impossible even to provide estimates of the number of internally displaced people in North Korea.

Responses to the problem of displacement

The international community has been slow to recognize the complexity of the situation. Rather, attention has been focused on general food aid distributions through the PDS. These efforts are beneficial: without widespread food distributions, displacement and starvation would undoubtedly be even more profound. However, the problems of the internally displaced are absent from the international community's agenda, the only channel through which this sensitive matter could be initially addressed. Without the overt support of the political actors who are now focused on the four-party talks (People's Republic of China, South Korea, USA and North Korea), humanitarians will continue to be unable to address the needs of displaced people. The most urgent needs that remain are to engage the North Korean government in negotiations for access to restricted areas to ensure that food and relief assistance reach the most vulnerable; to coordinate relief operations effectively under the difficult environment of a totalitarian state; and to alert the world to the plight of those who suffer in North Korea.

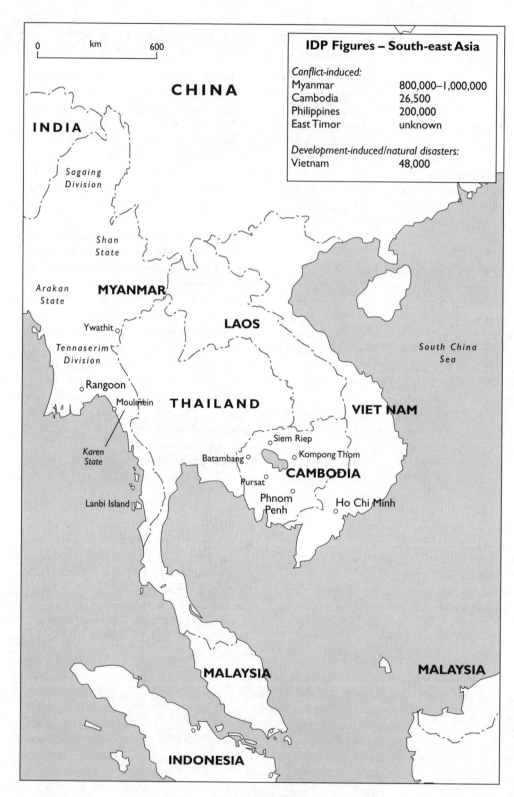

IDP Figures – South-east Asia

Conflict-induced:
Myanmar	800,000–1,000,000
Cambodia	26,500
Philippines	200,000
East Timor	unknown

Development-induced/natural disasters:
Vietnam	48,000

Map 7: South-east Asia

Southeast Asia

Overview

Southeast Asia, one of the poorest regions in the world, has witnessed some of the largest mass migrations this century as a result of internal conflict and human rights violations: the causes are undemocratic political systems; religious and ethnic intolerance; and poverty, landlessness and unemployment.

In Vietnam, a policy of introducing a market economy has resulted in economic growth, which has led to increased urbanization and displacement to economic development zones of more than 100,000 families. The Vietnamese government continues to repress domestic dissent and to restrict basic political and religious freedoms. UNHCR reported few protection problems for the 100,000 returning Vietnamese refugees. Nevertheless, poverty continued to force many thousands to migrate in search of work and some 48,000 people were displaced by natural disasters.

In mid-1997 Cambodia's northwest was once again a battlefield between the rival Cambodian forces of the two co-premiers. By September 1997, between 30,000 and 40,000 refugees had crossed into Thailand, with 15,000 people gathering at the border and another 10,000 displaced further inland. Meanwhile, unknown numbers of returned refugees had not yet found homes and remain displaced within the country.

Human rights abuses in Myanmar (Burma) and refugees fleeing to Thailand and Bangladesh present a number of dilemmas for the international community. Forced relocations, political persecution and forced labour have resulted in an estimated one million IDPs. In July 1997, Myanmar was admitted into the Association of Southeast Asian Nations (ASEAN), though this was not contingent upon an improvement in its human rights record.

There are an estimated 600,000 Myanmar illegal immigrants in Thailand. Those who remain along the border inside Thailand are not recognized as refugees and are often subject to border incursions from the Myanmar military. The Shan, unlike other Myanmar minorities have been prevented from entering Thailand and seeking asylum, as is their right under international law. In northern Myanmar, some 200,000 Rohingya Muslims have repatriated from Bangladesh in the last two years. About 10,000 of them sought asylum in Bangladesh, but were threatened with forced return.

Since Indonesia invaded East Timor in 1975 about 200,000 Indonesians have been settled there, causing widespread displacement of East Timorese people. Immigrants now make up about three-quarters of the capital's population and one-quarter of the total population. Human rights violations have been condemned by the UN Commission on Human Rights and guerrilla warfare continues against the Indonesians.

The people of the Philippines have suffered 20 years of civil war between the government and ethnic minorities. In 1997, approximately 189,000 people were displaced, either by counterinsurgency military operations or urban development projects. President Aquino's administration has not brought the peace or reduced the government forces' violations of human rights, as hoped.

Cambodia
Chris Dammers

Cambodia's long history of conflict and dislocation continues. By the end of 1997 about

25,000 people had been internally displaced, almost entirely in the northwest of the country. However, if the long-term displaced and returning refugees unable to return home are included, the number of IDPs would be considerably greater.

A five-year civil war led in 1975 to the victory of the Khmer Rouge under Pol Pot, whose rule led to the deaths of up to a million people through warfare, starvation and murder. The Khmer Rouge period witnessed massive internal displacement, including wholesale depopulation of urban areas: about 350,000 Cambodians fled the country, mainly to the border regions of Thailand. These refugees lived in camps throughout the 1980s, when Cambodia's Vietnamese-backed regime (1979–93) faced international isolation. Their repatriation under United Nations auspices took place in 1992 and 1993, following the Paris Peace Accords and in anticipation of the 1993 elections.

Although not generally classified as internally displaced people in official statistics, a significant proportion of these returnees were both unable to return to their original homes and have undergone further displacement. Many have continued to suffer impoverishment and disadvantage because of the difficulties of reintegration. Although intended under UN guidelines to return to their places of origin, many did not do so, the principal reason being the unavailability of suitable land. Sometimes designated land was not made available, or was unsuitable for agricultural use. Sometimes the land was in insecure areas, and/or was sown with landmines or suspected of being so. Moreover, economic opportunities for the landless in rural areas are often very limited. In addition, returnees were often subjected to suspicion or antagonism, usually as a result of their perceived political affiliation, which further inhibited their reintegration. Such factors often led to further migration or displacement. Secondary migration was also undertaken by returnees who were looking for lost family members with whom they wished to settle. This pattern of migration actually facilitated the process of reintegration. Though research has been limited, studies have shown that in some areas such secondary internal migration ran at levels of 50 per cent or more.

The 1993 elections led to *de facto* power sharing between the royalist FUNCINPEC – Front uni national pour un Cambodge indépendent neutre pacifique et coopératif (United National Front for an Independent, Neutral, Peaceful and Cooperative Cambodia) and the former ruling communist party, the Cambodian People's Party (CPP). The Khmer Rouge, which boycotted the elections, continued military operations from bases along the Thai border, a primary cause of further displacement in the following years. Patterns of displacement have been complex and fluctuating, relating to the variations in the extent of the fighting, which was often over access to resources. A peak was reached in late 1994, with 164,000 people internally displaced according to Red Cross figures, though around two-thirds of these were able to return home in 1995.

The complex, shifting and often temporary patterns of displacement and internal migration in many parts of Cambodia are reflected in major inconsistencies in available statistics on IDPs, which should be treated with considerable caution. Much depends on definitions employed: since a high proportion of Cambodians have been displaced at one time or another, it is difficult to say at what point they are sufficiently reintegrated into their communities to cease being considered displaced. For example, thousands of people displaced in the province of Kompong Speu in 1993 were dropped from most statistics once their displacement was considered permanent in what became a comparatively stable region. However, many returned to their original districts in the province during the second half of 1997. IDPs in Cambodia, even when their displacement has been long term, may face problems similar to those described above for returnees, though with little prospect of acquiring land, and less access to relief and rehabilitation assistance.

In July 1997, the CPP launched what amounted to a coup against its FUNCINPEC partners in government, leading to further extensive fighting between troops loyal to each party. By September 1997, as many as 40,000 people had been displaced over the border to Thailand: press reports of 60,000 refugees were almost certainly exaggerated and the real figure may be nearer to 30,000. By early 1998, only 3500 of these had returned to Cambodia, though the numbers unable to return to their original homes is not known.

Fighting escalated again in December 1997, with further displacements reported. In January 1998, the Cambodian Red Cross estimated figures for IDPs by province: Battambang (11,104) Preah Vihear (8977); Siem Riep (3627); Bantay Mean Chey (1806); Pursat (555); and Kompong Thom (393). The total came to 26,462. Despite repeated initiatives to broker cease-fires, in advance of elections planned for July 1998, conflict, instability, dislocation and displacement looked set to continue in Cambodia in 1998.

East Timor
Chris Dammers

Portuguese settlement in East Timor dates back to the sixteenth century, and colonial rule continued until after the 1974 coup in Portugal. Only then did political parties emerge in East Timor. The two main parties advocated independence, a prospect that had majority support. The rivalry between them, combined with Indonesian intervention and incursions, and the departure of the Portu-

guese, led to conflict in 1975. FRETILIN (Frente Revolucionária do Timor-Leste Independente/Revolutionary Front for an Independent East Timor) emerged in control of most of the territory and declared East Timor independent soon afterwards. Nine days later, in December 1975, Indonesian troops invaded, with the backing of the USA, Australia and Japan.

The Indonesian army perpetrated appalling atrocities – as many as 80 per cent of the adult male population of the capital city of Dili were killed, many by summary execution. A high proportion of the urban population fled to the mountainous interior, which was controlled by FRETILIN guerrillas. In the early years of the ensuing war, up to a third of the population of 600,000 died as a result of the conflict, bombing, disease and famine. By 1980, Indonesia had gained control of most of the territory, but guerrilla resistance has continued ever since. From 1987, the resistance forces were led by FALANTIL (Forças Armadas de Libertação Nacional de Timor-Leste/Armed Forces of National Liberation for East Timor) representing a coalition of nationalist parties among whom FRETILIN remains dominant.

Most of those who survived these years and returned from the mountains, or were displaced from their homes by the bombing raids, were resettled in 'guided villages', located by roads and subjected to Indonesian surveillance and control. These villages often had little agricultural land attached to them, and during the early years of the war were extremely badly hit by famine and disease. Although more recently some people have been allowed to return to highland villages, much of the territory remains depopulated.

Some agricultural land abandoned during the war was never rehabilitated. As much as 90 per cent of the livestock of the country was lost during the early years of the war, further contributing to the loss of productive land, since the rotational rice cultivation practised in parts of East Timor depends on cattle and buffaloes trampling the fields during the dry season. Some of this land has been allocated to immigrants.

The promotion of immigration to East Timor is part of a wider 'transmigration' policy of the Indonesian government to settle people from densely populated regions of Indonesia in more sparsely inhabited areas of the country, which in their view includes East Timor. The policy has caused further displacement, land alienation and economic disadvantage for the East Timorese. Political circumstances, exacerbated in 1997 by the acute economic crisis facing Indonesia, make the policy particularly problematic in East Timor.

Though independent research is almost non-existent, and official figures are highly unreliable, some estimates put the number of immigrants since the formal incorporation of East Timor into Indonesia as high as 200,000 people, about a quarter of the present population. Only a few thousand of them have received official government sponsorship since East Timor was declared part of the 'transmigration' policy in 1980.

The immigrants are primarily farmers from Java and Bali, entrepreneurs from Sulawesi, and a variety of migrants from West Timor. Immigrants probably comprise three-quarters of the population of the capital Dili. The Sulawesi immigrants appear to attract particular hostility, often manifesting itself as religious antagonism – 90 per cent of the population of East Timor are Roman Catholic, whereas Indonesia is a predominantly Muslim country. The migrants from West Timor, on the other hand, often speak Tetun, the *lingua franca* of East Timor, and usually share the religion of the East Timorese. However, as Indonesians, they usually favour the incorporation of East Timor into Indonesia, and support for such migration is also seen as politically motivated.

Thousand of hectares of land have been allocated to 'transmigrants' without any compensation being given to the original landowners. Mostly, these have been rice fields given to Javanese and Balinese farmers, notably in the districts of Maliana and Kovalima. More generally, displacement can be the result of economic marginalization, though detailed information is unobtainable. Displacement is only one component of wide-ranging abuses of human rights and political freedoms. It contributes, however, to the resentments of East Timorese, and so to the apparently indefinite postponement of an acceptable political settlement for the territory.

In April 1997 the UN Commission on Human Rights voted in support of a resolution condemning the human rights violations in East Timor. Meanwhile, East Timorese guerrillas launched attacks on Indonesian military and police targets. The military responded with an intensive operation throughout the country called Operation Extermination resulting in hundreds of arrests and about 40 summary executions. Violations occurred in the districts of Dili, Baucau and Viqueque, causing the displacement of suspects.

Myanmar
Pamela Harris

Ethnic minorities make up approximately one-third of Myanmar's population of 45 million. For the past 50 years they have been fighting for greater autonomy from the central Myanmar government. A military coup in 1962 led Burma, as it was then known, to become isolated from the world under the rule of the Burma Socialist Programme Party (BSPP) in a one-party system totally dominated by the military. Following nationwide pro-democracy demonstrations in 1988, the State Law and Order Restoration Council

(SLORC) staged a coup to take over the governing of Myanmar, reinstating martial law and imposing restrictions on opposition to the government. The SLORC renamed itself the State Peace and Development Council in November 1997. Human rights violations, including forced relocations of rural and urban populations, have, according to Human Rights Watch (Asia) increased in intensity since the SLORC seized power from the BSPP in 1988. Amnesty International has documented torture, ill-treatment and extrajudicial killings during this time. Elections held in 1990 when the National League for Democracy (NLD), headed by the Nobel peace prize laureate Aung San Suu Kyi, won a landslide victory have never been honoured.

MYANMAR: SLORC troops destroyed these people's village in March 1997, so they fled and built a shelter in the forest. The baskets on their backs contain all they still possess (PHOTO: KHRG).

Cease-fire agreements with ethnic minority resistance armies have not ended human rights violations but have, in some instances, increased the incidences of forced labour, portering and relocation. This is due to the expanded presence of SLORC soldiers in areas previously under control of ethnic minority groups. Cease-fire agreements have not resolved political grievances, for the SLORC refuses to include political solutions in negotiations. Since 1989, the SLORC has reached individual cease-fire agreements with 16 armed ethnic minority groups. The Karen National Union (KNU) is one sizeable group not to have agreed to a cease-fire to date. The cease-fire with the Karenni National Progressive Party (KNPP), agreed in March 1995, broke down after three months and talks are again underway. Armed elements dissatisfied with cease-fire arrangements in Shan state have also led to the renewal of armed activity. Lasting political solutions in Myanmar have so far proved to be elusive.

Despite repeated condemnation of Myanmar by UN agencies, international policy towards Myanmar has polarized. The effects of recent US economic sanctions and the European withdrawal of GSP privileges have been partly offset by Myanmar's recent admission into the Association of Southeast Asian Nations (ASEAN) in July 1997.

Internal displacement in Myanmar mostly results from systematic patterns of human rights abuse associated with the conflict in ethnic minority areas. Many refugees have initially been internally displaced and have subsequently managed to flee. Some people upon reaching an international border have been denied access to asylum and have been forced to remain internally displaced; others have migrated to forest areas to avoid persecution and the harsh conditions of refugee camps. The two main reasons for forced migration are to gain control of the population – through conflict in territories held by the ethnic minority groups and counter-

MYANMAR: IDPs in transit in the south of the country hoping to reach Bangladesh
(PHOTO: Y Saiti/UNHCR).

insurgency strategies involving relocation programmes – and development programmes that violate human rights. There is often a great overlap between these two areas. The forced recruitment of porters for offensives and for development projects is another cause of displacement. Top-down development programmes in which people are relocated so that they can provide forced labour, relocation of people to 'satellite towns' and forced relocation for tourism projects are also cited.

The following is not a comprehensive account of IDPs within Myanmar: it is a record of known instances during the last two years.

Lack of access means that it is difficult to estimate the number of IDPs inside Myanmar, though it is clear that the numbers of refugees in Thailand, China, India and Bangladesh are small by comparison.

Gaining control

In February 1997 a dry-season offensive by the SLORC's army, the Tatmadaw, began against the Karen in southern Karen state and Tennaserim division. This has caused at least 50,000 people to remain internally displaced. Some 20,000 have sought asylum in refugee camps in Thailand and an unknown number of people have entered Thailand as migrant workers.

In the south of Karen state the prominent considerations appear to have been to eliminate the logistical abilities of the KNU and the establishment of a permanent SLORC presence in order to exploit the numerous economic opportunities for trade between Myanmar and Thailand. Since June 1997, a Thai policy to deny access to asylum for new arrivals from these areas has resulted in unknown numbers of people remaining internally displaced in areas of great insecurity. Geographical enclaves, not yet under SLORC control but vulnerable to further armed conflict, have provided temporary shelter for the now much fragmented Karen. Many people are still scattered, hiding in forests without adequate food or access to medicines.

As a result of this offensive, people coexisting with the Karen have also been forced to flee to Thailand or to relocate internally. Muslim people targeted by the SLORC in former KNU held areas, have seen their mosques destroyed, materials from these mosques looted and the Koran ripped up in the streets before forced to flee.

The conflict continues in the northern part of Karen state where, despite nominal SLORC control, systematic relocation of villages is depopulating entire areas. Since March 1997, at least 93 villages have been completely destroyed. With the exception of villages close to Papun, people have not been given orders to relocate; rather they have just had their villages destroyed. Refugees continue to reach Thailand from this area while others have been deterred by the distance, landmines or the belief that Thailand will not grant them asylum. The displaced people in this area are living on rice stocks previously hidden in the forests, roots and leaves while they attempt to remain 'invisible' to the authorities. They have little access to medicine and many have died of treatable diseases.

Between September 1996 and January 1997 people were forced to relocate in the Tennaserim division, some on more than one occasion, from about 70 villages. Motives for this forcible relocation seem to have centred around the ability of the SLORC to control the area, and use the scattered people for forced labour on army bases and roads. This situation of generalized violence includes some 20 documented cases of murders and of confiscation of land and rationing of the villagers' rice. It has been estimated that some 25,000 civilians have been affected by these forced relocation orders.

The control of people invariably involves a counterinsurgency strategy known as the 'four cuts' – food, finance, intelligence and recruitment – used by successive Burmese military regimes since the mid-1960s. The aim is to sever links between civilians and the military forces in opposition to the central government. Forcible relocation of people acts as an effective method of breaking these links and enables the SLORC to consolidate its control over these fragmented communities. People are sent to particular relocation sites or have scattered after being served relocation orders, giving only a few days notice; these areas then become free-fire zones. In recent years, large numbers of Kachin, Shan, Karenni, Mon and Karen people have been forcibly relocated due to the 'four cuts'. The enforcement of these relocation campaigns are invariably brutal.

Relocations of this nature in Shan state have been particularly brutal since March 1996. In an area of approximately 5000 square miles, the SLORC has relocated, at gunpoint, more than 100,000 people from 600 villages in 45 main relocation sites. In 1997, a renewed relocation programme has meant that many of these villagers have been relocated more than once; in March 1997 alone, approximately 12,500 people moved for a second time and in April the SLORC proceeded to burn down 1000 houses in a relocation site. It is estimated that more than 200,000 people in Shan state have been relocated since March 1996. The increase in brutality during 1997 has involved large numbers of extrajudicial killings; in July, for example, 96 people were reportedly killed *en masse*.

Between April and July 1996, between 20,000 and 30,000 people were ordered to relocate from the villages between the Pon and Salween rivers in Karenni state. They were ordered to move to Shadaw and Ywathit, both of which are close to SLORC army camps. A further large forced relocation campaign occurred in 1997.

Conditions in these relocation sites in Karenni state have been severe. During 1996, in Shadaw, no food, building materials or shelter were provided; 200 people died of disease; people were forced to work and beatings were witnessed. Since 1997, it has been possible to buy passes to leave these relocation sites between sunrise and sunset to forage for food, but many people caught outside the camps have been arrested and tortured, even with passes. Villagers on multi-day passes who try to get to their home villages risk being shot on sight because all these areas are free-fire zones.

In northwest Myanmar the 'four cuts' policy is also used to destroy links between the civilian population and the Chin National Front (CNF) and Naga resistance forces. Amnesty International reports that 'thousands of ethnic Chin from Chin state and western Sagaing division in northwest Myanmar have fled to Mizoram state in northeast India to avoid forced labour and the *tatmadaw*'. Relocation campaigns are now being initiated along the Indian border.

Portering

The practice of forced recruitment of porters for the military is another cause of displacement. During the 1997 offensive against the Karen, large numbers of porters were conscripted for this operation from as far away as the outskirts of Rangoon. People were taken from their cars on the road leading to Moulmein, from cinemas and shops. If porters manage to escape they may find themselves far from their homes with, potentially, no option to return for fear of repercussions.

The controversial Unocal/Total Yadana gas pipeline project in the Tennaserim division has created conditions whereby the SLORC providing 'security' in the area has caused great hardship for porters forced to work on this project. Internal displacement has continued during 1996 and 1997 due to this forced portering. Referring to allegations in 1991 and 1992 a recent hearing in a US federal court heard that the 'plaintiffs essentially contend that Unocal ... is knowingly taking advantage of and profiting from SLORC's practice of using forced labour and forced relocation'.

Tourism and 'development'

The overlap between gaining control of people, and projects carried out in the name of national development is well illustrated by the case of a nature reserve and the demarcation of islands as national parks. It is not known just how many people have been relocated with these projects as a primary cause given the counterinsurgency operations carried out in these areas. Villagers in Tennaserim division in late 1996 reported that they were forcibly relocated when the land was declared a forest conservation area. The New York based Wildlife Conservation Society, the Smithsonian Institute in Washington and the Worldwide Fund for Nature (WWF) International in the UK have each been in contact with the SLORC regarding this potential tourist attraction: 'a unique million-hectare biosphere, the Myinmoletkat Nature Reserve'. The Smithsonian and WWF-UK have since denied any project collaboration.

The islands off the south coast of Myanmar are now being developed for tourism. Some of these islanders have been forced to flee and relocate under conditions of extreme brutality. In one incident in September 1996, 140 people were killed on Lanbi island to make way for an 'eco-tourism venture' to be known as the Lanbi Island Marine National Park.

All over Myanmar, 'development' projects such as the widening and construction of roads, bridges, railways and embankments are under way. People are often forced to relocate from the routes of these projects; they seldom receive compensation for the loss of their homes and are forced to work on these projects. This excessive forced labour then denies them the ability to sustain their families. Examples include the Ye-Tavoy railway and the extensive road network being constructed in Tennaserim division. Human rights reports from Sagaing division during 1996 on the border area development programme often cited relocation, loss of homes and lack of compensation as additional obstacles to sustaining livelihoods. Women and children often undertake the forced labour because their men are vulnerable to accusations of assisting insurgents, being beaten or being taken as porters.

'Urban Development Programmes' that involve the residents of a designated area having to move to 'satellite towns' at short notice have been cited as a form of forced relocation in urban centres: no comprehensive data are available. It has been reported that the authorities have first disconnected the electricity and water supplies at the old settlements and then razed them to the ground. Compensation or assistance to build new homes is rarely offered and the new sites afford little infrastructure such as sewage, clean water or access to health facilities. Once registered with the local authorities in these 'satellite towns', people are denied permission to move.

Impacts

Since 1988 over one million people have been forcibly relocated, without compensation, to new towns, villages or relocation camps in which they are essentially detained. The central government does not acknowledge IDPs and few statistics are available. People in Myanmar rarely flee in large numbers as in other situations; usually they move in small groups of a few families. They flee in silence, not wishing to be identified as displaced, fearing execution or persecution.

As the central Burmese authorities seek to control the people, particularly in the ethnic states, relocation takes on a number of dynamics. The degree of coercion, the scale and variety of reasons for relocations all need to be considered. The fragmentation of communities, the splitting of families, the individual losses associated with relocation and the mistrust generated by people relocated cannot be underestimated. In Shan state there have been cases of repercussions on ethnic villages due to the level of violence the SLORC has perpetrated against the Shan.

It has been pointed out by a Mon human rights group that 'despite the NMSP–SLORC cease-fire agreement the SLORC army has not abstained from forcible relocation and displacement of the Mon villages in the region.' The 10,000 Mon who, under Thai military pressure, 'spontaneously repatriated' in 1996 did so with no UNHCR assistance or monitoring. These 'returnees' moved to designated sites only a few kilometres inside Myanmar, due in part to fear of returning to their villages of origin. No international agency with a mandate for protection has access to these areas.

Some relocations also appear to be ethnically motivated. Amnesty International is concerned about widespread forcible relocations, often accompanied by death threats, ill-treatment, harassment and intimidation, which appear to be carried out solely on account of the ethnic origin or perceived political beliefs of those who are relocated. In addition, people are forced to remain in life-threatening conditions in the relocation sites, which include overcrowding, and a lack of sanitation and safe drinking water. Forced relocation is being used to change the ethnic balance in politically sensitive areas, especially in the Arakan state where many Muslim communities have been compelled to move. The problem is not new; it originates mainly from the absence of a political solution dating back to colonial times and before.

Access to health facilities in the ethnic relocation sites is minimal and for those who hide in the forests it is non-existent. Access to work, other than forced labour, is limited and food is often rationed. In urban areas such as Rangoon, rural workers migrating to the city in search of work are living in improvised shacks. The 'satellite towns' offer little in terms of infrastructure, access to clean water, sewerage or medical facilities.

Within Myanmar, responses to IDPs are bound up with the numerous regulations and restrictions imposed by the SLORC. Even UN agencies, mostly based in Rangoon, are denied permission to enter the border regions where the people affected by offensives, counter-insurgency operations or forced relocations are mostly found. Very few NGOs choose to operate in Myanmar, partly because of the human rights abuses, but also because they believe that without a political solution, corruption is unavoidable. Permission to operate is dependent on negotiating a memorandum of understanding with the SLORC and operational difficulties have been encountered by NGOs in the past. Current assistance is limited to specific areas where the government allows the international community access.

Violations of international norms and standards are countless. Even conventions ratified by the Myanmar government are regularly violated. Groups of civilians are directly affected by offensives and counter-insurgency operations that contravene Article 3 of the four 1949 Geneva conventions ratified by the government in 1992. Individuals or families are forced to flee the excessive forced labour, which contravenes ILO Convention (No 29) on forced labour, which Myanmar ratified in 1955.

In practice, there is no international agency with responsibility to assess the extent or to address the needs of IDPs inside Myanmar. No international human rights monitor is granted access to Myanmar, even on a periodic basis. The UN special *rapporteur* on Myanmar has never been granted permission to visit. There are few places in the world with so little scrutiny of the treatment of IDPs.

The Philippines
Chariza T Medina-Salgado

The costs of more than 20 years of armed conflict in the Philippines have been high. Human rights continue to be violated by government forces against the people, under the framework of militarization and 'development' projects. Internal displacement of families dates back to Spanish colonial times when thousands of Filipino families fled their homes in fear of their lives. This persisted during the American and Japanese occupations of the late nineteenth and early twentieth century and continued during the Marcos era. Between 1972 and 1984, during the height of the Marcos dictatorship, one million families were displaced by armed clashes between the military and rebels.

The Philippines are predominantly Catholic, and it was reported that in 1975 500,000 Muslims were forced off their land. Up to 300,000 refugees, mostly Muslims, now live in Malaysia.

After the people's revolt in February 1986, which toppled the Marcos administration, the Filipino people hoped that President Corazon C Aquino would bring them peace. However, less than a year later the Aquino administration openly declared war against the insurgents and military operations were intensified. School buildings and churches were filled again with fleeing families. During the height of Aquino's 'total war policy', more than a million Filipinos were displaced.

In Mindanao, there was increased fighting

between Moro rebel groups and government forces, with armed clashes. The government's medium-term development plan is also causing a rise in the number of internally displaced people and homeless families.

Between January and December 1997, there were 550 recorded incidents of displacement, not counting those caused by natural disasters: 31,564 families or 189,000 people throughout the country were displaced by counterinsurgency operations or by the demolition of urban shanties for the construction of government development projects. This was a 51 per cent rise over the 1996 figure. Most of the families whose homes were demolished and who also lost their jobs or livelihood, came from Mindanao. However, there may be other IDPs who have not been counted because of the lack of access to certain areas, particularly in the interior. Although there is a slight decrease in the number of displacement incidents, from 38 to 26, the number of affected people remains high.

Mindanao had the highest number of displacement incidents in 1997, with the largest number of displaced people: 24,459 families. Five incidents in Metro Manila affected about 5300 families. Two incidents were documented in Luzon, affecting 1305 families, and one in Visayas, which affected about 500 families.

Armed conflicts

Counterinsurgency operations and related military activities remain the leading cause of displacement. Though most families are exposed to difficulty and hardship even before their displacement, those affected find themselves deprived not only of shelter but also of food and clothing, and they have a decreased capacity to support themselves.

In Mindanao, the displaced families are usually herded into relocation centres where they are concentrated in cramped makeshift shelters. The inadequate food, clothing and shelter, combined with overcrowding and poor sanitation, causes epidemics of disease, particularly among children.

In the confusion and fear that accompanies forced displacement, families are often separated, or relationships become strained. Fathers, husbands or brothers leave their families to look for work elsewhere. So the burden of keeping the rest of the family together and providing for their basic needs is left to the women. Children from affected rural communities, prevented from going to school by armed clashes between government troops and Moro rebels, had their schools used as evacuation centres for the displaced. Sometimes, clothes and other material goods are stolen during military operations in their villages and houses burned. Farm animals and poultry disappear and crops are wasted because peasant farmers are not allowed to return to harvest them. Agrarian reform, the cornerstone of Aquino's stated policy was diluted after going through a legal assembly made up principally of landowners. President Aquino's family own plantations and oppose any changes to the country's agrarian economy. Sharecropping and renting provides 80 per cent of the country's employment, whereby peasants must give landowners two-thirds of their crops or pay high rents. Rapid deforestation means that available land is decreasing fast: in the 1950s, 75 per cent of the land was forested, by 1990 this had fallen to 24 per cent.

Active volcanoes are a major cause of displacement in the Philippines. In 1991, Mount Pinatubo erupted, killing 700 people, flattening an entire village and forcing the evacuation of more than 300,000 people. The US Air Force base was completely buried under the ashes and the USA abandoned it, leaving 40,000 Filipinos out of work.

Development or demolition?

In Metro Manila, alternative housing has not been provided for the victims of demolition.

Those few who were relocated complained of inappropriate sites that lacked basic facilities such as potable water, electricity or proximity to schools, hospitals or employment.

The government denies the alarming annual increase in the numbers of internally displaced people in the Philippines. Only when it takes note of their rights and needs will the problem begin to abate.

Vietnam
Ophelia Mendoza

There are two forms of internal displacement in Vietnam: those who move either by choice or by force because of economic development projects, and those who have to move because of natural disasters.

In 1986, the government of Vietnam launched the *doi moi* reform process, which aimed to reorient the Vietnamese economy away from central planning towards the market. This controlled transition towards a market economy led to remarkable economic growth with an annual average per capita income increase of 7–8 per cent; there were steady decreases in the inflation rate and high rates of growth in gross domestic product. However, this economic development has not been equally distributed, resulting in a widening gap between regions, socioeconomic classes and ethnic groups. The Political Bureau of the Communist Party of Vietnam has openly recognized this problem. These economic disparities have given rise to migration movements, especially from rural to urban areas. At present, Ho Chi Minh City accommodates an estimated one million migrants from other cities and provinces. In the past, Vietnamese people could not move from one province to another without a permit. Residents are still given priority when applying for employment, which makes

migrants a vulnerable group and more likely to be unemployed or underpaid. In response to this problem, the government has moved many city dwellers to new economic zones. From 1975 to 1990, 84,000 families from Ho Chi Minh City were moved to these new economic zones. From 1990 to 1997, 3200 families settled in the provinces of Binh Phuoc, Lam Dong and Dac Lac. City authorities are planning to move an additional 33,000 households consisting of about 165,000 people to new economic zones in neighbouring provinces over the next four years.

The government has clear plans for those who have to be relocated to economic zones. In addition to incentives such as land and house allocation, the state will provide capital and technical assistance to farming production and will build food and farm produce processing plants. Settlers are reorganized into zones to facilitate farming production and the building of roads, electricity, water, schools and medical facilities. Economic migrants may not fall within the working definition of IDPs, for theirs may be considered development-induced displacement, but the extent of displacement and the manner in which the government addresses the needs of internally displaced people are not well documented. Documentations of human rights violations related to the process of displacement are even harder to come by. The state's complete control of all forms of media has to be considered in assessing the real status of IDPs in Vietnam.

The presence of a UNDP-funded disaster management unit, which has developed an information system operating throughout the country, has meant that natural disasters in Vietnam, such as typhoons, flashfloods and cyclones, are well documented. The damage inflicted by Typhoon Linda on 2 November 1997 resulted in 473 deaths, 3020 persons missing and 77,307 houses destroyed. Altogether, 9610 households consisting of approximately 48,050 people were evacuated in 1997, but the areas most greatly affected were the Mekong River Delta and the northcentral coastal part of the country. Natural disasters in Vietnam in 1997 included 560 people killed on land and at sea; 3076 missing; 9610 households evacuated and an economic loss of nearly US$ 4 million.

The launching of *doi moi* has strengthened Vietnam's links with the international community, bringing the country increasing international assistance. For Typhoon Linda, donations amounting to nearly US$ 6 million were received from foreign governments, international NGOs and charities. In 1997, there were 181 NGOs operating in Vietnam, of which at least six were working with refugees and IDPs. The UNHCR's work focuses on returnees rather than on IDPs.

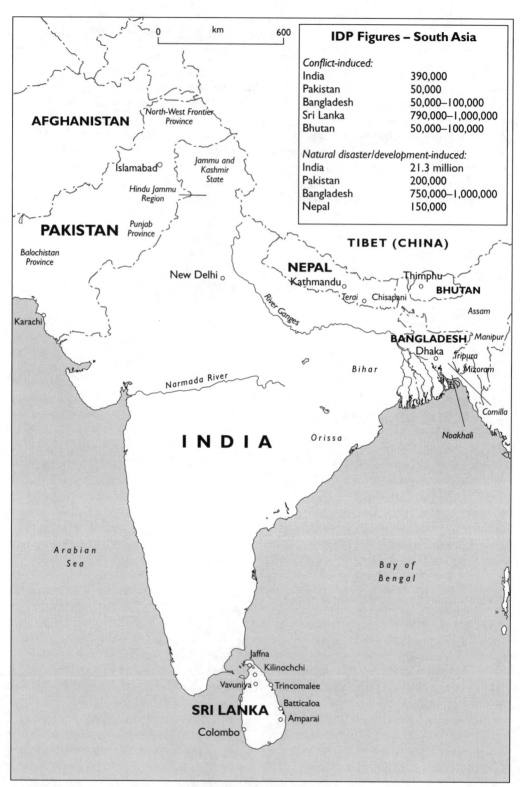

IDP Figures – South Asia

Conflict-induced:

India	390,000
Pakistan	50,000
Bangladesh	50,000–100,000
Sri Lanka	790,000–1,000,000
Bhutan	50,000–100,000

Natural disaster/development-induced:

India	21.3 million
Pakistan	200,000
Bangladesh	750,000–1,000,000
Nepal	150,000

Map 8: South Asia

South Asia

Overview
Sumit Sen

Forced migration in modern South Asia began with the partition of India in 1947. The transfer of power to independent India and Pakistan was followed by the transfer of 20 million people, with the governments of India and Pakistan undertaking to rehabilitate the displaced people. However, 50 years after independence, the plight of refugees and IDPs in South Asia is unenviable. Migration into South Asia has taken place from Afghanistan, Tibet and Myanmar. The continuing civil war in Afghanistan has discouraged repatriation; China's occupation of Tibet causes regular exoduses into Nepal and India; and the Myanmar military junta has renewed the flight of Rohingyas into Bangladesh. In addition, movements within the region include more than 1.5 million Tamil, Chakma, Lotshampa and Bihari refugees. There are no regional or national legal mechanisms for protecting displaced people, the level of government assistance is minimal, and access for the UNHCR or ICRC is either restricted or denied.

There are far more IDPs than refugees in South Asia. Apart from Tamil, Chakma and Lotshampa people displaced by ethnic unrest, the majority are victims of natural and man-made disasters. Natural and man-made disasters are widespread in India, Bangladesh and Nepal, and persecution of minorities leading to displacement is prevalent in Sri Lanka, Pakistan and Bhutan. UNHCR and the special *rapporteur* have a regional approach to IDPs in Sri Lanka. In encouraging regional settlements, UNHCR has facilitated a 'Draft Regional Declaration on Refugees in South Asia', with preparatory discussions. Generally, however, the governments concerned are suspicious of regional initiatives on refugees. With the exception of Tamils in Sri Lanka, only national NGOs have had a role in advocacy and assistance programmes for IDPs. Any regional initiatives for IDPs would be considered a violation of national sovereignty.

A significant number of people in South Asia are displaced by development projects. The World Bank withdrew its funding to the Narmada river project in India when it gained an international reputation for being a large-scale development project that submerged land and had displaced more than a million people. There is often a failure to consult the people affected by projects that violate their human rights. Traditional smallholders lose their land and livelihoods and thus require equivalent land and cash. However, the quantity and quality of compensation leave much to be desired. As a result of inadequate data, the provisions for resettlement and rehabilitation have not adequately addressed the real needs of those affected. In particular, national policy initiatives have failed to recognize that not even the IDPs' previous standard of living is achieved. Further, development projects may affect the livelihoods of people who are not immediately displaced by them but who risk becoming IDPs in future if their situation is ignored.

The South Asian region should be seen within a dynamic geopolitical context. Emergency situations beyond the region, especially in Myanmar, Tibet, Afghanistan, Tajikistan, Uzbekistan and Turkmenistan, influence population movements. Home to over 25 per cent of the global population with 50 per cent of the world's poor, the governments of South Asia need consistent and predictable policies for IDPs. Governments need to cooperate with the UNHCR and ratify the 1951 Refugee Convention and 1967 Protocol. The human rights treaties need incorporation and implementation for effective national protection, rehabilitation and resettlement policies for forcibly displaced people.

Bangladesh
Sumit Sen

Population displacements in Bangladesh are a regular feature and result from both natural disasters such as cyclones, tornados, riverbank erosion and drought; and governmental policies such as the dispossession of Chakma tribal land and forced settlements.

Bangladesh has one of the largest deltas in the world, with a catchment area of 660,000 square miles and a rural population density of 2000 per square mile. It is estimated that riverbank erosion alone displaces nearly one million people a year. This high frequency of displacement encourages people to move only short distances, and studies have shown that 88 per cent of displaced households remain within two to ten miles of their previous settlement. This is compounded by the absence of resources to move greater distances, the pull factor towards kith and kin, and the wish to return to their original homes. However, local powerful interests often acquire the emerging riverside land following flooding, with the displaced people as losers. The IDPs add to numbers of landless in Bangladesh, estimated at half the rural population.

In May 1997 a tropical cyclone hit the Bangladesh delta, damaging 500,000 houses and affecting two million people. Temporary displacement of several hundred thousand people was reported. Then, in September 1997, a cyclone in the Chittagong totally destroyed 92,000 dwellings and caused

widespread crop damage. The International Red Cross helped evacuate 750,000 people from the storm area. Sophisticated early warning systems meant that the death toll was low – between 30 and 60 people were killed compared 138,000 in 1991, when the country's last major cyclone struck.

Pressures on land have resulted in government policies in which organized population transfers and relocations involve the use of force and other human rights violations. While IDPs in squatter settlements live in constant fear of eviction by domestic agencies like the Bangladesh Water Development Board, government policy has concentrated on interdistrict population relocation. The most significant relocations were from Dhaka, Noakhali and Comilla to the Chittagong Hill Tracts (CHT). The resettlement plan for some IDPs became a policy of displacement for many others, for government planning resulted in evicting local people.

The current settlement of Muslims in the CHT has caused the relocation of the Chakma tribal population. Long-standing ethnic conflict has resulted in an estimated 50,000 remaining in camps in India and 20,000 in Myanmar. The 'detribalization' of CHT and the internal displacement of Chakmas began with the Kaptai dam project in Rangamati in 1960, which submerged 40 per cent of the cultivable land and left over 100,000 people displaced. In response, the tribal people formed an organization, Shanti Bahini, to fight for their rights. Conflict accelerated with an excessive military and paramilitary presence, and in 1976 the civil administration was disbanded and the region was designated a military zone. There is reportedly one member of the security forces for every 20 hill people.

Over the years, the government has completely altered the demographic composition of the CHT. The 1991 census showed that in 1983 the Bengali Muslim population in the CHT formed 45.2 per cent of the total CHT population, having risen from 2.94 per cent in 1941, 6.29 per cent in 1951, 11.77 per cent in 1961, 22.83 per cent in 1971 and 35.81 per cent in 1981. Chakma refugee leaders in India contend that the population transfers are aimed at changing the character of the CHT to that of the dominant Bengali Muslim culture.

Government resettlement programmes for Muslims in the late 1970s and early 1980s displaced thousands of hill people. Shanti Bahini oppose the settlements, and argue that Muslims could not have been settled without the support of the armed forces. Tribals, some as refugees in India and the majority as IDPs in Bangladesh, have stated that Bengali Muslims attacked them and killed their friends and family. The illegal land grabbing began with intimidation and coercion, and culminated in brute force. Along with the settlers, the military forces took over land. Any representation to the civil and judicial authorities provided little respite.

The tribals in CHT have been persecuted with sexual attacks and rape; women have been forced into marriage, men beaten and children traumatized. In consequence, refugees from CHT in India have been extremely reluctant to return. Although a renewed phase of repatriation was negotiated for the end of November 1997, not all refugees have returned. The fear of the Chakma refugees is justified, for the Bangladesh government has not done enough to ameliorate the situation. Both India and Bangladesh have refused to give UNHCR access to the refugees to determine if the return is voluntary, so repatriation takes place without any monitoring. UNHCR, mandated with the international protection of human rights of displaced people, is the agency best suited to help the Chakma refugees in India to return to Bangladesh.

Bhutan
Sumit Sen

For a country of such a small size and population, Bhutan generates a significant number of refugees and IDPs. The government's conservative and traditionalist policies have led to human rights violations and harassment of certain groups with the aim of displacing them and acquiring their property. Many of those displaced find refuge in Nepal and India. Given the severe restrictions imposed on access to international organizations, the true picture of the plight of IDPs in Bhutan is extremely difficult to ascertain. However, information provided by Lotshampa refugees in Nepal gives some insight into the situation. Bhutan has not yet accepted important treaties, including the two human rights covenants. The forced migration of Bhutanese citizens of Nepalese origin, the Lotshampas, began with the forced assimilation by the Bhutanese state machinery in 1990. The Bhutanese were traditionally resident in northern Bhutan, with the south being administered by the Dorji family based in Kalimpong. Lotshampas have immigrated to Bhutan since the end of the last century and settled primarily in southern Bhutan. They have contributed substantially to the national economy of Bhutan. Although opposition groups claim that Lotshampas make up over 50 per cent of the 700,000 population, excluding the refugees in Nepalese camps, Bhutanese government figures state that they are less than 25 per cent of the population, which they estimate at 1.4 million. Interestingly, both figures lead to approximately 350,000 Lotshampas, excluding the 100,000 refugees. The Bhutanese minister of home affairs, Dago Tshering, said: 'It must be made very clear that such people's [Lotshampa refugees] family members [in Bhutan] will be held fully responsible [for their anti-Bhutan agitation] and will forfeit their citizenship.' Bhutan's ruling regime has carried out its threat on numerous occasions, has denationalized its citizens and has displaced them. Recently, they turned their attention to southern Bhutan's remaining intelligentsia. In January 1998 a further 219 Nepalese-speaking civil servants were sacked. The displacement of them and their families will follow. Deserted villages are being resettled by 'genuine' Bhutanese from the north.

The forcible imposition of the Druk language, dress and culture on Lotshampas and the acquisition of their lands by the army and civil officials has led to internal displacement. Cultural oppression and crushing of pro-democratic movements have resulted in the government forces attacking unarmed civilians, conducting house to house searches without warrants, beating up men, raping women, and burning down entire villages. This has resulted in thousands of IDPs, though their number is indeterminable, due to the government's strict control of entry to the country. For example, only 3000 tourists are allowed in each year.

King Wangchuck and his ruling regime are about to embark on a programme of rapid industrialization with a hydroelectic dam, expansion of the only airport and the introduction of television. India supports Bhutan, a strategic buffer zone against China.

The plight of IDPs is linked to a more general need for governmental transparency and international access. Improvements in this respect would include access for the international media and human rights observers; a reduction on expenditure for the machinery of internal oppression (police and defence forces); free association for pro-democracy movements; and a fundamental review of the rights of minorities.

India
Omprakash Mishra, P V Unnikrishnan and Maxmillan Martin

Ethnic conflict based on demands for secession or greater autonomy has generated significant internal displacement in India's northeast region. In May 1996 many Adivasis (loosely called Santhals) of Assam were displaced. While the majority of the displaced Adivasis (about 80,000) have returned to their villages, 70,000 of them remain in relief camps and rehabilitation centres. About 30,000 non-tribals, or 'outsiders' who dominate trade and the professions and control prime urban property, mostly Bengalis, were uprooted by violence in Tripura in early 1997. Also, the continuing clashes between Nagas and Kukis in Manipur have moved the two population groups. The 255,000 Kashmiri Pandits who were forced to flee the Kashmir Valley in 1990, and the 15,000 Reang tribals who fled western Mizoran bring the number of conflict-induced IDPs in India to approximately 390,000.

Jammu and Kashmir
Almost the entire minority Hindu community of Kashmir valley in the Jammu and Kashmir state was forced to flee when the region came under the control of many secessionist groups during 1989/90. The displacement of the Pandits occurred after select killings of community members and widespread anarchy. The secessionist movement in the valley, which was earlier led by secular groups, passed into the hands of the fundamentalist forces. Consequently, 'Kashmiriyat' – a concept of ethnic identity distinctive of the valley and uniting Muslims and Hindus – came under serious attack with the ascendancy of fundamentalist secessionist groups such as Hizbul-Mujahidden. Approximately 250,000 Pandits fearing for their life migrated

to the predominantly Hindu Jammu region, New Delhi, and other parts of the country. Despite the installation of a popularly elected government in October 1996, no progress has been made to return or resettle the displaced Pandits. In March 1997, seven Pandit men were killed by the militants, starting yet another exodus of the few Pandits who still lived in the valley after the main community had migrated in 1990. The militants gunned down three Pandit schoolteachers in Udampur district in June 1997. Pandits are now reluctant to return to the valley. Some people are now demanding a 'homeland Panun Kashmir' – a separate enclave for Pandits within Kashmir.

Most of the displaced people, largely Hindus but including about 3000 Muslim and Sikh families, are living in Jammu and Delhi. Out of a total of 49,760 registered displaced families, 28,561 are living in Jammu region; 19,339 in Delhi; and the rest in other parts of the country. Many families, however, are not registered. Moreover, thousands of applications for registration are pending before the authorities in Delhi. The Delhi administration has fixed Rs 1800 (US$ 51.50) as maximum relief payable to each displaced family. However, only about one-third of the registered families are paid the relief amount, which may be less for smaller families and is reduced after a death in the family. Basic pay is being given to those who were employees of the state government. Many are living in miserable conditions in camps scattered throughout the Delhi and Jammu region. Over the years some people have found employment in the urban areas.

Assam

India's northeast has ethnic conflicts of various types, resulting in numerous IDPs. Large-scale violence in the Kokrajhar, Bongaigaon and Dhubri districts of Assam in May 1996 against Adivasis, mainly Santhals, rendered more than 150,000 people homeless.

The violence, involving plunder, arson and massacre, was the third major riot against the non-Bodo communities in the proposed Bodo Autonomous Council area of western Assam which was settled as part of an agreement in 1993. Since the Bodos are not in a majority in a large number of villages in the council area, the Bodo Liberation Front (BLF) and All Bodo Students Union (ABSU), which are spearheading a movement for a separate Bodoland, targeted non-Bodo communities to spark off an exodus.

The affected Adivasis were sheltered in 58 relief camps, mostly in Kokrajhar district. As the situation has normalized since December 1996, many people have been moved from the relief camps to the rehabilitation camps. Since then more than half of the IDPs have returned to their villages. About 45,000 of them remain in rehabilitation camps and the rest are still in the relief camps. The prospect of settlement of those in the relief camps is remote, since many were living in unregistered villages in reserve forest areas, and the Guwahati High Court has banned their resettlement in these areas.

The administration has provided the affected people with inadequate relief. Since December 1996, even food rations have been discontinued for those who have been moved to rehabilitation camps. A rehabilitation grant of Rs 10,000 (US$ 285.71) per family has been provided to some of the affected people, but most have only received grants of between US$ 85.71 and US$ 114.29.

Tripura

In Tripura, tribal militants of the National Liberation Front of Tripura (NLFT) and All Tripura Tiger Force (ATTF) have adopted the strategy of engineering internal displacement by targeting non-tribals, mostly Bengalis, to express their resentment of the 'domination of outsiders', and to bolster their demand to convert the Tripura tribal areas autonomous district into a full tribal state. Recent violence forced out about 30,000 non-tribals from their villages in the Khowai subdivision. Most of these people have found shelter in government-run relief camps where they lack adequate rations and security. The tribal militants even attacked Gouranga Tilla relief camp in February 1997, killing 32 people. In March, the inmates of the relief camps organized a procession to protest against inadequate security in the camps and government attempts to persuade the inmates to return to their villages. Starting from Paharampura, near the border, the protesters attempted to cross over to Sylhet in Bangladesh to seek refuge there.

Manipur

Severe ethnic strife between Tangkhul Nagas and Kukis in parts of Manipur has resulted in large-scale movements of two population groups. More than 1000 people have been killed since July 1992. The Senapati, Chandel, Churachandpur and Ukhrul districts are particularly affected. Insecurity has forced Kukis to leave many Naga-inhabited areas. Similarly, non-Kukis are migrating to Mizoram from the Churachandpur district. Though the ethnic conflict has generated large-scale relocation of population, figures are not available. The continuing clashes between the Paites and Kukis in Manipur since July 1997, and the possibility of violence between Nagas and Meiteis triggered by demands for a 'Unified Nagaland', may provoke more internal displacement.

Bihar

Various armed extreme leftist groups, commonly termed Naxalites have taken control of many villages spread in different parts of Bihar state. Espousing the cause of the landless poor, forcibly redistributing excess land owned by the rich, these groups have gained some support. However, extortions, kidnappings and random killings are common; deaths from Naxalite violence in 1997

amounted to 100 villagers, 192 Naxalites and five policemen.

In another part of Bihar in December 1997, 59 men, women and children were shot dead by a 250-strong private army of landlords. The group hit socially lower castes and, fearing reprisals, about 200 upper-caste men fled their homes, leaving behind their women and children.

Shillong, the capital of Meghalaya, is witnessing a slow but continuous outflow of non-tribals or outsiders. This is secured through intimidation and force by the local militant groups in rural and urban areas.

Mizoram

During October 1997, about 15,000 Reang tribals, fearing persecution and threats to their life from a militant group of the ethnic majority Mizos, fled from western Mizoram. They have taken shelter in north Tripura and border villages in Assam. The Mizoram government alleges that Reangs, in pressing for an autonomous district council, are resorting to violence under the leadership of the Bru (Reang) Revolutionary Army and this has impaired ethnic harmony. The displaced Reangs are surviving on wild plants with little access to water. The Assam and Tripura governments have expressed their helplessness in meeting the Reangs' food and medical requirements. Some of the people who were repatriated returned to their makeshift camps after alleging non-cooperation from the administration and local people. Negotiations for repatriation of the displaced Reangs are continuing, but the damage to ethnic harmony between Mizos and Reangs seems irreparable.

Development-induced displacement

The absence of a national policy for resettlement and rehabilitation makes it difficult to count development-induced IDPs in India. Natural disasters and 'planned forced eviction' have created more than 21.3 million IDPs, where according to government figures, fewer than one-quarter have been rehabilitated.

While the national disaster management division of the Agriculture Ministry records specific information on casualties, crop loss and houses destroyed, the number of IDPs due to the disaster is not recorded. Many IDPs, especially poor and marginalized farmers, go to the cities and become casual labourers or even beggars. Only a few return to their original homes. Statistical data on interstate displacement have a low priority in census reports. Figures are based mainly on the estimates of NGOs and independent researchers. While official government figures are often underestimates, figures given by special interest groups tend to be inflated.

According to the Indian Social Institute figure, the 21.3 million development induced IDPs include those displaced by dams (16.4 million), mines (2.55 million), industrial establishments (1.25 million), and wildlife sanctuaries and national parks (0.6 million). Large-scale development projects such as mines and hydroelectric projects are located in remote villages, hills and forests, often tribal habitats. Tribal people make up 40 per cent of the total number of IDPs, though only 8 per cent of the total Indian population. No figures are available for the urban displacement caused by building public services and infrastructure.

When the Indian government drafted a national rehabilitation policy in 1994, it accepted a figure of 15.5 million as the total number of development displaced people, with 74.52 per cent of the total number of IDPs still awaiting rehabilitation. It added: 'In the absence of a detailed subject-specific study, it is not possible to outline the problem of displacement in all its dimensions. It is not even possible to arrive at an approximate figure of displacement for the country as a whole.'

Though the government document contended that IDPs often found their own means without state support, forced displacement sets in motion a succession of events, which may lead to years of economic deprivation and psychological trauma. Studies in the north Indian state of Bihar, where millions were displaced by industries, mines and dams, have shown that many displaced families of tribal cultivators ended up as casual labourers, with lower standards of living. Uprooted from kin and their forest-based livelihood systems, traditional cultivators lose their identity and means of living. Oxfam India believes that the present method of compensating only those who have lost material assets is not equitable, leaving out the landless, women and children. In the eastern state of Orissa, those displaced by the Hirakkud dam between 1949 and 1958 got too little cash compensation and their descendants are still fighting for proper compensation. Official records show that 110,000 people were affected and that more than 6000 received no compensation. Many IDPs live on land belonging to government or private owners, and face eviction if it falls within a reserved forest area. About 100 Hirakud families have been displaced for the third time to make way for different development projects. The construction of high dams and irrigation structures have been India's greatest cause of displacement. IDP protests at incomplete or badly implemented rehabilitation work continue.

Floods, droughts, cyclones and earthquakes strike various states of India, affecting an average of 63 million people every year. The economic loss due to disasters in India approximates US$ 1.6 billion every year. Flood alone displaces more than 30 million people. India is prone to annual cyclones hitting the east coast states of Orissa and Andhra Pradesh, damaging 30,000 hectares of paddy fields, killing hundreds of people and blowing away homes. In addition, of the total cultivable area of India, an estimated 68 per cent is drought prone and earthquakes are frequent in the Himalayan region and the Deccan plateau in south central India.

The 1996 monsoon floods killed 1962 people and affected more than 50 million. Flash floods in the western state of Rajasthan in June 1996 alone damaged 119,000 houses and affected more than 1.2 million people. In 1996/7, more than 29 million people were affected by drought in 33,357 villages spread across four states, while more than 2.6 million were affected by cyclones and depressions. The government and other independent reports estimate casualties in terms of the total affected, but none of these estimates indicate the total number of IDPs.

Nepal
Sumit Sen

Nepal provides asylum to Tibetan and Lotshampa refugees. Most Tibetan refugees eventually find permanent asylum in India, but about 88,000 Lotshampas (Nepalese-origin subjects of Bhutan) are in various camps in Nepal. The displaced people who have failed to gain international attention are those affected mainly by development projects, landslides, droughts and earthquakes; they are reported to number more than 150,000.

The Kulekhani hydroelectric project is located about 40 kilometres from Kathmandu, and was planned to generate 60 MW of electricity. The project was initiated in 1963, and construction began in 1976. Funding by the World Bank, UNDP, OPEC, the EC, the Japanese government and the Kuwait Fund totalled $105.4 million. Although it was completed in 1980, IDPs are still waiting for adequate compensation and resettlement.

The project area was under traditional agriculture in plots of 0.5 hectares each. Although the government of Nepal did suc-

cessive revisions on the rate of compensation for land, standing crops, schools and temples; common resources of fodder, fruit trees and bamboo bushes were not taken into account. Project officials state that the displaced people were either offered 'land-for-land' or a 'cash payment', but IDPs maintain that government efforts to inform them of available land similar to theirs were inadequate. IDPs had to look for comparable land at their own expense.

The land of the Tamang ethnic group was the first to be acquired, with only cash as compensation. The women, being active in agriculture, protested actively because they could foresee that the absence of land would lead to their displacement.

Displacement was particularly severe in the regions of Hetuada-Ramnagar, Bastipur, Trisuli, Chisapani and Bhorle, where the majority of IDPs have yet to achieve their previous social and economic standards. Traditionally farmers, they maintain that their main crop used to satisfy all needs including medical care and travel. Now, their incomes are insufficient because they have to farm lands of much lower productivity. Cash compensation without adequate vocational training for the IDPs has resulted in greater poverty. With the dispersion of the internally displaced, even travel expenses to maintain family and social links prove beyond their means. Nepal has failed to provide displaced children with educational facilities, or employment for displaced adults.

The assistance and protection of IDPs in Nepal is subject to the vagaries of bureaucracy and is clearly inadequate. The government department responsible for implementing a development project is also charged with rehabilitating the IDPs. For the Kulekhani project, the agreement between the World Bank and government of Nepal stated that reponsibility to rehabilitate IDPs belonged with the electricity department. However, the department has neither the technical nor administrative capacity required for this function. It could do so only with the cooperation of the departments of housing and physical planning and of forestry. Since it was not the mandate of these departments, the department of electricity approached the Resettlement Agency, which refused to resettle IDPs from development projects because its responsibility related only to the landless or victims of natural calamities.

The flood problem is mainly restricted to the Terai region. Nepal has about 6000 rivers and four mega basins of Mahakali, Karnali, Gandaki and Kosi. Towards the end of the monsoon season in September devastating floods occur. The Himalayan mountains of Nepal are affected by the glacial lake outburst floods. These occur when the moraine dam breaks after glacial melt and heavy rain, causing avalanches, landslides and rendering fertile land uncultivable. The average annual loss to local people is estimated at US$ 250,000.

In the absence of horizontal planning between ministries, the protection of IDPs is inadequate and *ad hoc*. Since Nepal is embarking on development projects with consequent human displacements, the government and international funding agencies should review their compensation and rehabilitation policies.

Pakistan
Sumit Sen

Estimates vary greatly, but internal displacement affects about 250,000 people in Pakistan, including the victims of natural disasters. Although the Pakistan government has not ratified the 1951 Refugee Convention, it is a member of the UNHCR executive committee. While Pakistan hosts South Asia's largest refugee population from Afghanistan, Iraq, Somalia and Iran of about 867,500, the government has exacerbated displacement by not allowing 250,000 Pakistani citizens to return home from Bangladesh.

The separation of East Pakistan in 1971 to form the independent nation of Bangladesh was accompanied by persecution of the pro-Pakistani Bihari minority in Bangladesh by the Bengali majority. The Biharis claim that several thousand of them were killed by Bengalis prior to the Pakistani army's ruthless intervention in March 1971. While civil unrest continued and faced with continued persecution, the Biharis remained in camps in East Pakistan during all of 1971. Although 25 years have elapsed, the Biharis still remain in those same camps, amid squalor, disease, deprivation and poverty. When Bangladesh emerged as an independent state, Pakistan promulgated restrictive policies, whereby the majority of the Biharis who were denied entry to Pakistan remained displaced.

While Pakistan has provided asylum to Iranians, Burmese, Sri Lankans, Somalis and three million Afghans, there is still a lack of coherence over the goverment's policy towards the Biharis. Over the years, Nawaz Sharif's government has made some efforts to resettle them, while the Pakistan Peoples Party (PPP) has contributed to prolonging their displacement. Since the Biharis were given the option to return to Pakistan and since they still consider themselves to be Pakistanis, Pakistan needs to respect and restore their basic human rights.

The large number of Afghan refugees in northwest Pakistan has resulted in internal displacement. The Afghans control a substantial portion of the transport business, and may be active in arms and drug dealing. Local conflicts between Afghans and Pakistanis have resulted in some forcible evictions, and oustees have had to move to other provinces. There has been an increase in religious and political violence with Sunni–Shi'a sectarian killings becoming a particularly acute national security issue. In late 1997, 1600 members of a tribal group in the Punjab province were forced out of their homes by a coalition partner of Prime Minister Nawaz Sharif because they had voted against him. Elsewhere in Pakistan there were reports of two Christian villages being burned down as part of age old interreligious rivalry between Muslims and Christians. In Baluchistan, resentment is growing among members of the Raiji tribe of Baluchistan who allege that the leader of the Bugti tribe ordered 200 families to leave their homes and fired mortars at them after they voted against him in the general election. These displaced people have taken refuge at Valana, where there is no electricity or water, and many have only wild food from the nearby forests to eat. They state that petitions to the prime minister and other authorities have brought no respite.

The Pakistani authorities maintain that there are as many as 10,000 Kashmiri refugees from India living in eastern Pakistan. Fighting between Indian government forces and the pro-Pakistan Kashmiri Muslim separatists continues. Whether some of these people are refugees or IDPs depends on the status of Pakistan-occupied Kashmir (PoK), which is the disputed swathe of territory between India and Pakistan. As estimated 250,000 Kashmiri (Pandits) have been displaced inside India, Fewer are displaced in Pakistan, although access to PoK is severely limited and bombardment of civilian centres is common.

With regard to disaster mitigation, the second flood protection sector (FPS) project, funded by the Asian Development Bank and implemented by the Federal Flood Commission, has emerged as a key element. Flood protection features in the ninth five-year plan, which is under preparation and reportedly suggests removing the 'unprotected' riverside population. The Pakistan government is advised to rehabilitate the IDPs and protect their human rights.

Sri Lanka
Koenraad van Brabant

Internal displacement in Sri Lanka is linked to the ongoing ethnic conflict. Ethnicity entered Sri Lankan political life immediately after independence in 1948. The Sinhalese people, whose cultural revival dates back to the late nineteenth century, are the majority in the country (approximately 74 per cent). With independence from Britain in 1948, they could reassert a political majority. One of the first acts of the Ceylonese government was to deprive most of over a million so-called 'Indian Tamils', who had come to the island in the nineteenth century, of citizenship and voting rights. In the following decades, until 1984, several hundred thousand of them were 'repatriated' to south India. Most of the remaining 'Indian Tamils' (approximately 5.5 per cent) are concentrated in the plantation sector. But the continuing unwillingness of Sinhalese politicians to accommodate minority rights led in 1976 to a more radical demand from the longer established 'Ceylon Tamils' (approximately 12.5 per cent) for a separate state, 'Tamil Eelam'.

The ethnic tensions escalated into violent riots in 1956, 1958, 1971, 1977 and 1981. The particularly gruesome riots of 1983 signified a turning point. Tamil militancy was radicalized into an armed struggle, for which India, with its 70 million Tamils in the southern state of Tamil Nadu, had been providing support since the mid-1970s. Since then there have been three major upsurges in the war. The waves and intensity of displacement coincide with these cycles of violence. The first Eelam war ended in 1987 when India intervened just as the Sri Lankan army was preparing to enter the northern city of Jaffna, the Sri Lankan Tamils' political and cultural centre. India sent up to 50,000 troops to monitor the subsequent Indo–Sri Lankan peace accord.

SRI LANKA: A primary school for returnees and IDPs near Madhu (PHOTO: H. Davies/UNHCR).

The Liberation Tigers of Tamil Eelam (LTTE), however, opposed India's political decision-making, and started an effective guerrilla war against the Indian Peace Keeping Force (IPKF). The latter withdrew in 1990. Meanwhile, the Sri Lankan government had its hands free to crush an armed youth insurgency in the mainly Sinhalese south of the island.

In 1990, the LTTE initiated the second Eelam war with government forces, in which heavy fighting continued until the end of 1993. In that confrontation, the LTTE extended its territorial control over most of Sri Lanka north of Vavuniya, but was pushed back into the bush in the eastern districts of Trincomalee, Batticaloa and Ampara. The new People's Alliance government that came to power in August 1994, initiated a multi-pronged approach to end the ethnic conflict, involving peace talks with the LTTE, a package of rehabilitation and reconstruction of the

north and east, and proposals for political devolution that would grant the Tamils in the north and possibly the east, more autonomy. The peace talks were not, however, well managed and levels of distrust were apparently too high. In April 1995, the LTTE initiated the third Eelam war, which still continues.

The current government's moves to end the ethnic conflict and the fact that the LTTE has initiated a new cycle of violence, have generally led to a shift in the position of Western governments. Previously, there had been strong international criticism of the perceived intransigency of the United National Party (UNP) government with regard to minority demands, its atrocious human rights record, and its suppression of youth insurgency in the south. The LTTE lost political support in India when it fought the IPKF but especially when in 1991 it assassinated Prime Minister Rajiv Gandhi in Tamil

Nadu. One consequence is that, unlike during the first and second Eelam wars, few Tamils have been able to seek political asylum abroad during the third Eelam war.

Patterns of displacement

Almost 25 years of violence have led to major population movements in and from Sri Lanka. Since the second Eelam war in the early 1970s, some 500,000 Tamil asylum seekers joined the estimated 300,000 who in the 1970s and 1980s had moved to the West as legal economic migrants. During that phase of violence, tens of thousands also took refuge, sometimes for the second time, in Tamil Nadu in south India. In 1994, some 10,000 were repatriated, but an estimated 50,000 remain in south India. During the successive ethnic riots, Indian Tamils from the plantations in central Sri Lanka fled, and resettled in the north and east of the island. The army's occupation of the islands off Jaffna in 1991 created many IDPs in the north. In late 1990, the LTTE had expelled approximately 75,000 Muslims from the north it had come to control. Another 50,000 left the eastern province after LTTE attacks on Muslims. Most of these settled 'temporarily' in the districts of Puttalam and Anuradhapura. Most Sinhalese had already left, or been forced to leave the north.

In the eastern districts, successive governments have manipulated the state-sponsored irrigation and agricultural development schemes (which involve resettling Sinhalese from the densely-populated south) to alter the ethnic balance. Notably, the huge Mahaweli irrigation scheme to increase the amount of land under irrigation in the east and north, received financial backing from several Western governments. The Muslim minority (about 7.5 per cent) was dragged into the ethnic conflict between Tamils and Sinhalese during the second Eelam war. The LTTE attacked Muslims and the army used many of them as 'homeguards'. As a result, especially in the early 1990s, armed extremist groups of Tamils, Muslims and Sinhalese attacked each other's villages. While the history of land settlement and land ownership in eastern Sri Lanka has been 'over-ethnicized' (changes caused by the various ethnic groups' different economic strategies are downplayed), since the second Eelam war the army has deliberately and almost permanently displaced Tamils in the east to strengthen the political and economic position of the Sinhalese. Historically, the three ethnic groups have coexisted. Although mono-ethnic villages have existed for a long time, the violence has encouraged segregated patterns of residence. Inevitably, ethnic violence has generated suspicions and conflicts over property, though the tradition of tolerance and mutual acceptance has not been destroyed beyond repair. Notably in the east, the army has been very heavy-handed with regard to displacement. There have been numerous instances of 'forced' resettlement or of resettled villagers being told to remain in their villages and not flee again to the towns, notwithstanding renewed insecurity. The main influence on people's movements has been the threat to withhold the government's vital food rations. This goes against government guidelines that stress voluntariness. Unfortunately, these guidelines, articulated in the early 1990s, were never formalized into government policy or as an administrative circular.

In turn, Sinhalese villagers from the so-called 'border areas' especially in the north-central province and Pollonaruwa district, have become displaced by LTTE attacks. In mid-1995, the government forces shifted the theatre of war from the east to the north. In the face of a sustained army offensive towards Jaffna city, virtually the whole urban population, some 400,000 people, fled and became internally displaced. When the army subsequently extended its control over the whole of the Jaffna peninsula, about 200,000 came back under the authority of the government and most of these eventually returned to Jaffna. Since then, the theatre of war has been in the Vanni, a collective name for an agricultural and forest area comprising four districts between the Jaffna lagoon and the town of Vavuniya. IDPs from Jaffna city and Vanni residents joined the existing large numbers of IDPs previously displaced from plantations and from the islands off Jaffna. In May 1997, the situation worsened as a result of the army's slow advance from Vavuniya to establish a land route to the north.

Depending on the levels of violence, government figures of IDPs in the 1990s fluctuate between 500,000 and one million for a total population of 18 million. At the end of 1997, there were 787,877 officially recognized IDPs. Most of these (635,752) are self-settled or stay with friends and relatives. The remainder (152,125) tend to be temporarily accomodated in 'welfare centres', which are mostly public buildings such as schools or temples. The majority of IDPs are on the Jaffna peninsula and in the Vanni.

Institutional framework for assistance to IDPs

Unusually, the Sri Lankan government recognizes its obligations to IDPs. Its economic blockade against LTTE-controlled areas has affected health services, water and sanitation, the functioning of trade and markets, agricultural production and fishing. But registered IDPs who are deemed to be living below the poverty line do qualify for food rations and food stamps. Throughout the years of violence, the government has maintained a skeleton administration in LTTE-controlled areas, which has been effective in registering IDPs and managing humanitarian assistance provided by the government. In the areas under its control, IDPs and resettled families have also been able to get some government assistance for shelter. In principle, returnees from abroad and resettling or relocating IDPs can benefit from government grants and loans (Unified Assistance Scheme) to help make

them self-sufficient. In practice, poor management has reduced the scheme's effectiveness.

On several occasions, the government has set up rehabilitation and reconstruction programmes to which the international community has given financial and other support. Following the Indo–Sri Lanka peace accord of 1987, a ministry of reconstruction and rehabilitation was created to provide an institutional focus and extra capacity. The continuing violence, insecurity and organizational problems have, however, hampered the original programme. During the peace talks in the autumn of 1994, World Bank sponsored consultants drew up a new comprehensive and detailed reconstruction and rehabilitation programme, the implementation of which was once more impeded by a renewed cycle of fighting.

One of the major criticisms of the first seven-year (1987–94) emergency rehabilitation and reconstruction plan (ERRP 1) was its lack of participatory involvement of the target groups and intended beneficiaries. Participatory approaches were one of the strong recommendations of the comprehensive assessment exercise that should have resulted in an ERRP 2. Components of that assessment and draft plan found their way into programmes for the rehabilitation and reconstruction of the Jaffna peninsula in 1994 and 1996. The institutional framework for the government's decision-making with regard to the areas of the north, now back in its control, is the Resettlement and Rehabilitation Authority for the North (RRAN). The Ministry of Ethnic Affairs and National Integration, created in 1994, has an important role to play in peace-building initiatives.

One of Sri Lanka's characteristics is that its repatriation, resettlement and relocation programmes have been ongoing, although the conflict itself has not abated.

Given that most IDPs are self-settled or staying with friends and family, it is necessary to recognize the massive 'hidden relief' operation of Sri Lankan host families. The government's efforts are further complemented by the programmes of some 40 to 50 national NGOs. The scale of most of these is small, and there is a great variation in skill and competence. There are ten international NGOs working with IDPs, most of which also have development programmes in the south.

The ICRC has been operating in Sri Lanka since 1989. Its large-scale operation involves visiting detention centres, tracing missing people, dissemination and relief, mostly in health, water and emergency shelter. The rationale for UNHCR's presence in Sri Lanka derives from returning refugees. But it has also been active in providing assistance to IDPs, for example through its 'open relief centres'. These 'safe havens', initiated during the second Eelam war, provide protection and an abode for short-term displacement due to military actions, and a mechanism for decentralized relief.

Restrictions imposed by the Indian government have sometimes made it difficult for UNHCR to assess the voluntary nature of repatriation from that country, resumed in 1992. In anticipation of tens of thousands of returnees from Tamil Nadu, UNHCR started 'quick impact' or 'micro-projects' to help them and their host communities with reintegration. In 1993, an agreement was signed with the Sri Lankan government to allow the UNHCR to provide assistance to IDPs who live alongside returnees. During the third Eelam war therefore, UNHCR became a major player in emergency relief and logistics for IDPs and returning refugees. UNICEF has been actively providing assistance in conflict affected areas, especially in water and sanitation, with some health, and education for peace. Unlike UNHCR, UNICEF, at least until 1997, had no operational presence in the north, but worked through government structures.

International agencies trying to provide humanitarian assistance in the LTTE-controlled areas have often found their operations severely hampered by endless bureaucratic and logistic obstacles. A major problem in coordinating humanitarian assistance has been the government's reluctance to develop an institutional mechanism for information exchange and coordination with the international humanitarian agencies. The advocacy efforts of operational humanitarian agencies therefore tended to focus on access more than on entitlements. International political actors have been reluctant to put pressure on the government on issues of relief assistance and protection. Some Western governments have repatriated rejected asylum seekers, which has caused concern.

The experience of displaced people

The government security forces (police, army and paramilitary special task force) have an appalling record of human rights abuses. There has been less harrassment, sexual abuse, intimidation and torture (and fewer disappearances) during the third Eelam war than during the second, but such behaviour has not stopped. Abuses by the security forces are now more closely monitored and sometimes investigated, but the perpetrators are seldom brought to justice. Also, the LTTE has used indiscriminate violence against Tamils of a different political stance and civilians in the border villages, and has perpetrated terrorist bomb attacks in Colombo and Kandy. The LTTE continues to use child soldiers and does not allow Sri Lankan and international human rights organizations to work in areas under its control.

Notwithstanding the comparatively high level of official assistance, the reality for most IDPs has been impoverishment and disrupted lives and aspirations. Many survive on combinations of rations, an occasional pension, remittances from relatives in Western countries or non-skilled migrant workers in the Middle East, casual labour, petty trading, sexual services, non-commercial fishing, a goat and a kitchen garden. As such they have joined the group of often well-educated unemployed people living close to, or under, the poverty line.

As in the south, the war in the north and east has resulted in a significant number of female-headed households who try to cope, materially and psychologically, in many ways. Where the war increased food insecurity, women and the elderly often reduce their food intake on behalf of the children. Displaced women, certainly in LTTE-controlled areas, often have reduced access to health services and there are few facilities for their children's emotional and educational needs. The aid agencies have paid very little attention to the disabled and their special needs. There is, on the other hand, a recognition of the widespread prevalence of psychosocial trauma, and a number of projects are being implemented to try and meet some of these needs.

IDP Figures – Central Asia

Conflict-induced:
Afghanistan   1,450,000
Tajikistan   600,000 (but almost
                     all returned by
                     October 1997)

Map 9: Central Asia

Central Asia

Overview
William Maley and
Shahram Akbarzadeh

From the late 1930s to the late 1970s, central Asia was a stable part of the world. Its stability was fatally undermined by a communist coup in Afghanistan in April 1978, followed 20 months later by the Soviet invasion of Afghanistan. This not only led to significant forced migration from and within Afghanistan but contributed to the changes in the USSR once Mikhail Gorbachev became general secretary of the Communist Party in March 1985, which culminated in the disintegration of the Soviet Union in late 1991. The decomposition of Soviet power deprived the Afghan communist regime of vital support, and that regime in turn collapsed in April 1992.

In 1992, post-communist Afghanistan and post-communist Tajikistan both slid into civil war, which led to the internal displacement of a large number of people. Virtually all IDPs in Tajikistan have now returned to their places of origin. In Afghanistan, heavy fighting has continued on various fronts, most recently in September–October 1997, between the ultra-fundamentalist Taliban movement (predominantly ethnic Pushtun), supported by Pakistan and Saudi Arabia, and a range of groups opposed to it on sectarian, ethnic and ideological grounds. As a result, approximately 445,000 people have recently been internally displaced (although the rapidly-changing military situation means that the position of IDPs remains exceptionally fluid), in addition to an estimated one million long-term IDPs. Adding together these figures suggests a total for central Asia of 1.445 million internally displaced people.

While Afghanistan and Tajikistan share a border, this has not led to a regional approach to the two countries' internal displacement problems. The proximate causes of forced migration in each of these states are local; and for administrative purposes, Tajikistan is still treated by many agencies as part of a larger bloc comprised of the states of the former USSR, while programmes in Afghanistan tend to be managed from the Pakistani cities of Peshawar and Islamabad. While central Asia is now a very different region politically from what it was ten years ago, from the point of view of humanitarian relief operations it continues to be divided along the lines that divided it before the Soviet Union broke up.

In the 1920s, the central Asian republics of Kazakhstan, Kyrgyzstan, Tajikistan, Turkmenistan and Uzbekistan appeared for the first time on the world map. This created homelands for the major ethnic groups in central Asia and was hailed by Soviet policymakers as fulfilling the age-old aspirations of the local people. However, the process did not give rise to ethnically homogeneous societies. All five central Asian republics contain large ethnic minorities. Interethnic strife shook Kyrgyzstan, Tajikistan and Uzbekistan on the eve of the Soviet collapse. With the exception of Tajikistan, no serious interethnic tension has been reported in the past five years. The central Asian republics have retained their Soviet-drawn borders and have also inherited Soviet economic and environmental legacies. The environmental repercussions of the cotton monoculture, imposed forcefully on Uzbekistan and Turkmenistan, have been a serious cause of internal displacement.

Afghanistan
William Maley

Afghanistan has approximately 445,000 recently displaced people. The bulk of these are victims of the Taliban seizures of the Persian-speaking cities of Herat in September 1995, and Kabul in September 1996. However, approximately one million people were displaced during earlier phases of the Afghan conflict, and their situations shed light on various difficulties in defining internal displacement.

The Soviet–Afghan War (1979–89) created significant internal as well as external displacement. In 1988, the UN estimated the number of IDPs in urban centres and remote rural areas at more than two million. Anecdotal evidence of massive increases in the population of Kabul suggested that it was the main point to which IDPs fled, an understandable destination since it was the most heavily protected of all Afghan cities. However, two other forms of internal displacement deserve to be mentioned.

The first relates to pastoral nomads, estimated in 1979 to number 800,000. Such nomads normally fall outside the definition of IDPs, and some nomadic groups, such as the Zala Khan Khel, opted for external exile. Others remained in Afghanistan, but were prevented by landmines and other war-related factors from exploiting traditional pastures. To an extent therefore, they were 'internally displaced', although the diversity of the nomad economy makes it almost impossible to estimate the scale of the problem.

The second form relates to repatriating refugees from Pakistan and Iran who have been prevented by ongoing conflict from returning to their homes, and who are thus 'internally displaced'. The 1992/3 spontaneous repatriation of Afghan refugees from Pakistan was the largest and one of the fastest in UNHCR's history, but there is a dearth of reliable statistics on the exact scale and distribution of the problem of secondary internal displacement.

Number and location of IDPs

There are three major groups of IDPs in Afghanistan at present:

- IDPs in the Sar Shahi camp near Jalalabad, and elsewhere in the vicinity of Jalalabad itself;
- IDPs in northern Afghanistan, some in camps in the vicinity of Herat; and
- IDPs from the Shomali valley north of Kabul, the bulk of whom are currently located in the Kabul conurbation.

There are approximately 80,000 persons in Sar Shahi camp, which was established for victims of the rocketing of Kabul carried out by the forces of the Hezb-i Islami of Gulbuddin Hekmatyar between June 1992 and March 1995. Anecdotal reports suggest that half as many again may be living in the Jalalabad conurbation, making the total in the area 120,000.

Most of the IDPs in the Herat area are the victims of armed conflict around the province of Badghis, which broke out in October 1996. By late 1997, 5000 families, with an average of six members each, were receiving international assistance, the bulk of them in the Maslarkh camp. A further 4000 families were receiving help in the Pul-i Khumri area, and 4000 in the Panjsher valley, suggesting a total of 78,000 persons. Since mid-1997, there have been further displacements in northern Afghanistan as a result of the escalation of conflict between the Taliban and their opponents.

The largest displacements by far have been from the Shomali valley to the north of Kabul. These began following a Taliban assault on opposition positions, and reflected a systematic intent on the part of the Taliban

AFGHANISTAN: IDPs in Baghlan Province constructing a water tank for the camp
(PHOTO: A Hollmann/UNHCR).

to clear the area of potential opponents. In this writer's view, the flight of these IDPs was largely a result of 'ethnic cleansing'. By July 1997, 200,000 IDPs had entered Kabul from the Shomali valley and a further 47,000 were reported by UNHCR to have fled to the north, mostly from the same region. Some have since returned to the Shomali Valley following the recapture of the northern half of the valley by the Taliban's opponents.

Needs of IDPs

The population of Afghanistan is estimated to be 20.9 million, of whom 6.9 per cent are IDPs. Given Afghanistan's high level of impoverishment, low life expectancy and high infant mortality rates, not only the IDPs have urgent needs. The main needs of the IDPs are tents, drinking water, latrines and basic medicines: needs that the ICRC has largely

met for camp dwellers. IDPs in Kabul largely depend on support from extended families, but some benefit from WFP and ICRC subsidized bakery projects.

Gaps in assistance and protection

The Afghan state has largely disintegrated. None of the groups aspiring to exercise national power in Afghanistan has the capacity to provide assistance of any significance to IDPs. Some groups, notably the Taliban government, also lack the inclination to do so, since their main aim is not the improvement of citizens' lives in any practical sense, but rather the enforcement of idiosyncratic standards of moral purity. The lead role in assistance and protection of IDPs in Afghanistan is taken by the ICRC, which also attempts to disseminate the principles of international humanitarian law to Afghan combatants. However, civilian non-combatants continue to fall victim to the use of force by armed groups, especially in the form of aerial bombardments.

Conclusion

The main cause of internal displacement in Afghanistan has been war. At present the principal factor driving ongoing conflict is interference in Afghanistan by neighbouring states, most significantly in the form of Pakistani backing for the Taliban. Even if the Taliban were to control all major urban centres in Afghanistan, this would be unlikely to spell the end of conflict: indeed, it could be the signal for a change in the nature of the conflict, from an intra-elite struggle involving perhaps 100,000 armed fighters to a mass ethnic conflict with fighting at a local level between groups of differing ethnic identities. As long as outside interference in Afghanistan continues, the phenomenon of internal displacement and the burdens it places on donors will persist.

In February 1998, an earthquale shook the province of Takhar in northeastern Afghanistan. Killing almost 5000 people and leaving 20,000 homeless, this was one of the most severe natural calamities to have hit Afghanistan in recent years. The situation of the survivors is exacerbated by the winter climate and remote location; and Afghanistan's civil war. Although the area of the earthquake has been largely spared the consequences of the 18-year conflict, there is no national structure left to render assistance. Supplies have to be brought across front lines and across the border from neighbouring Tajikistan. Before the earthquake, Takhar was controlled by the northern coalition opposed to the Taliban government. A temporary cease-fire enabled access for some aid agencies but it is unlikely that this will hold. Thus, victims of this natural disaster find their fate tied to the civil war, with assistance and protection compromised.

Kazakhstan, Kyrgyzstan, Turkmenistan and Uzbekistan

Shahram Akbarzadeh

These four republics remain untroubled by armed conflict. However, they experience serious economic and social problems as a result of the break-up of the Soviet Union. The Soviet experience was associated with serious environmental degradation as a result of excessive use of pesticides and chemical fertilizers to sustain the cotton monoculture and the excessive use of the two major water-ways of Amu Darya and Syr Darya as irrigation canals. Consequently, only 10 per cent of the 78 cubic kilometres of water generated between Amu Darya and Syr Darya reach the Aral Sea. Since 1961, the volume of water in this sea has halved. The shrinking of the sea has precipitated a health crisis for the people living around it. Drinking water in adjacent territories of Kazakhstan (Kyzyl Orda and Aktubinsk regions), Turkmenistan (Dashkhavuz region) and Uzbekistan (Karakalpak Autonomous Republic) is high in saline. Pregnant women in these regions are advised against drinking it.

The Aral Sea is saturated with salt and chemical fertilizers, washed from excessively-treated cotton fields. This has caused the Aral fishing industry to disappear. The Aral Sea has become a health hazard and a source of saline contamination for all central Asians. Territories adjacent to the sea are often subject to storms, which carry salt and chemical mixtures from the dried-up sea bed. Such storms have become more frequent and have been reported in areas as far as Kyrgyzstan. Health hazards and declining living standards associated with the contamination of agricultural land around the Aral Sea have forced many rural families to relocate to areas further away from the Aral basin. There is no government-run programme to assist such relocations and the displaced people rely on personal contacts and resources to arrange their resettlement. This is treated as a matter of personal choice by the authorities. There is, therefore, no registration and no accurate information as to the size and the immediate needs of the environmentally displaced. No international organization is involved with the relocation of displaced Aral people.

Tajikistan
Shahram Akbarzadeh

Tajikistan is the only central Asian state to experience civil war accompanied by mass relocation of people in the aftermath of the Soviet collapse. Large-scale fighting broke out in late 1992 after a coalition government of opposition Islamic and democratic parties was resisted by armed militia groups. Armed bands, loyal to former President Rahmon Nabiev, clashed with armed opposition supporters in the southern parts of the republic. Regional administrators in the southern province of Kulob (now part of Khatlon) played a critical role in encouraging anti-opposition forces. Opposition forces were driven out of the capital Dushanbe in December 1992. Fighting continued in mountainous regions to the east of Dushanbe and on the Tajik–Afghan border, with different degrees of intensity.

The civil war in Tajikistan (1992–97) has been the cause of massive migration, both internal and external. The civil war displaced more than 502,000 people externally and more than 600,000 internally. By late 1997, all IDPs and most refugees were believed to have returned to their homes. The resettlement and reintegration of returning refugees and IDPs in Tajikistan has suffered from residual intercommunity feuds and the unwillingness of local authorities to protect the returnees. The weakness of the central government in relating to local administrators has hindered the government in Dushanbe from direct intervention on behalf of the returnees.

On 27 June 1997, under the auspices of the UN, a peace accord was signed between the government of Tajikistan and the United Tajik Opposition. This agreement brings over four years of bloody conflict to an end and promises to bring political stability to this republic. The establishment of the rule of law is hoped to contribute to the reintegration of the returnees.

The civil conflict in Tajikistan had an identifiable ethnic and regional component, and this continues to influence the reconciliation process. Many opposition leaders had originally come from the Autonomous Province of Mountainous Badakhshan (in the Pamir mountains) and the eastern valley of Gharm. The latter is regarded in Tajikistan as home to a religious population. In the 1950s and 1960s, the Soviet regime had relocated entire villages from Gharm to southern Tajikistan (Kulob, now part of Khatlon) as part of a general drive to bring more land under cotton cultivation. This relocation programme brought the local people, with a sizeable Uzbek minority, into contact with the culturally distinct Gharmis; while both the local population and the new settlers retained their regional affiliations. With the formation of opposition parties on the eve of the Soviet collapse, Tajiks were divided into pro- and anti-government camps. This was a convenient cover for family feuds and community disputes that had separated Gharmis from their host communities. By mid-1992, a Gharmi background was generally regarded as tantamount to political dissent, just as the Kulobi identity was interchangeable with a pro-government

TAJIKISTAN: Returned IDPs, Khatlon Province (PHOTO: A Hollmann/UNHCR).

stance. A similar association was made between the population of Badakhshan and the opposition parties. The predominance of the Ismaili faith in Badakhshan and the distinct vernacular language of Badakhshan have also contributed to the division between those of Badakhshani descent and other Tajiks.

With the intensification of armed clashes between pro- and anti-government forces in 1992/3 many Gharmi-populated villages in the south were targeted by Kulobi bands. A similar pattern became apparent in Dushanbe, where those with Gharmi or Badakhshani backgrounds were systematically attacked, sometimes murdered, by Kulobi bands. The Uzbek minority in the south tended to side against Gharmis and Badakhshanis.

The civil war produced a major humanitarian crisis. It claimed 50,000 lives and resulted in more than 502,000 refugees and 600,000 IDPs. By September 1997, all IDPs were believed to have returned to their homes. The steady flow of returning refugees and IDPs since 1994/5 was interrupted in the second half of 1996 by fighting in Tavildara, in the upper Gharm valley. Control over the settlements in the region changed hands four times. The escalation of fighting between May and December 1996 forced civilians to flee either to Dushanbe or to the Autonomous Province of Badakhshan.

In September 1997 the UN-sponsored joint National Reconciliation Commission held its first meeting to guide Tajikistan out of crisis. The commission formed four sub-committees, one of which is devoted to the resettlement of refugees (including the IDPs).

Number and location of IDPs
The exact number of IDPs is unknown because many of them rely on the support

and hospitality of friends and relatives in their place of refuge. In July 1995 Tajikistan's Ministry of Labour took over the registration of IDPs from the UNHCR. According to official Tajikistani records, by February 1995 only 25,833 IDPs were awaiting repatriation. A great majority of these had sought sanctuary in the northern Leninabad province, Dushanbe, Badakhshan and the Gharm valley.

The number of IDPs increased temporarily in the second half of 1996. According to an ICRC report in November 1996, around 15,000 people were forced to escape the fighting in Tavildara. This figure may have been higher, for many IDPs did not register with the ICRC or Ministry of Labour for fear of their names falling into the hands of the Tajik Ministry of Interior. Data used and published by international agencies in relation to the situation in the Gharm valley are highly suspect and should be treated cautiously.

The cessation of hostilities in 1997 and the recent peace accord appear to have encouraged repatriation. According to the IOM office in Dushanbe, 'there are no more IDPs in the country except the people who refuse to return and prefer to stay with their relatives.'

Needs of IDPs

Internal dislocation in Tajikistan took place against a background of general social, political and economic crisis. Economic crisis has become a familiar experience for all former Soviet republics. The crisis in Tajikistan, however, has deepened as a result of the civil war and massive dislocation of farming communities. Apart from the northern region of Leninabad, which remained peaceful throughout the conflict, the rest of the country lost its already limited ability to feed itself. Tajikistan depends on imported foodstuffs and experiences chronic shortages in staples such as flour, rice, oil and sugar.

Food shortages affected the IDPs more than other citizens of Tajikistan because they could not grow food on their private family plots. The most severe food shortage is in Badakhshan. The arrival of IDPs there in 1992/3 and 1996 made an already critical situation untenable. Badakhshan inhabitants and IDPs depend on food donated by the Aga Khan Foundation.

The resumption of hostilities in Tavildara in the second half of 1996 caused a fresh wave of IDPs to arrive in Badakhshan. The ICRC sent food parcels, basic necessities (warm clothes, shoes, blankets, ovens and fuel) and medical supplies to Badakhshan and the affected regions of the Gharm valley. Access to both destinations was restricted by the fighting in Tavildara and the treacherous terrain in Badakhshan. Food convoys to Badakhshan in late 1996, organized by the ICRC, had to take a detour via Kyrgyz territory to avoid fighting on the Dushanbe–Khorog highway. This detour through the high mountain passes of the Pamirs extended the six-to-eight hour journey to four days.

The cessation of hostilities in January 1997 opened the Dushanbe–Khorog highway to convoys of aid and IDPs returning to their homes. The government of Tajikistan, in coordination with the UNHCR, ICRC, OSCE, IOM and Human Rights Watch (Helsinki), has encouraged the return of refugees and IDPs. Latest reports claim that the repatriation is nearing completion, though a number of bomb explosions in Dushanbe in September 1997 caused temporary delays in the repatriation of refugees from Afghanistan.

Problems of resettlement

The resettlement of returning refugees and IDPs has been hampered by the question of safety. Fighting in Tavildara along the only road connecting Dushanbe to Khorog, the provincial capital of Badakhshan, was the main obstacle to repatriation in 1996. The dismantling of road blocks and check points in 1997 has allowed the return of IDPs from Badakhshan.

Since mid-1993, UNHCR, ICRC and other agencies have provided food and shelter to the displaced people and supported their return, aiding the survival of refugees and IDPs in harsh winter conditions. Once back at home, refugees and IDPs have had to cope with threats and intimidation by neighbours and local authorities. Members of the Gharmi community who had returned to their homes in the Khatlon province in 1995/6 complained of continued harassment by Kulobis. Returnees seldom sought justice against perpetrators of violence and harassment, as their complaints to local authorities were often ignored or ridiculed and they feared reprisal attacks.

Upon their repatriation, many returnees found their houses occupied by their Kulobi neighbours. In some cases the intervention of foreign aid workers on behalf of returnees in negotiations with local authorities and occupants resulted in the restitution of property. In other instances the returnees have had to buy their original property back. Shelter kits of timber, nails and asbestos sheets, provided by the UNHCR, offered temporary relief while houses were being rebuilt. According to the UNHCR, 18,500 houses in 170 villages had been reconstructed by mid-1996.

A major issue for the returnees in rural areas is the absence of income. The UNHCR has offered 'seed money' to returnees, aimed at initiating income-generating schemes. Many participants in such programmes were widowed women responsible for their families. They received wool, wheat and pregnant goats or sheep as part of UNHCR-run 'quick impact projects' to foster financial recovery. But the decreasing involvement of UNHCR in Tajikistan since late 1995, and lack of coordination with the UNDP have resulted in the suspension of these income-generating projects and the questioning of their economic viability.

Employment for the returnees has been a serious problem. Despite the government of Tajikistan's promises to reinstate them in their original jobs, returnees and IDPs have found local authorities less receptive to their employment needs. The general economic crisis and massive hidden unemployment have aggravated the situation, curbing the process of reintegration.

The Department of Refugee Affairs, which is attached to the Ministry of Labour, blames weak central control over local government for the difficulties of integrating returnees. Many of these authorities led armed militia groups against the opposition forces during the civil war and were directly responsible for the flight of refugees and IDPs. The government in Dushanbe has proved ineffective and has been unwilling to challenge local authorities lest it leads to further instability.

The UNHCR has been involved in providing aid to refugees and IDPs in the southern Khatlon province and in assisting their voluntary repatriation since March 1993. In 1995, it decided to scale down its involvement, citing the near completion of the repatriation process. The UNHCR's responsibilities have been taken up by other international agencies such as UNDP, which is responsible for the financial recovery of the returnees.

The OSCE mission in Tajikistan was established in December 1993 with a view to promoting human rights and advising the government on legislative reform. The OSCE mission reports violations of human rights to local and central authorities to ensure that crimes committed against the returnees are properly investigated.

Government

The current government of Tajikistan has repeatedly stated its commitment to the repatriation process. The Department of Refugee Affairs attached to the Ministry of Labour was established in July 1992, under the coalition government. This survived the change of government in December 1992 and is responsible for registering refugees and IDPs. In 1994, the government passed several laws on the reintegration of returning refugees and IDPs, which included financial support for resettlement and employment guarantees. However, the department's visibility and contacts with international organizations have not been translated into support and aid to the returnees.

The government operates under severe economic, political and military restrictions that have impeded large-scale assistance to the returnees. The weakness of the central government towards local authorities has also hindered the implementation of government policies on guaranteed employment and housing.

Matters have been made more complicated by local armed groups, nominally belonging to the government armed forces, which seriously challenged Dushanbe's control over Khatlon and western Tajikistan in 1996. In Badakhshan, the regional administration is largely independent of Dushanbe. The peace accord signed in July 1997, however, is seen by observers and aid workers as the most positive indication of the end of hostilities. It is hoped that political stability will enhance the power of the central government and extend the rule of law to outlying regions of the republic.

Conclusion

Political instability and a general social and economic crisis hamper the reintegration of returned refugees and IDPs. The current needs of the returnees are related to the general needs of their neighbours in conditions of economic collapse. The peace accord may afford the country a respite from fighting and a chance for economic recovery. The government of Tajikistan will no doubt use this opportunity to expand its control at the expense of local authorities, which will provide a chance for the implementation of government policies for the returnees.

International aid agencies and humanitarian organizations need to monitor human rights issues in Tajikistan, especially in the southern province of Khatlon, in order to promote and further the rule of law. In the past, the presence of foreign aid workers helped prevent the resumption of large-scale abuse. With the consolidation of the central government, aid workers will become more effective in this role. The anticipated political stability and growing government powers will give aid agencies and human rights organizations greater influence over the government of Tajikistan, which may no longer cite its limited authority for its inactivity.

IDP Figures – Russian Federation
and the Caucasus

Conflict-induced:
Russian Federation   90,000
  Chechnya   350,000
  Stavropol   100,000
  Krasnodar   60,000

Georgia   280,000
  South Ossetia   13,000
Armenia   75,000
Azerbaijan   550,000–612,000

Map 10: Russian Federation and the Caucasus

Russian Federation and the Caucasus

Overview
William Hayden

Since the breakup of the Soviet Union in 1991, the Russian Federation has had an explosive growth in refugees, asylum seekers and IDPs. Nearly 1.2 million persons from the CIS, east-central Europe, the Baltics and the periphery of the Russian Federation are registered as refugees or IDPs. The primary concentration of IDPs is in the north Caucasus region where intercommunal conflict and civil war in north Ossetia and Chechnya have forcibly displaced up to 600,000 persons.

Violent civil war and economic catastrophe have also generated a long-term humanitarian crisis in the Caucasus republics of Georgia, Armenia and Azerbaijan. As many as 1.5 million people have been forcibly displaced by ethnic conflict, and currently live in deplorable conditions that have been only partially ameliorated through the humanitarian assistance provided by the international community. The emergency conditions in which IDPs and refugees live are exacerbated by an economic crisis that has left the governments of the three republics with few resources to assist displaced people. This has also been aggravated by the lack of negotiated political settlement to the disputes, producing a regionwide state of political insecurity. International intervention in the humanitarian crisis affecting the region has been most robust in Georgia, with Armenia and Azerbaijan receiving far less attention. The continuing political instability, economic crisis conditions, and scarce resources for humanitarian assistance means that the IDP situation in the Transcaucasus will persist for some time to come.

Armenia
William Hayden

Since 1988, Armenia has experienced a protracted humanitarian emergency brought about by anti-Armenian pogroms in Azerbaijan; the December 1988 Spitak earthquake, which killed 25,000 people and left 300,000 homeless; and the ethnic conflict between Armenians and Azeris in the Nagorno-Karabakh region of Azerbaijan. Ethnic war in and around Nagorno-Karabakh caused large-scale population movement between Armenia and Azerbaijan, with approximately 350,000 Armenians fleeing Azerbaijan for Armenia and the entire Azeri population of Armenia, an estimated 190,000 people, being forcibly displaced from the country to Azerbaijan. Although large-scale fighting between Karabakh-Armenian forces and Azerbaijan government forces has stopped under the 1994 cease-fire, the parties involved have neither reached a political settlement to the conflict nor resolved the political status of Nagorno-Karabakh, despite negotiations sponsored by the OSCE Minsk group. Refugees and IDPs in both countries remain vulnerable.

In November 1997, there were an estimated 75,000 IDPs in Armenia according to official government figures. The majority of these people were evacuated from villages located along the border with Azerbaijan. Since the 1994 cease-fire has been relatively well observed, it is believed that many of these people have returned to their homes, for there is evidence of repopulation and agricultural activity. In addition to war-induced IDPs, there are also people still affected by the 1988 earthquake: an estimated 37,500–50,000 persons still live in temporary shelters and makeshift dwellings, and continue to require humanitarian assistance. Many of those people displaced by the earthquake were also displaced by war in Nagorno-Karabakh.

ARMENIA: IDPs in transit
(PHOTO: M Alford/UNHCR).

However, ethnic Armenian refugees from Nagorno-Karabakh are not recognized as IDPs and are classified as refugees under the 1951 Refugee Convention, since the international community still recognizes that Nagorno-Karabakh lies within the borders of Azerbaijan. While Armenia acceded to the 1951 Convention in 1993, the government has not promulgated any legal framework to implement it. The Armenian National Assembly passed a law on citizenship in 1995, establishing a waiver of the three-year residency requirement for citizenship for ethnic Armenians with permanent residence status. But that legislation has also not been implemented, and instead the Armenian government has classified these refugees as 'persons given temporary leave to remain'. The government, in concert with ethnic Armenian authorities in Nagorno-Karabakh, has conducted repatriation operations in which Armenians from that region have been voluntarily returned to the territory. There are no official figures available on the number of Armenian returnees to Nagorno-Karabakh, though there are estimates of between 35,000 and 50,000.

Armenia's natural and human-made humanitarian emergency is exacerbated by the precarious state of the economy. Low growth, inflation, high unemployment, the slow pace of infrastructure reconstruction and the role of the unofficial economy have all placed severe constraints on the government. With funding available for international humanitarian activities limited and few government resources at hand to offer assistance, the UNHCR is the only international agency with enough donor support to help IDPs and refugees. Fortunately, substantial private funds have been generated by the Armenian diaspora, either channeled into humanitarian relief through organizations such as the Hayastan All-Armenian Fund, the Fund for Armenian Relief and the Armenian General Benevolent Union, or in direct remittances to relatives from Armenians in Europe, Russia and the USA.

Overall, emergency relief provisions such as food, shelter, clothing and health care are the principal means of support to IDPs. There is evidence of a growing transition to sustainable community development and income-generation projects, but those are primarily benefiting villages and communities that suffered because of the general economic crisis that was worsened by the economic blockade by Azerbaijan and Turkey. Moreover, there is a significant shortfall in funding for self-reliance and infrastructure rehabilitation projects targeting IDPs and refugees. While humanitarian coordination among the Armenian government, UN agencies, NGOs and the Armenian diaspora community have improved considerably since 1988, the pressing needs of IDPs, either induced by war or by earthquakes remain.

Azerbaijan
William Hayden

Azerbaijan is the most economically depressed republic of the former Soviet Union. It is estimated that 60 per cent of the total population lives in poverty, with 20 per cent living in extremely impoverished conditions. This may change as a result of oil revenue. Since early 1990, there has been a continuous movement of forcibly displaced people in Azerbaijan and a large influx of refugees from Armenia and Uzbekistan. It is currently estimated that 11 per cent of Azerbaijan's population are either IDPs or refugees, although no international organization has ever collected formal countrywide information on their numbers. There is a general agreement that there are between 550,000–612,000 IDPs and 200,000–250,000 refugees, with the Azerbaijan government claiming that there are 196,845 ethnic Azeri refugees from Armenia and 51,649 Meskhetian Turks who fled from ethno-political violence in Uzbekistan.

The first displacement flow began with the expulsion of the entire ethnic Azeri population of Armenia (180,000–200,000) to Azerbaijan by early 1990. Intercommunal conflict between Armenians and Azeris was exacerbated by the entry of Soviet forces into Baku in January 1990, causing a migration of more than 100,000 ethnic Russians from Azerbaijan to the Russian Federation. Armenians also began to leave Azerbaijan, with approximately 279,000 fleeing to

Armenia and 44,000 to Nagorno-Karabakh. In the autumn of 1991, civil war broke out between Karabakh-Armenian forces and Azeri government forces, resulting in the entire Azeri and Kurdish population of Nagorno-Karabakh and the Lachin region fleeing the violence. Counterattacks by Azeri forces with help from Russian units, resulted in large numbers of Armenians being forcibly displaced from Shaumyan to north Nagorno-Karabakh.

By the beginning of 1994, when a cease-fire agreement with Armenia was implemented, war and political chaos in Azerbaijan had enabled Karabakh-Armenians to occupy Karabakh and six districts of Azerbaijan adjacent to that disputed region. The Azeri IDPs have sought shelter in makeshift camps, railroad cars, roadside dugouts and abandoned public buildings. In cities such as Imishli and Beylagan, it is estimated that IDPs who fled the fighting now constitute as much as 50 per cent of the total urban population. Most IDPs are located in the frontline districts, many in cities such as Agdzjabedi, Fizuli, Agdam, Yevlax, and in Baku and Sumghayit. According to the DHA, the IDP population is currently sheltered in organized camps (60,000), public buildings (300,000), and makeshift temporary shelters (252,000). The Azerbaijan government is planning a countrywide census in January 1999, which will also cover IDPs. However, given the precarious conditions that they are living in, the UNHCR intends to undertake a countrywide reregistration of IDPs beginning this winter in order to facilitate provision of humanitarian assistance and development of self-reliance projects.

IDP conditions
The displaced people in Azerbaijan are by far the most vulnerable demographic group in the country. Over and above the general economic crisis affecting the entire population, IDPs face specific problems associated

AZERBAIJAN: IDPs in Yevlak (PHOTO: R Redmond/UNHCR).

with long-term displacement, including chronic food shortages, lack of potable water and adequate sanitation, deteriorating public health conditions (particularly affecting children and pregnant women), high rates of malnutrition, psychosocial problems, inadequate shelter and criminality (especially in the organized camps). Conditions worsen during the colder winter months. USAID, UNHCR and ECHO have undertaken a number of house-building and shelter rehabilitation projects, including mud, brick, limestone and prefabricated wooden structures, with improved water and sanitation. To date, close to 1900 shelters have been constructed for IDPs, and an additional estimated 18,240 IDPs are benefiting from rehabilitated rooms. However, the uncertainty of fiscal resources for various shelter programmes means that many IDPs will have to suffer through another

winter of deplorable conditions.

Most of the basic humanitarian needs of IDPs and refugees are being inadequately met because of severe funding constraints for both intergovernmental and non-governmental organizations. Substantial shortfalls in the UN Consolidated Appeal, along with severe cutbacks in ECHO funding of emergency programmes, will result in an overall decline in humanitarian activities, including transition programmes for self-reliance and sustainable development. US NGO activities funded by USAID are still affected by the US congressional ban on aid to Azerbaijan enacted in 1992 (Section 907 of the Freedom Support Act), undercutting the effectiveness of humanitarian assistance. Although Section 907 was not applicable to Azerbaijani NGOs, their limited number and operational incapacity does not enable Azeri NGOs to assume a larger and more effective role in the humanitarian field.

Economic restraints

Economic factors such as the slow pace of agricultural land privatization, the collapse of the industrial sector, high unemployment, the lack of a political resolution to the conflict over Nagorno-Karabakh and mine contamination prevent any large-scale return of IDPs to their former homes. With low agricultural production of basic foodstuffs and steadily increasing prices, most IDPs will continue to depend on emergency food aid. The Azerbaijan government has been slow to dismantle state control of urban grain distribution and pricing. This further reduces the domestic food supplies already limited by constraints on farmers producing and selling at market rates. Food vulnerability will continue to be a pressing condition for the displaced people and other impoverished groups.

There have also been no effective improvements in the state-run health-care system, which is failing to deliver adequate basic services. Humanitarian medical assistance has filled some gaps in public health care, especially with service to vulnerable IDPs in areas such as vaccine-preventable diseases and women's reproductive health. Nevertheless, the number of persons suffering from tuberculosis has increased dramatically due to the poor performance of the national health care system. The WHO, ICRC, MSF-Holland and MSF-Belgium are collaborating with the government to improve public health policy and care provision for TB victims, many of whom are found in IDP camps.

Georgia
William Hayden

Since 1989, Georgia has been racked by a series of politically, socially and economically disruptive internal conflicts: the ethnic conflict between Ossetians and Georgians over the political status of the South Ossetian Autonomous Oblast (1989–92); the power struggle between former President Zviad Ghamsakhurdia and his supporters and the political opposition over control of the government of the newly independent state (1991/2); and the civil war between the central government of President Eduard Shevardnadze and ethnic Abkhaz secessionists over the northwest Black Sea region of Abkhazia (1992–94).

Upwards of 300,000 people were forcibly displaced by the three civil conflicts, generating a large-scale humanitarian crisis that was also exacerbated by the collapse of the Georgian economy. In December 1996, the Georgian Ministry of Refugees and Accommodation reported that there were 272,359 registered IDPs in Georgia, including 261,052 from Abkhazia and 10,897 from south Ossetia. The south Ossetian committee on migration and nationalities also reported at the end of 1996 that there were 12,951 IDPs in south Ossetia, although that figure has not been independently verified. At this time, there are no figures on IDPs in Abkhazia. The majority of IDPs are ethnic Georgians, with the largest concentrations according to the UNHCR located in Samegrelo (123,538) and Tbilisi (74,692). These IDPs have been living in less than adequate conditions in hotels, former hospitals and schools, camps and other temporary shelters that lack adequate water, sanitation, structural integrity, heat and living space.

Although cease-fires were mediated under Russian Federation auspices in Abkhazia and south Ossetia, including the deployment of a CIS peacekeeping force (CISPF) and UN monitors (UNOMIG) in Abkhazia and a small OSCE monitoring mission in south Ossetia, political settlement of the disputes has been slow to come. The lack of political resolution has protracted the humanitarian crisis, and although the international community has stabilized the short-term assistance needs of

IDPs, a long-term solution to Georgia's humanitarian problems rests on a negotiated settlement to the question of Abkhazia and South Ossetia's political status vis-à-vis Georgia. The international community has also stepped up its involvement, as Russian mediators have been complemented by the OSCE, and the 'Friends of Georgia' group (USA, UK, France, Germany and Russia), in efforts to broker a political settlement.

However, the secessionist Abkhaz leadership seems determined to achieve independence from Georgia. The intention has been declared of replacing the CISPF with its own force, if the CISPF mandate is not renewed and leaves Abkhazia. This has provoked concerns among the Georgian IDPs from Abkhazia and their political representatives, who are discontented that a solution has not been achieved that will allow them to return home. These circumstances have delayed the implementation of the IDP and refugee repatriation provisions of the April 1994 quadripartite agreement signed by Georgia, Abkhazia, Russia and the UNHCR. That agreement planned for a return of 100,000 IDPs, with 80,000 ethnic Georgians returning to the Gali district and 20,000 Russians, Armenians and other ethnic groups returning to other places in Abkhazia. By the end of 1997, only 311 IDPs have been returned under UNHCR auspices, although an estimated 25,000–35,000 Georgian IDPs have spontaneously returned without assistance to the Gali district.

Yet, because of high insecurity in the Gali region, and the failure of the CISPF to control and stop the activities of Abkhaz paramilitaries, many Georgian IDP returnees have faced continued intimidation, including arson, robbery, torture and murder. The insecurity in the Gali district is compounded by a significant number of landmines, with estimates as high as 700,000. Mine contamination, along with a high degree of insecurity, has compelled organizations such as the ICRC to pull out of Abkhazia.

There is also evidence of Georgian paramilitaries crossing into Gali to attack ethnic Abkhazians. Continuing tensions have motivated Georgians from Abkhazia, led by Tamaz Nadareishvili, the chairman of the so-called Abkhaz parliament-in-exile, to call for a resumption of military operations to restore Georgian central government control over the breakaway region. Any large-scale voluntary return of Georgians, supported by military force, would seriously undermine ethnic Abkhaz control, since they constituted less than 17 per cent of the prewar population (and only 1.8 per cent of the Georgian population based on 1989 census figures).

Humanitarian needs

The majority of the approximately 280,000 IDPs in Georgia continue to require humanitarian assistance. Although there is evidence of economic recovery in Georgia, assistance in the areas of food security, shelter, public health, community services, income generation, sanitation, education and capacity building are needed. The international and Georgian humanitarian community have implemented new projects and continued with existing efforts in 1997 to address the pressing needs of this most vulnerable part of the Georgian population. However, as of May 1997, the UN consolidated appeal has only received US$ 11,898,162 out of a requested US$ 29,868,021, with only US$ 5,758,309 available for IDPs. A lack of public and private funds necessary for humanitarian relief will mean that most vulnerable IDPs will be maintaining a survival existence. The positive benefits of economic recovery are not reaching IDPs, with many experiencing great hardship coping with the negative effects of market liberalization and privatization.

To help counter these conditions, the IOM has been assisting the Georgian government in developing institutional capacity for more effective migration management,

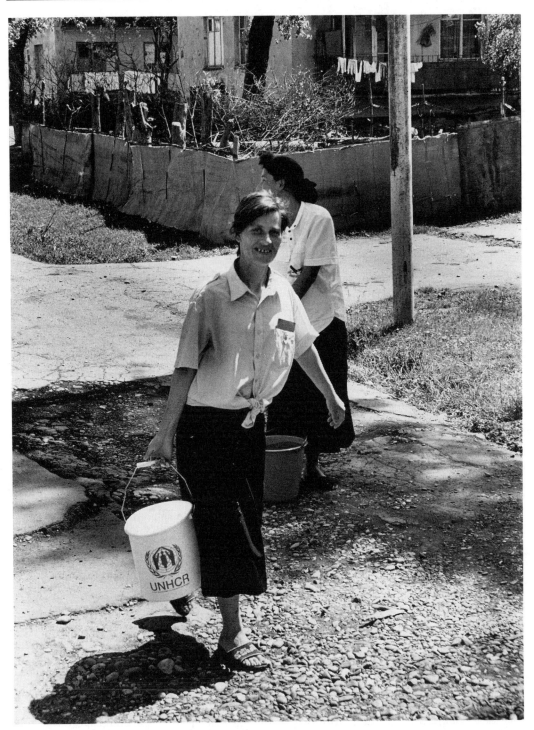

GEORGIA: IDPs from the Abkhazia region (PHOTO: R Redmond/UNHCR).

implementation of migration policy, development of legislative participation in IDP policy, and increasing government capabilities in legal, social and humanitarian protection of IDPs. These projects include such government agencies as the Coordination Bureau for International Humanitarian Aid (CBIHA), Ministry for Refugees and Accommodation, Ministry of Labour and Social Welfare, the State Border Guard Services and the Department of Statistics.

From relief to development

International humanitarian efforts in 1997 are continuing the shift from relief-oriented activities to sustainable development programmes targeting income generation, microfinance, agriculture and small business development that will enable IDPs to use their skills and limited assets to make their own living. This is especially critical for establishing linkages that enable IDPs to participate in larger economic recovery processes, since return to their former residences in Abkhazia or south Ossetia is not possible in the short term. Nevertheless, the beneficial impact of sustainable development projects will not be experienced immediately, necessitating continued emergency relief assistance in the form of food aid, health care, housing, clothing, fuel and winter support. This is also the case for Abkhazia and south Ossetia, which are not benefiting in any real sense from economic recovery, and have large vulnerable groups, especially women, children and the elderly.

International and indigenous NGOs are expanding their assistance to IDPs in places such as Achara, Imereti, Kvemo Kartli, Mtskheta-Mtianeti, Racha-Lechkumi, Samegrelo, Samtske-Javakheti, Shida Kartli and Tbilisi. The Norwegian Refugee Council, IRC, Oxfam, MSF-Spain/Greece, Action internationale contra la faim (ACF), Lazarus/International Orthodox Christian Charities, Counterpart, Salvation Army, IFRC and Nuova Frontiera are involved in supplying humanitarian relief, IDP shelter rehabilitation, public health and medical services. They are also assuming primary roles in community development, small business development and income generation. This crucial work will lay the basis for sustainable self-sufficiency as IDPs are incorporated into local economic life and establish permanent homes. While most IDPs would like to see peaceful political settlements that would enable them to return to their former homes, the present reality of non-resolution makes it both a survival and an adapative necessity to build new lives where they now live. However, the Georgian government is not in favour of integrating IDPs.

Nevertheless, most IDPs experience minimal benefits from these interventions. This is due to several factors, but primarily to economic marginalization and the limited resources of humanitarian agencies. Most IDPs, even with the help of income generating programmes, survive with odd jobs and selling goods and personal belongings at local markets. But many IDPs cannot find work and no longer have personal assets to sell. Moreover, in Samegrelo, the food sector activities of NGOs such as ACF and IFRC have been substantially reduced or even stopped, leaving 123,538 IDPs with little or no food aid.

Internally displaced children suffer from a lack of education and physical and mental health care. A number of NGOs and UNICEF have been involved in developing and implementing educational programmes and other support activities, such as play groups, which are targeted at children in communal centres where IDPs are living. Health care support for IDPs, especially children, infants and pregnant mothers, has been negatively affected by the fragile and insecure state of the Georgian health care system, which relies in substantial part on international support. Diphtheria, measles, pneumonia, acute respiratory infections, diarrhoea and tuberculosis have high rates of incidence among these IDPs.

Russian Federation
William Hayden

The revised law of the Russian Federation on forced migration, adopted on 20 December 1995, is confusing. It defines IDPs as either Russian citizens forced to flee their homes in the Russian Federation or Russian citizens who have been forced to flee their homes in another country and seek haven in Russia. Many ethnic Russians who fled from the conflict in the north Caucasus have sought a safe haven in other parts of Russia, with Moscow being a primary migration point. Other non-Russian ethnic people fleeing generalized mass violence have usually sought refuge with relatives or other ethnic kin in and around the areas of conflict. These persons have generally not undertaken registration or protection with the Russian Federation Migration Service (FMS).

Its decentralized nature is supposed to bring the FMS closer to its beneficiaries, but it adds to the complexity and difficulty IDPs have in obtaining adequate information or access to FMS services necessary for registration, assistance and relocation to a temporary residence. This is also com-pounded by rules implemented at the local level, which impose constraints that evoke the worst aspects of the Soviet-era *propiska* or residency permit. In the north Caucasus, where there is a large-scale IDP crisis, the international humanitarian community has played a beneficial but limited role in assisting persons displaced and affected by violent conflict.

Since the eruption of intercommunal conflict in October 1992 between north Ossetians and Ingushetians in the Prigorodnyi

district of north Ossetia, and the war between Chechen separatists and the Russian Federation in Chechnya in mid-December 1994, several hundred thousand persons have been internally displaced in the north Caucasus region. According to the FMS, 600,000 persons belonging to Chechen, Russian, Ingush, Ossetian and other ethnic groups were displaced in and around Chechnya, Dagestan, Ingushetia, Kabardino-Balkaria, Stavropol, Krasnodar and other locations around the Russian Federation.

Long-standing tensions between Ossetians and Ingush stemming from the deportation of the Ingush by Stalin were exacerbated and exploded into conflict after the arrival in Prigorodnyi district of approximately 16,000 south Ossetian refugees, fleeing civil war in the south Ossetian autonomous Oblast in newly-independent Georgia. Although fighting was short lived, an estimated 500–700 persons were killed and, with the help of Russian units, most of the ethnic Ingush population of the district and north Ossetia (ranging from 34,000 to 64,000) were forcibly displaced to the neighbouring autonomous republic of Ingushetia. North Ossetian authorities also claimed that up to 9000 Ossetians were displaced from the Prigorodnyi district to other areas of north Ossetia. According to Human Rights Watch, Helsinki, by mid-1994 the number of south Ossetians refugees in Prigorodny district had increased to 43,168.

Chechnya uprising
Following intervention by Russian Federation forces in Chechnya against separatist forces led by Dzokar Dudaev, up to 400,000 people were initially displaced, with the ICRC estimating 260,000 displaced throughout Chechnya, 100,000 to Ingushetia, 30,000 to Dagestan, and 5000 each to north Ossetia and the Stavropol region of the Russian Federation. Fighting throughout Chechnya during the period of the conflict (December

RUSSIAN FEDERATION: Chechen IDPs in north Ossetia (PHOTO: T Bolstad/UNHCR).

1994 to August 1996) caused an estimated 60,000–100,000 casualties, the majority being civilian non-combatants, and created frequent and large displacements, placing great pressure on local resources in Chechnya and the neighbouring region.

During August 1996, the FMS reported that it had registered 198,000 more displaced people who fled Grozny just before and during the offensive in which Chechen separatists regained control of the mostly destroyed city. The UNHCR also reported that during the two weeks prior to this fighting, 20,000 displaced fled to Ingushetia and 5000 to Dagestan.

An accurate count of both registered and unregistered IDPs in the north Caucasus region has been difficult to obtain, principally because of the fluidity of IDP movements and the refuge and support offered by extended family ties. The FMS estimates that 350,000 ethnic Russians were forcibly displaced from Chechnya (which according to a 1989 census would be more than the ethnic Russian population of Chechnya), with approximately 100,000 IDPs in Stavropol, 60,000 in Krasnodar, and the remainder in other regions of the Russian Federation. Most ethnic Russians want to settle permanently in other locations in the Russian Federation. The FMS has made several public statements on the urgent problem of finding accommodation for ethnic Russians from Chechnya in other parts of Russia.

According to the different figures of UNHCR, OCHA and the ICRC, there are as many as 300,000 Chechen IDPs in Chechnya, 25,000 in Ingushetia (along with 30,000 Ingush IDPs), and 40,000 in Dagestan. Ethnic Chechens generally did not register with the FMS and, combined with the limited operations of the international community in

Chechnya, this has made it difficult to determine exact figures and locations of IDPs. However, regardless of absolute accuracy, these numbers indicate that a substantial proportion of the north Caucasus population has been forcibly uprooted since 1992. The situation has also been aggravated by the devastation of local economies and infrastructure, continuing political instability, human rights protection problems, persistent operational difficulties, and insecurity faced by international humanitarian organizations in delivering assistance to the displaced.

International response

The cessation of hostilities in Chechnya in August 1996, initiated through the efforts of Alexandr Lebed, opened the opportunity for expanding the institutional response to the IDP crisis in the region. From early 1995, a limited number of humanitarian NGOs, the ICRC and IOM were operating inside Chechnya. However, because of hazardous security conditions, most of the relief and assistance, including operations by UNHCR, WHO, WFP and the DHA, targeted the displaced in the neighbouring republics of Dagestan, Ingushetia, north Ossetia and the Russian regions of Stavropol and Krasnodar. Although security conditions after August 1996 were still precarious, UN agencies, the ICRC, and international and local NGOs stepped up their activities to assist IDPs and other vulnerable persons.

However, humanitarian assistance has been hampered by the increase in intimidation, kidnappings and other attacks against expatriate and local humanitarian staff, culminating in the December 1996 murder of six ICRC expatriate delegates in Novye Atagi. This attack caused the ICRC, UN agencies and most international NGOs to terminate their operations in Chechnya for the first few months of 1997. The UN also held back its consolidated inter-agency appeal for 1997 until February. Security in the region

has not improved. In August 1997 four French humanitarian workers from Equilibre were being held in Dagestan, one French member of MSF-France had been abducted in Ingushetia, and two British aid workers had been kidnapped in Grozny. In February 1998, the head of the UNHCR's operations was kidnapped in Vladikavkaz.

The DHA reported that US$ 11 million of humanitarian assistance had been collected by October 1997 from contributions in direct response to the 1997 consolidated inter-agency appeal for the 'return and integration of displaced persons from Chechnya' and outside the UN framework. These funds are being used by UN agencies, ICRC, ECHO and NGOs for IDP food, housing, mental and physical health rehabilitation, war-affected children, sanitation and other infrastructure rehabilitation projects. However, only 48.5 per cent of the total needs of UN agencies have been met, especially the requirements of UNICEF, WHO and WFP.

This lack of donor response will be a major constraint to assistance targeting vulnerable women, children and the elderly. International humanitarian agencies also experience difficulties in clearing supplies through Russian customs, and the Chechen government has few resources, so IDPs will continue to subsist in fragile and vulnerable conditions.

Returnee programmes

By the end of August, UNHCR had facilitated the return of 15,000 IDPs in Dagestan to Chechnya, who were supplied with 'returnee packages' containing three-months food supplies, domestic items and plastic sheeting. UNHCR also assisted in the return of 1100 IDPs from Ingushetia and 100 from Kabardino-Balkaria to Chechnya. However, there have been considerable difficulties in returning Ingush IDPs to the Prigorodny district in north Ossetia. Eight villages were designated for returnee movement under a 20 April 1996 agreement between Ingushetia and north Ossetia, which was reconfirmed in a 4 September 1997 general treaty signed by Ingush President Aushev and north Ossetia President Galazov. Nevertheless, at the end of July 1997 a mob of north Ossetians attacked the Ingush returnee camp at Tarskoye in Prigorodnyi, destroying or damaging all 84 container houses provided by the FMS.

As of October 1997, only four of the eight designated villages cleared for Ingush returnees were considered safe. In August 1997, only 89 Ingush people were able to return to the Kartsa and Chermen villages with UNHCR assistance. That leaves a further 17,000 Ingush IDPs who qualify to return to the eight designated villages. Moreover, 11,000 Ingush IDPs from Prigorodnyi come from villages not covered by the April 1996 agreement between Ingushetia and north Ossetia. In 1997, returnee operations in Ingushetia and north Ossetia were unsuccessful, primarily because of unresolved tensions between the two ethnic groups, which were heightened by the presence of 29,000 registered and 10,000 unregistered south Ossetian refugees from Georgia.

Conditions for returnees
Conditions in Chechnya for the return and integration of IDPs are no better. They are particularly deplorable in the larger cities of Grozny and Gudermes, which suffered extensive damage to buildings and infrastructure. The conditions are exacerbated by the non-functioning of public and social services, and will severely affect the elderly and women and children located in and returning to urban areas. Grozny's water and sanitation system was virtually destroyed during the war, with Number 1 pumping station now serving as the main watersource, while contaminated water and other waste are collecting in the damaged sewerage system. IDPs returning to Grozny and Gudermes must rely on the inadequate services provided by

international agencies, since the government of Chechnya does not have the resources to commit to large-scale rehabilitation of services. The ICRC has played an important role in providing public health resources through the rehabilitation of the Number 4 and Number 9 hospitals, and in funding and supplying a visiting nurses' programme for the homebound and elderly managed by local branches of the Russian Red Cross. Outside urban areas, many small villages have suffered damage that will affect the successful return of displaced people. The HALO Trust, a British NGO involved in mine clearance and awareness training, estimates that 20,000 hectares of farmland are contaminated or believed to be contaminated by mines and unexploded ordnance. Villages, fields, wooded areas, riverbanks and roadsides are also contaminated with mines. Because of these conditions, the UNHCR estimates that the remaining 75,000 Chechen displaced outside Chechnya will not return, choosing instead to remain with relatives. UNHCR activities are being reoriented towards resettling and integrating those persons.

Protection of human rights
The government of Chechnya currently has few resources to undertake the immediate and long-term activities necessary for addressing the IDP crisis. Although the Russian Federation government promised in August 1997 that US$ 120 million would be made available to Chechnya for economic assistance and reconstruction, few funds have been released. Moreover, a vacuum still exists in human rights protection. The government of Chechnya still does not have the institutional capacity to monitor adequately and redress human rights violations, and the Russian Federation has made no contributions to assist Chechnya other than denouncing the 3 September 1997 public execution in Grozny of two people convicted of murder. Human rights protection activities by international

organizations are limited to reports released after events have occurred, or to restrained protests by humanitarian agencies in the field or the OSCE assistance group. Throughout the conflict, the most successful efforts at denouncing and publicizing human rights violations in Chechnya, whether committed by Russians or Chechens, has been the work of the Memorial Human Rights Centre, a Russian NGO based in Moscow. Substantial work remains to be done in this area, and is mainly hampered by institutional incapacity and political disinterest, both international and domestic.

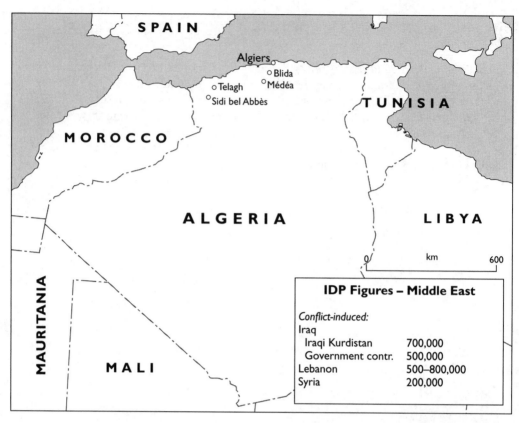

Map 11: Middle East and North Africa

Middle East and North Africa

Overview
Chris Dammers

Overall prospects for internally displaced people in the Middle East deteriorated during 1997. Conflict and instability continued to generate new displacements in Iraq and Algeria. The return of people displaced for more than a generation in Cyprus and Syria seemed no nearer. Only in Lebanon was some limited progress made with rehabilitation and return.

In Iraq, fighting continued in Iraqi Kurdistan, with more than 700,000 people estimated to be displaced by the end of 1997. In government-controlled areas, displacement is harder to assess, but may reach 500,000 people if those displaced by the draining of the southern marshes are included.

Comparative stability continued in most of Lebanon, though not in the south. Though reconstruction continued, reconciliation and rehabilitation are proving to be more difficult. The return home of over half a million internally displaced people proceeded only slowly in 1997. South Lebanon remained unstable, though was spared any repeat of the massive displacements of 1996.

In Algeria conflict, human rights violations and displacement continued unabated in 1997. Though documentation is limited, tens of thousands of people are known to have been temporarily or permanently displaced in recent years.

In Syria, those displaced from the Jawlan by Israel in 1967, may now, together with their descendants, number 200,000 people. The stalled Israeli/Palestinian peace process means that they too have almost no chance of returning in the foreseeable future.

The situation of four million Palestinian refugees deserves recognition; restriction and displacement within their host countries, and the semi-permanent nature of their exile, makes their situation analogous to that of IDPs. Prospects of a permanent Israeli–Palestinian settlement, on which overall regional stability is so dependent, receded in 1997.

Algeria
Chris Dammers

Algeria has witnessed extraordinarily high levels of political violence and human rights abuse since 1992, when the government cancelled elections the FIS (Front islamique du salut/Islamic Salvation Front) seemed certain to win. Although estimates vary greatly, most observers put the number of people killed in the last five years at more than 50,000. In the same period, tens of thousands of people are believed to have been temporarily or permanently displaced as a result of the violence, though documentation has been almost non-existent. As many as 400,000 may have left the country altogether.

Ostensibly the primary violence is between government forces and extremist Islamist groups, notably the GIA (Groupe islamique armée/Armed Islamic Group). However, in numerous civilian massacres the precise circumstances and the motives of the perpetrators have been difficult to establish. Some of the killing seems designed largely to discredit opponents, with government forces disguising themselves as Islamists and vice versa. Journalism, or serious human rights work, is a dangerous profession in Algeria, and most information is tightly controlled by the government.

If anything, conflict and violence

escalated in 1997. Local elections in October 1997, boycotted by the main opposition parties, appear to have had little impact on the underlying conflict. The elections did provide a rare opportunity for international journalists to visit the country. Though having to work under government supervision, most found disturbing evidence of security force collusion even in the massacres whose aftermath they were invited to witness.

Displacement caused by fear of attack would be still greater if the timing and location of massacres were predictable. Displacement has been greatest from some of the worst affected areas, notably the 'triangle of death' on the Blida plain south of Algiers, a region including villages and shanty towns politically hostile to the government, and from which migration to Algiers has been significant. Some reports have claimed that displacement, eventually to be followed by land appropriation by officials or army officers, may even be a motive for the atrocities. Bulldozing of shanty towns has also reportedly displaced thousands.

Though precise information is impossible to obtain, the following examples, cited by the Algerian Refugee Council, give some indication of the scale and extent of displacement.

- Médéa is believed to be an important base for the GIA. An estimated 200,000 people are said to have left for nearby Algiers, or to have fled abroad.
- Blida was the scene of some of the worst massacres. An estimated 50,000–100,000 people have fled, mainly to Algiers nearby.
- In Ouled Allel about 15,000 were evacuated – almost the whole town.
- In Larba about 5000 were displaced – 20 per cent of the population.
- In Telagh (between Sidi bel Abbès and Oran) 3000 people were displaced following government bombardments in 1993.

- In Sidi Moussa town, Cheraga, near Algiers and Bouïnane, 8000 people were displaced. In Les Eucalyptus, 500 people were displaced following a massacre attributed to GIA.
- Ouled Beni Messous (suburban Algiers) was the site of double displacement: many had sought refuge there, then fled again following further massacres.

Economic interest, support for the government and fear of Islamist forces have limited international concern about the appalling events in Algeria, though some initiatives were taken in response to new waves of civilian massacres at the end of 1997 and beginning of 1998. However, thousands more people were displaced by these and prospects for a resolution of the conflict are no nearer.

Iraq
Chris Dammers

Over the last 40 years the most extensive conflict within the borders of Iraq has followed the ethnic division in the country between Arabs and Kurds. Conflict between opposing Kurdish factions has also been considerable. To a lesser extent conflict has also followed the confessional division between Sunni and Shi'a Muslims.

Conflicts leading to displacement within Iraq have been triggered and fuelled by regional and global conflicts: notably hostilities between Iraq and Iran, and the Gulf War of 1991, as well as tensions between Turkey and its neighbours and direct intervention in Iraq by Turkey and Iran.

Since 1991 Iraq has been divided into those areas controlled by the government, and regions in the north and northeast of the country that have been under the control of Kurdish parties. Displacement is considered

IRAQ: IDPs near Ranya (PHOTO: A Roulet/UNHCR).

first, within these Kurdish-controlled regions, and second from and within government-controlled territory.

Displacement in Iraqi Kurdistan

Iraqi Kurds number about 4.2 million people, about 22 per cent of the population, and have traditionally inhabited the north and north-east of the country (Iraqi Kurdistan). The Assyrian Christian minority of about 250,000 people also lives mainly in Iraqi Kurdistan and has been caught up in the conflict and displacement there, particularly in 1987/8 and 1991.

In recent years much of Iraqi Kurdistan has been controlled by Kurdish political forces. The principal parties have been the Kurdish Democratic Party (KDP), associated with the Barzani clan and dominant in the north of the country, and the Patriotic Union of Kurdistan (PUK), associated with the Talabani family, which is dominant in the northeast. Sometimes the KDP and PUK have collaborated, but more often have opposed each other.

In the 1960s, Iraq witnessed several changes of government and fluctuating conflicts in which the Barzani and to a lesser extent the Talabani militias played a significant role. In 1970, 300,000 people were reported displaced in Kurdistan, the result of fighting between Kurdish militias and the government, as well as between the militias themselves. By 1975, when the government defeated Barzani's KDP, as many as 600,000 were displaced, 250,000 over the border to Iran. The Iraqi government forcibly relocated perhaps 1400 villages and 300,000 people, mainly to 'strategic hamlets' designed to facilitate government containment and control. Along the Iranian border depopulation was almost total, with villages bulldozed to prevent return.

The Iran–Iraq war (1980–88) completed the displacement of much of Iraq's Kurdish population. Towards the end of the war, following increasing collaboration between Iran and Kurdish guerrilla forces, the Iraqi regime pursued its genocidal *Anfal* policy, killing between 50,000 and 200,000, and destroying about 3000 Kurdish villages and hamlets. Their inhabitants – over half a million people – were deported to new 'collective settlements' away from border or mountain areas, or to detention camps in south and west Iraq. Others fled to Iran. Many of these people have been displaced more than once since then. In 1997 those displaced during the mid-1970s and late 1980s numbered 375,000 in the governorates of Dohuk and Arbil; figures for the third Kurdistan governorate of Suleimaniyeh were unavailable.

The Gulf War from January to March 1991 led to further massive displacements. The cease-fire between Iraqi and Allied forces was immediately followed by uprisings in the Kurdish north and Shi'a south of Iraq. Kurdish guerrillas briefly occupied the whole of Iraqi Kurdistan, but the reoccupation of most of the region by Iraqi government troops led to as many as two million people fleeing to Iran, Turkey, and those areas still under Kurdish control. These areas soon included the 'safe haven', initially patrolled by Allied troops, comprising those parts of Iraqi Kurdistan adjacent to the Turkish border. Most of the cross-border refugees later returned to areas under Kurdish (and/or Allied) political control, which expanded greatly following the substantial withdrawal of Iraqi troops in October and November 1991.

Fighting between Iraqi troops and Kurdish militias, between Turkish forces and Kurdish militias, and above all between the Kurdish militias themselves, has continued intermittently ever since the Gulf War. This has almost always been accompanied by temporary or permanent civilian displacement.

Since 1994, displacement has most commonly followed conflict between the two main Kurdish parties, the KDP and the PUK, usually along the border between their respective territories: in and around the city of Arbil and along a fluctuating front line from Arbil to the Iranian border. People identified with one party (an identification generally based on clan loyalty rather than ideology) living in territory controlled by the other feel highly vulnerable and have frequently been displaced.

In 1996, an alliance between the KDP and the Iraqi government allowed the KDP to capture Arbil, Suleimaniyeh, and much of the rest of Iraqi Kurdistan. Fear of Iraqi troops led to many inhabitants of Suleimaniyeh city and governorate fleeing in advance, mainly to Iran or the border regions; estimates of numbers involved vary but were probably around 80,000, of whom perhaps half crossed into Iran. Many returned when it became clear that Iraqi government involvement was much less in Suleimaniyeh than in Arbil; and nearly all did so when the PUK regrouped and recaptured Suleimaniyeh in October. However, in early November, the ICRC was still assisting 5000 internally displaced people in the Zaleh area near the Iranian border, and 2000 in Arbil.

UN figures for those displaced by the fighting in 1996 and the first half of 1997 were: Dohuk governorate 13,281; Arbil governorate 67,283; and Suleimaniyeh governorate 38,453 (total 119,017).

Turkish incursions and the PKK
Despite increasing hostility from the KDP, guerrillas of the PKK (Kurdistan Workers' Party), which pursues a separatist guerrilla war in Turkey, have established bases in northern Iraq. These have been the target of frequent Turkish bombardments and incursions, with major invasions taking place in October 1992, March 1995, June 1996, May 1997 and September/October 1997. Fighting between the PKK and KDP has continued intermittently since 1995, and was a significant factor in the displacements of late 1997. Turkish bombardments and incursions from May to July 1997 were accompanied by

fighting between the KDP and PKK. Further attacks from September to November led to renewed conflict between the KDP and PUK, with credible PUK claims that the Turks were supporting the KDP, as well as reports that the PKK was gaining support among Iraqi as well as Turkish Kurds.

A WFP survey conducted in August 1997 reported 1291 people still displaced from the border regions of northern Iraq affected by the Turkish incursions. In November, a UN security report revised this to '600 families'.

Iranian incursions and the KDPI

A parallel situation, though on a smaller scale, has existed on the Iranian border, with guerrillas of the Kurdish Democratic Party of Iran (KDPI) being bombarded by Iranian troops, generating displacement of both Iranian and Iraqi Kurds. Iranian conflict with its own Kurdish separatists has not, however, precluded cooperation between Iran and the PUK, especially when the rival KDP has allied itself with the Iraqi or Turkish governments. Indeed, the events of 1997 generated common interests between the KDP, Iraq and Turkey on the one hand and the PKK, PUK and Iran on the other, which proved quite capable of translating into unlikely alliances on the ground.

Returning refugees from Iran

Despite the renewed fighting, improved economic prospects following the 'oil for food' dispensation and new trading opportunities between Kurdish- and government-controlled areas led to continuing repatriation of Kurdish refugees from Iran, whether from the major displacements of 1974/5, 1988, 1991, or subsequently. UNHCR reported 2747 returning refugees in the first six months of 1997; but since these were all UNHCR registered refugees, the real figure is likely to be considerably higher. Other reports speak of refugees returning at the rate of 11,000 a year.

Many of these returnees, however, are unable to return to their original homes, which may have been destroyed, and have merely graduated from being 'refugees' to being 'internally displaced'.

Displacement from and within government-controlled areas of Iraq

The strategic city of Kirkuk, which is surrounded by oil fields, has traditionally had a mixed Turkoman, Kurdish and Arab population. Although long claimed by Kurds as part of Iraqi Kurdistan, it lies outside the 'Kurdistan Autonomous Region' delineated in 1975. Of the cities captured and then lost by Kurdish forces in the uprising of 1991, only Kirkuk subsequently remained under permanent Iraqi government control.

Most Kurds fled Kirkuk when it was retaken by Iraqi government troops following the Kurdish uprising in 1991; about 140,000 are thought to remain in Kurdish-controlled areas, fearful of returning because of the persecution and displacement of Kurds remaining in the city. Turkomans (Turkish-speaking Iraqis), who number up to a million, live mainly in the lowland and urban areas of northern Iraq, but used to be predominant in Kirkuk. They too have been subject to repression, with many reportedly moving under pressure to Baghdad, though figures are unavailable. Shi'a Turkomans have been particularly vulnerable. Arab families from central and southern Iraq have been settled in Kirkuk, part of government efforts to 'Arabize' the city.

While Kirkuk has been the most seriously affected, other parts of northern Iraq under government control have seen similar displacements, for example of Kurds from the predominantly Arab city of Mosul.

Thousands of non-Kurdish opponents of the Saddam Hussein regime have also sought refuge, or a base for continuing their opposition, in the Kurdish-controlled regions of Iraq, particularly since the Gulf War. The entry of Iraqi government troops and agents into these regions in 1996 left them particularly vulnerable – many were captured or killed, particularly in Arbil. In late 1997, the Iraqi National Congress reported that around 2000 non-Kurdish political displacees were still sheltering in PUK-controlled regions, mainly in Suleimaniyeh. Many reportedly had difficulty finding work, and were often regarded with suspicion (as potential government agents) by the PUK authorities.

Faili Kurds, most of whom are Shi'a, form a distinctive group of displaced people in Iraq, many of them twice displaced and now back in their country of origin. Unlike most Iraqi Kurds, until the early 1970s they lived mainly in central and southern Iraq, many of them in Baghdad. At that time, perhaps 130,000 Failis were deported to Iran by the government of Iraq on the pretext that they were not Iraqi citizens, thought in fact it was because their loyalty was considered suspect. Most had lived in Iraq for generations, but in Ottoman times had not registered as citizens in order to avoid conscription. Since the 1970s, most of the Faili Kurds have lived in Iran. However, since 1981, some have returned to Kurdish-controlled northern Iraq, where they are not necessarily welcome.

In the south of Iraq a combination of administrative neglect and political repression had long reinforced migration to the towns and cities (especially Baghdad) as well as to Iran. The Shi'a uprising following the Gulf War led to an estimated 60,000 refugees fleeing to Iran, as well as many more fleeing to those areas of the marshes in central southern Iraq, which remained outside government control. The draining of the marshes has facilitated the establishment of government control of this region – which was limited even before the Gulf War – a process accompanied by further displacement. Most of an estimated 500,000 'Marsh Arabs' have been displaced, or have had to abandon their traditional livelihoods. Large numbers of

villages, particularly in the Al-Nasairiya, Al-Amarah and Basra districts, have been destroyed. Lawlessness and instability remain a feature of many areas. Reports of politically-motivated attacks on government troops have continued, but have generally proved impossible to confirm.

Forced displacement as a response to perceived political opposition would appear to be widespread in contemporary Iraq, though documentation is patchy. The Organization of Human Rights in Iraq reported the following examples of displacement in 1997:

- 440 Kurdish families displaced from Khanaqin, Diyala governorate, to Kurdish-controlled regions, in February and March;
- 20 Faili Kurd families moved from Khanaqin to Fullajah, Arramadi governorate in February and March;
- many Faili Kurds displaced from Khanaqin to Najaf; and
- enforced population exchange in July between 100 Faili Kurd families in Tuz Khurmatu, south of Kirkuk, and Shi'a Arab families from the south of Iraq.

Prior to the Gulf War, the 'Bidoon', most of whom are of Iraqi origin, were stateless residents of Kuwait. Their name is Arabic for 'without' – that is without nationality. They numbered about 250,000 and most had been born in Kuwait, or had lived there for a long time. Since the war around half of them have fled from or been expelled from Kuwait, mostly to Iraq. Though they are refugees, their statelessness, their displacement and their Iraqi connections mean that their status has much in common with that of other 'internally displaced' people. Detailed information on their situation in Iraq is, however, unavailable.

The Gulf War led to the intensification of chronic conflict and instability in Iraq. Economic sanctions have added a new dimension of poverty, malnutrition and disease for millions of Iraqis. The easing of sanctions in 1996 led to some degree of amelioration of conditions for the civilian population in both government- and Kurdish-controlled regions of Iraq. However, renewed confrontation between Iraq and the UN from late 1997 could reverse this process.

The conflicting interests of Iraq, Iran and Turkey, combined with lack of respect for human rights and Kurdish aspirations in all three countries, are a potent recipe for continued instability, conflict and further displacement in Iraqi Kurdistan. The highly centralized government in Iraq has survived through a pervasive emphasis on security and ruthless suppression of its opponents; its demise, though no more likely now than in recent years, could once again unleash conflict and displacement throughout the country.

Lebanon
Chris Dammers

Since the founding of the state in 1920, Lebanese society has been organized on confessional lines, which have been formally incorporated into the country's political structures. Muslims constitute the majority of the population, divided into Sunni and Shi'a groupings. The principal denominations of the once politically dominant Christians are Maronites, Greek Orthodox and Greek Catholics. Other minorities include Druzes, Alawis, Armenians and Kurds. Palestinian refugees comprise about 10 per cent of the population.

From 1975 to 1991, Lebanon witnessed persistent internal conflict, fomented by wider regional conflicts, which resulted in the fragmentation of the country. In the civil war (1975/6), Maronite-dominated militias and army units fought an alliance of the Palestine Liberation Organization (PLO) and the Lebanese National Movement (LNM), whose constituency was largely among the Lebanese Muslims and Druze. The armed Palestinian presence in Lebanon was a major catalyst for the war. The intervention of Syria, initially on the side of the Christian militias, imposed something of a stalemate, consolidating the cantonization of the country into confessional districts. Syria has remained the dominant force in Lebanon ever since.

Before 1975 many parts of Lebanon had predominant confessional groupings, but settlement patterns were complex and intertwined. The civil war led to the wholesale expulsion of Muslims from regions controlled by Christian militias, and substantial displacement of Christians from regions controlled by the PLO and the LNM. Most of these 'population exchanges' took place in and around Beirut, and probably led to the long-term displacement of between 250,000 and 300,000 people, the great majority Muslims.

The later phases of the war saw many Christians displaced from the Shouf, the mountainous region to the southeast of Beirut. The Bekaa region in the east of the country, and to a lesser extent the north of Lebanon, also saw displacement, largely of Christians to areas controlled by the Christian militias, particularly Zahleh and Beirut. An estimated 650,000 Lebanese left the country altogether during this period (a disproportionate number of them Christian), of whom perhaps half returned during the comparative calm of 1977.

Israeli invasions: 1978 and 1982
The Israeli invasion of 1978 displaced about 200,000 Lebanese (mostly Shi'a Muslims) and 65,000 Palestinians from the south of the country. Although most of this displacement was temporary, some became effectively permanent, with many people resettling indefinitely, particularly in the southern suburbs of Beirut. Israel established a sizeable 'security zone' adjacent to its northern border, which it jointly controlled with a surrogate

militia, which later became the South Lebanese Army. UN troops established a buffer zone to the north of the Israeli-controlled area. This situation has essentially continued ever since (though the configurations of Israel's opponents to the north have changed) and has been a recipe for almost permanent instability with several large-scale if mainly temporary displacements.

The Israeli invasion of 1982 was on a very much larger scale than in 1978, leading to the occupation of the whole of the southern half of Lebanon, up to and including Beirut. Though directed primarily against the PLO, the invasion also aimed to restructure Lebanese politics. Virtually the whole of the country was affected, with bombardments extending to the far north and to the Bekaa. The war saw further displacements from south Lebanon and from west Beirut, which was besieged for more than two months.

The 'war of the camps' and the 'war of the mountain'

The aftermath of the 1982 invasion saw further conflict, mainly between Shi'a militias and Palestinians (who were increasingly besieged in their camps), as well as between Christian and Druze militias in the mountains east and southeast of Beirut (Bhamdoun, Aley and the Shouf). Massacres and atrocities were committed on all sides. The outcome of the latter conflict in particular was further displacement and cantonization, with many Christians (some of whom had been displaced earlier and had returned after the Israeli invasion) expelled from Druze-dominated areas, and later too from other areas further south.

By 1986, an estimated 225,000–300,000 people had been displaced by the 1982 Israeli invasion and its prolonged aftermath.

The 'last round'

The fragmentation of Lebanon into confessionally based districts was accompanied by growing Syrian hegemony (except over the border districts controlled by Israel). The Syrians, like the Israelis before them, aimed to reconstitute the country politically, efforts that eventually bore fruit in the Ta'if accords of 1989. A key aspect of these accords was the abolition of the constitutional Christian domination of parliament and state. Though divided among themselves, many Christian politicians (and the militias under their control) were hostile to Syria and opposed the Ta'if accords. In 1989 and 1990 there was heavy fighting between Christian militias and Syrian troops, and between the militias themselves, leading to further extensive displacement, estimated at about 150,000 people. These displacements were mainly from and within the Christian areas comprising east Beirut and the region to the east and north. The defeat of the forces of General Aoun, later followed by the 1992 elections, seemed to many to herald the end of a decade and a half of civil war. Freedom of movement returned to the country, but most of the displaced found they could still not go home.

The south

Though most of Lebanon is making rapid progress with reconstruction, and slow but definite progress with reconciliation and return, the problems of the south remain unresolved, since they are linked to the stalled Israeli–Palestinian peace process and to continuing hostility between Israel and Syria. While the Palestinians are no longer a significant political force in Lebanon, their former role in confronting Israel and its local allies has been taken by Hizballah, an Islamist militia supported by Syria and Iran. The result is continuing instability, with south Lebanon constantly subjected to conflict and the forced displacement of its people.

In April 1996, following Hizballah rocket attacks on northern Israel, Israel launched extensive air raids and rocket attacks on

Beirut and on a reported 54 villages in southern Lebanon. Estimates of those displaced, many from Beirut itself, were put at 600,000 by the government, but 400,000 or fewer by most independent sources. An informal cease-fire was declared after 16 days and most of the displaced people returned home. Undoubtedly, some stayed on in Beirut or in areas they considered safer, but the long-term impact of such large-scale temporary displacement is not so much the immediate creation of permanent IDPs, as that of accelerating rural–urban drift and depopulation of the south, which has seen neither peace nor stability for more than 20 years.

Palestinians in Lebanon

Since Palestinians in Lebanon are classified as refugees, they would fall beyond the scope of this survey. However, since most were born in Lebanon (or Jordan), and most of those born in Palestine left their homeland half a century ago, they can be considered indefinite residents, even though such residence is by no means accepted as permanent and remains insecure. Their situation is part of the problem of internally displaced people within Lebanon. Despite many being confined to refugee camps, Palestinians have also been displaced within Lebanon, and involved with the displacement of others. For example, in July 1997, 53 Palestinian families were reported to have resisted eviction from premises they had occupied in Mieh Mieh near Sidon after they had in turn been displaced from the nearby refugee camp. The squatters demanded compensation equivalent to what would have been available had they been Lebanese displaced, to which they were not, however, entitled. More generally, their situation contributes to the climate of injustice and discrimination, which undermines efforts at reconciliation in Lebanon as a whole.

Lebanon now: reconciliation and return?

Though figures are contested, between 15 and 25 per cent of Lebanon's population of about 3.2 million people (excluding Palestinians and non-Lebanese nationals) can be classified as long-term displaced. Probably the majority of the adult population has been subjected to temporary displacement at one time or another, for many several times. The social and psychological costs of upheaval on this scale are enormous.

In 1996, the Ministry of Displaced cited a figure of 90,000 families (more than 500,000 people), of whom 70,000 were said to be seeking return. Of these 70,000 families, 45,000 were said to be illegally occupying other people's accommodation, largely of those who had been displaced. While such official figures may in general be too low, the figures for those genuinely wishing to return to their original homes are probably too high. Much of the displacement has been to urban areas, particularly Beirut, a long-term trend greatly reinforced by the extended periods of conflict and instability.

Large numbers of displaced people do not want to return home because economic, social and/or security conditions are better for them in their new locations. Difficulties over repossessing property, or confusion over legal mechanisms and reparation procedures, remain major obstacles. Mistrust between confessional groups has been greatly exacerbated by 15 years of conflict. At a local level, antagonisms generated by specific episodes may be severe; as a result 'home' may be precisely the place where a displacee might feel most insecure. Many may wish to regain their property without physically returning to their former homes. According to press reports, by early 1997 less than 12 per cent of those displaced had returned to their homes, though official figures are higher.

According to an assessment by the Lebanese NGO Forum, slow progress and widespread dissatisfaction among both the displaced and the politicians attempting to represent them have characterized the return. Obstacles cited include:

- wastage of funds, particularly associated with lack of accountability for money allocated through the national fund for the displaced;
- imbalances in the distribution of compensation money;
- attempts to evict people from illegally occupied houses without corresponding provision for their resettlement elsewhere; and
- political tensions and controversies between government officials.

An example cited of political interference in the return of the displaced is the support, early in 1997, of the speaker of parliament and head of the Shi'a Amal movement, Nabih Berri, for 150 displaced people illegally occupying the houses of other displaced people in the Maramel district of Ouzai, south of Beirut. This led to the indefinite postponement of their eviction, as well as of the return of those originally displaced from their homes. Such political interference is widely seen as relating to the confessional affiliation of those concerned. Incidents such as these illustrate that Lebanon is still embroiled in confessionally-based politics, despite the objectives of the new constitutional dispensation.

In January 1997, following pledges to upgrade the priority given to the return of the displaced, the government allocated 64,000 million Lebanese pounds (about US$ 42 million) to the Central Fund for the Displaced. However, widespread criticism of inequitable allocation of funds continued. A dispute between Prime Minister Rafik Hariri and Minister for the Displaced Walid Jumblatt, following what the former saw as the squandering of funds during the recent return of families in the Kfar Nabrakh region

in the Shouf, led in mid-1997 to the virtual suspension of disbursements from the fund.

Those displaced by the 'war of the mountain' have seen some of the most systematic (as well as comparatively well documented) efforts at reconciliation and return. It also seems likely that fewer displaced people here than in other rural areas have become *de facto* urban migrants. Official figures at the end of August 1997 indicated that of the 20,000 families (more than 100,000 people) displaced in the districts of Baabda, Aley and Shouf (the majority of them Christians), about 31 per cent had returned. However even if these figures are accurate, they can be assumed to be among the highest levels of return in the country.

Huge problems remain. The nature of the conflicts in many places have left a legacy of bitterness, which takes time and determination to overcome. Demographically, much of Lebanon remains cantonized into confessional areas. Uncertainties and inconsistencies about access to compensation generate further delays. Against this stands the determination of many Lebanese to overcome the conflicts of the past, a determination reinforced by policy – if not always practice – at an official level. Though frequently criticized as inadequate, available resources are very much greater than in most places aspiring to reconstitute societies fractured along the lines of ethnicity or religious affiliation.

Continued conflict and instability in south Lebanon, and the unresolved question of the large numbers of Palestinian refugees, have repercussions for wider national initiatives of reconciliation, including the return of the displaced. Many of those displaced from the south are reluctant to return, and consequently to vacate property belonging to others who have been displaced. This has a serious knock-on effect on the prospects for overall return. Similarly, if less directly, the strategy of containment of Palestinians in Lebanon through restrictive legislation and denial of human rights is likely to have a destabilizing effect in the long term, retarding efforts to move away from the conflicts and divisions that have plagued the country for so long.

Syria
Chris Dammers

In 1967 Israel occupied much of the Jawlan district of the country, commonly if somewhat misleadingly referred to as the 'Golan heights', displacing almost all the population, including the inhabitants of the large town of Quneitra. The numbers of those displaced have always been disputed, varying from Israeli estimates of 75,000 to Syrian figures of 155,000. Syria claims that those displaced and their descendants now number nearly half a million. A more realistic figure may be 200,000. About 15,000 Syrians, mainly Druze villagers, have remained under Israeli occupation; most have resisted the offer of Israeli citizenship. The formal annexation of the Jawlan by Israel in 1981 (in violation of the fourth Geneva Convention), to which the present Israeli government is fully committed, make the prospects for return of the displaced remote.

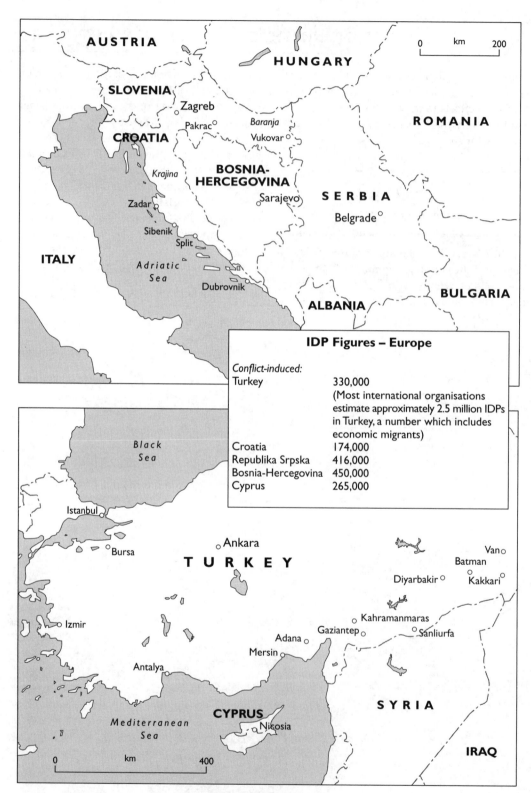

IDP Figures – Europe

Conflict-induced:

Turkey	330,000
	(Most international organisations estimate approximately 2.5 million IDPs in Turkey, a number which includes economic migrants)
Croatia	174,000
Republika Srpska	416,000
Bosnia-Hercegovina	450,000
Cyprus	265,000

Map 12: Europe

Europe

Overview
Paul Stubbs

If the successor states of the former Soviet Union are excluded from our definition of 'Europe', then there are two major areas where internal displacement exist and may continue to exist in the future: Bosnia-Hercegovina, Croatia, Cyprus and Turkey. None of the other countries in Europe have significant numbers of IDPs apart from displaced Romani people.

The break-up of Yugoslavia involved large-scale conflict, which may only have ceased temporarily. In Croatia, the possibility of renewed conflict over the government's resumption of control of eastern Slavonia seems to have diminished but cannot be ruled out. While NATO troops keep an uneasy peace in Bosnia-Hercegovina, renewed clashes between and within its different ethnic and administrative areas are possible in the medium to long term. The former Yugoslav Republic of Macedonia remains 'unstable in a stable way' with clashes between ethnic Macedonians and ethnic Albanians, as well as problematic relations with all its neighbours, particularly Greece. Above all, Kosovo, a province of Serbia within the rump of the Federal Republic of Yugoslavia, remains a major potential area of conflict. In Kosovo, 90 per cent of the original population is ethnic Albanian, but fervent ethnic Serbs have been joined by increasing numbers of Serb refugees from Croatia and Bosnia, leading to perceived insecurity for the ethnic Albanians.

The break-up of Yugoslavia poses problems in defining who are IDPs and who are refugees. While the boundaries of the successor states, as recognized internationally, broadly follow the boundaries of the post-1945 federal republics, this does not coincide with many of the realities on the ground. Most importantly, within Bosnia-Hercegovina, Republika Srpska is administratively linked to Serbia proper, while Croat-controlled Herceg-Bosna is similarly linked to Croatia. Indeed, many ethnic Croats who were technically refugees have obtained Croatian citizenship. Increasingly, the resolution of Serb/Croat relations seems to involve allowing each ethnic group to have dual citizenship, of the country in which they live, and of their nominal 'ethnic homeland'. The implication of this is that many people who would, in other cases, be refugees, begin much more to resemble IDPs. Most importantly, the crisis of forced migration in the region can only be resolved through regional agreements.

Similarly in Turkey, regional issues, as well as economic underdevelopment, remain crucial even in the absence of continued military activity by Kurdish nationalists. In Cyprus, about 265,000 people were displaced in 1974 and still have little prospect of return.

In early 1998, ethnic violence in the Yugoslav province of Kosovo created more than 23,000 refugees and displaced people, mostly ethnic Albanians. Dozens have died since the beginning of 1998 in clashes between Serbian security forces and the ethnic Albanian Kosovo Liberation Army. Hundreds fled abroad to Albania, Macedonia and Turkey, while some 5000 fled to the neighbouring Yugoslav province of Montenegro. The remaining internally displaced people settled in Albanian families in and around Kosovo's capital, Pristina.

Bosnia-Hercegovina
Paul Stubbs

Conflict raged in Bosnia-Hercegovina from April 1992 until a cease-fire was called in September 1995. A general framework agreement (the 'Dayton Agreement') was signed in Dayton, USA on 21 November 1995 and subsequently in Paris, France by the presidents of Bosnia-Hercegovina, Croatia and Serbia. The causes and development of the conflict are beyond the scope of this report. Describing the conflict as a 'civil war' is inadequate, given the political and military involvement of neighbouring states, notably Croatia and Serbia who are 'parties' to the peace agreement. Similarly, the 'ethnic' nature of the conflict is sometimes overstated, though peace plans, from Vance–Owen to the Dayton Agreement, recognize three 'ethno-religious' protagonists: Bosnian Croats, predominantly Roman Catholic (17 per cent of Bosnia's population at the 1991 census); Bosnian Serbs, predominantly Orthodox (32 per cent); and Bosniacs, who are Bosnian Muslims (44 per cent). The remainder of Bosnia's 1991 population (totalling 4.36 million) was made up of those who described themselves as 'Yugoslav' (5 per cent) and 'other ethnicities' (2 per cent).

The Dayton Agreement secured the continuation of Bosnia-Hercegovina as a sovereign state within internationally recognized borders, but gave this state and its revolving presidency only limited powers. *De facto*, most power resides in the two entities that make up the state: the Federation of Bosnia-Hercegovina, which controls 51 per cent of the territory, effectively a Bosniac–Croat federation that is further divided along ethnic lines at the cantonal and municipal levels; and Republika Srpska (the Serbian Republic), which controls 49 per cent, itself increasingly split between the western part

loyal to Republika Srpska President Plavsic, and the eastern part loyal to Bosnian presidency member Krajišnik and, ultimately, to indicted war criminal Karadzic. The two entities are divided by an inter-entity boundary line (IEBL), which, on the whole, runs along the cease-fire line. In places, this is a highly visible line with the Dayton Agreement securing demilitarized 'zones of separation'; in others it is virtually invisible. Two significant territorial exchanges were agreed: Sarajevo became reunified within the federation, and Mrkonjic Grad and its surrounding areas were handed over to Republika Srpska. The strategically important town of Brcko remained Serb-held pending final arbitration, which, in February 1997 was again postponed until March 1998. The Dayton Agreement provided for a strong NATO peace implementation force (IFOR), which later became the peace stabilization force (SFOR), together with a civilian office of the high representative (OHR).

Only a few people continued to live in their own homes throughout the war. Between 200,000 and 300,000 (5–7 per cent of the population) were killed and between 2.4 and 2.7 million (55–62 per cent) were displaced. Annex 7 of the Dayton Agreement is an 'Agreement on Refugees and Displaced Persons', which provides for the safe return of refugees and IDPs to their homes and restoration of their property, or compensation where this is not possible. Although the 'early return of refugees and displaced persons is an important objective of the settlement of the conflict in Bosnia and Hercegovina', the Dayton Agreement has had little impact on statistics of the displaced. By April 1997, 17 months after the signing, only about 250,000 forced migrants had returned to their homes, while a further 80,000 had been displaced as a consequence of the agreement's clauses relating to exchanges of territory between the entities. By December 1997, approximately 400,000 people had returned home.

BOSNIA-HERCEGOVINA: IDPs in the Kozovac Collective Centre, Prijedor
(PHOTO: A Hollmann/UNHCR).

A recent UNHCR report suggests that 30 per cent of Bosnia's population has been internally displaced as a result of the war. Currently, estimates suggest a total IDP figure of 866,000 (or 20 per cent of the prewar population). This is made up of 416,000 IDPs estimated by the Republika Srpska authorities to be residing in that entity, and 450,000 IDPs estimated by UNHCR and the authorities to be in the Federation of Bosnia-Hercegovina. While a full census is due to be carried out in 1998, the total figure of 866,000 may be relatively accurate, although there is considerable disagreement about the breakdown between the entities.

The internally displaced population can be further subdivided as follows:

1. *Inter-entity displaced* are the largest number of IDPs, those who left their

homes during the war and now find the place where they used to live assigned to the 'other' entity (for example non-Serbs find their former homes are now part of Republika Srpska). Their forced expulsion, termed 'ethnic cleansing', was an explicit war aim and paper guarantees of 'freedom of movement' are unlikely to alter their situation in the near future. Consequently, they remain unable or unwilling to return to places governed by the same authorities who caused them to flee in the first place. Many left so-called 'safe areas' that were overrun despite international community guarantees and long after Western countries closed their doors to Bosnian refugees. The most dramatic such exodus was from Srebrenica in eastern Bosnia, which was overrun by Serb forces on 11 July 1995. Some 6000 Bosniac males appear to have been killed in the following days, and over 30,000 people fled to Tuzla and its environs from where, in municipal elections held in September 1997, they elected one of many 'councils in exile' in Bosnia-Hercegovina.

2. *Intra-entity displaced* are within the Bosnia-Hercegovina federation and were displaced during the bitter Bosniac–Croat war that raged in Hercegovina and central Bosnia from April 1993 until the Washington Accords, which established the federation in March 1994. While the accords stopped the fighting, they neither reversed 'ethnic cleansing' nor led to the abolition of the Croatian para-state of Herceg-Bosna. This 'state' continues to retain a separate identity, though such symbols as telephone codes, motorcar registration plates and currency are integrated with those of Croatia proper. Notwithstanding pilot projects to promote 'minority return' within the federation, this group of IDPs resembles those who are inter-entity displaced. Some people could return to areas where they would be in the majority, but are prevented from doing so by the absence of any physical or social infrastructure. Even if minority return were to become politically feasible, the tremendous costs of reconstruction and economic regeneration would pose considerable obstacles.

3. *Displaced returnees* are relatively few so far, but are likely to grow as there is pressure on Bosnian refugees to return from western European countries where they have temporary protection. Various push–pull factors, including a few cases of forced repatriation, have produced newly displaced people.

UNHCR figures suggest that 1.2 million citizens of Bosnia-Hercegovina sought refuge abroad and only about one-third of these have found, or are in the process of finding, a 'durable solution', including 88,000 who repatriated to Bosnia-Hercegovina in 1996. This leaves a refugee figure of 815,000 still in need of durable solutions. The total number of refugees and displaced people from Bosnia-Hercegovina, therefore, is 1.68 million – 39 per cent of the prewar population. There are few systematic data comparing and contrasting refugees and IDPs, though some generalizations can be made. On the whole, the refugees who left Bosnia-Hercegovina did so earlier in the war rather than later (when the exit doors were firmly closed). They tend to be urban, more cosmopolitan in outlook and better educated than their internally displaced counterparts. The presence of large numbers of rural IDPs in the urban centres has been a cause of continuing tension in Bosnia-Hercegovina (the two groups were relatively impermeable before the war) and has contributed to the continued dominance of the three ethnically-based nationalist parties.

UNHCR figures also show the slow pace of 'minority return' as a proportion of total return. In 1996, a total of 226,000 people had returned to their homes (27 per cent returning to Republika Srpska and 73 per cent to the federation). Of these, only 9400 or 4 per cent were returning to places where they were in the minority. This failure of minority return clearly results from continuing human rights abuses, discrimination, harassment and in some cases the use or threat of force. However, the role of international agencies in pressurizing overstretched local authorities to expedite minority return, and emphasizing the 'ethnic' dimension at the expense of all other variables, has also played a role. Above all, the high costs of clearing mines, rebuilding houses and the social infrastructure, and regenerating the economy continue to place huge obstacles in the way of return. With increasing donor fatigue, it seems unlikely that these problems will be resolved in the short or medium term. The cost of restoring damaged or destroyed houses to their prewar level alone is estimated at somewhere between US$ 3000 million and US$ 4000 million. After the Dayton Agreement, donor commitments to housing reconstruction totalled only US$ 693 million. The need for cash is matched by the need for a code of practice for reconstruction programmes, both to avoid duplication of donor efforts and competition, and to ensure that programmes are based on need rather than donor priorities. Without this, and many other policy and practice shifts, the future for IDPs in Bosnia-Hercegovina remains bleak.

Croatia
Paul Stubbs

Following its declaration of independence in 1990 after democratic elections, full-scale war broke out in Croatia in late 1991. Ethnic Serbs in particular areas joined forces with the Serb-dominated Yugoslav People's Army. The shelling from the sea of the southern city of Dubrovnik, and the siege and subsequent fall of the eastern city of Vukovar, focused the world's attention on Croatia. While the aggression failed either to reverse independence or secure the continuance of a larger Yugoslavia – indeed there was some question of whether this was ever an explicit or realizable objective – it did succeed in splitting the country into those areas controlled by the Croatian government and those controlled by the 'rebels', which became the self-styled Republic of Serbian Krajina (RSK).

At the end of 1991, the Vance–Owen peace plan set up four United Nations protected areas or 'UNPA zones' corresponding to the main areas of rebel control. These were Sector East,

in eastern Slavonia including Vukovar; Sector West, in western Slavonia bordering Bosnia, including Oku ani and part of Pakrac; Sector North, the northern part of former Vojska Krajina (Military Frontier) west of Karlovac; and Sector South, also part of the old Krajina, a large sweep of territory including the RSK 'capital' Knin. An explicit war aim was the expulsion of the non-Serbian population from these areas. According to the Croatian government, the number of IDPs in Croatia reached its peak on 22 November 1991, at 536,000. However, this figure seems excessively high and may include many who were counted twice or returned fairly quickly. UNHCR figures suggest that by late 1992, Croatia had 265,000 IDPs, which, together with 350,000 refugees from the fighting in Bosnia-Hercegovina, meant that more than 15 per cent of the population consisted of forced migrants.

Over the next five years, the Croatian government gradually recovered control of some of the territory. By the end of 1994 about 45,000 IDPs had returned to their homes in areas that were now under Croatian control, including Dubrovnik, Zadar, Šibenik, Split and parts of Pakrac. A similar number of IDPs returned home in 1995. By the end of the year, according to government figures, Croatia had some 180,000 IDPs. As a result of military action in May 1995 (in western Slavonia) and in August 1995 (in 'Krajina'), these territories were returned to Croatian government control in a matter of days: this led to the exodus of a large number of ethnic Serbs – 12,000 from western Slavonia and up to 200,000 from the 'Krajina'. In the aftermath of the actions, particularly in the Krajina area, many Serbs who stayed were killed, particularly older people. By the end of the year, only Sector East remained under 'rebel' Serb control.

For a number of reasons, the reintegration

of these areas into Croatia did not lead to a large-scale return of IDPs to their homes; the government estimated that about 85,000 returned in 1996 – a figure that seems high from anecdotal evidence. Having suffered heavy damage during the initial fighting and then years of neglect, these areas had by now lost most of their original inhabitants and the prospects for return, reconstruction and economic regeneration were poor. In addition, with the exception of some 'model' reconstruction programmes, few international agencies were offering large-scale support, in part at least because they had diverted the main focus of their activities to Bosnia-Hercegovina. The Croatian government was also unhelpful, preferring paternalistic loan schemes to more imaginative projects and dealing very slowly with requests from ethnic Serbs to return, implicitly making it clear that they wished these areas to be largely mono-ethnic. The Serbs who did return faced systematic discrimination and, sometimes, open harassment or worse. In addition, the areas were being repopulated by ethnic Croats from Bosnia-Hercegovina, themselves often poor and unskilled, whose presence caused a degree of resentment among the local people.

Few people have been able to return either to or from east Slavonia, although the reintegration of the area into Croatia, which was part of the Erdut and Dayton agreements of late 1995, appears to be proceeding satis-factorily. Under the agreements, the area came under the control of a United Nations transitional authority (UNTAES) for a one-year period, extendible by a further year if either side (the Croatian government or the 'rebel' Serbs) requested it. The process was completed in January 1998, though the area had been formally reintegrated in July 1997 with local elections taking place and reintegration of physical infrastructure and the public, economic and educational sectors, continuing. East Slavonia could hold the key

to the resolution of the IDP crisis in Croatia. Some 80,000 IDPs wish to return to the region, while between 60,000 and 80,000 of its present inhabitants are themselves displaced from other parts of Croatia. Many of these have arrived via Serbia or Bosnia, after the Croatian actions of 1995. Alternatively, the reintegration of east Slovania could trigger a new refugee crisis with many thousands leaving their homes and heading for Republika Srpska in Bosnia-Hercegovina, or Serbia proper. More than 50,000 people had left by January 1998 and 6000 or 7000 remain. The view that the Serbian political leadership in the area wants Serbs to stay but has 'neither the experience nor intelligence to inspire' and that the Croatian authorities are keen to observe the letter if not the spirit of the Erdut and Dayton agreements, seems most accurate. Prospects for peaceful reintegration avoiding mass flight appear better in the Baranja area than in the area surrounding Vukovar.

To obtain a reliable current figure for IDPs in Croatia, therefore, one must add IDPs in east Slovania, many of whom have not obtained Croatian documents or citizenship, to the total for Croatian government-controlled areas. The Croatian government's figure of 114,000 IDPs in Croatia should probably have a further 60,000 added to it. In the absence of reliable data from Sector East, it is very difficult to judge the accuracy of this figure. While the formal preconditions exist for the return of all IDPs in Croatia, and of refugees from Serbia, progress remains painfully slow. Many local NGOs are active in a range of civil initiatives, including human rights and psychosocial projects, but few have reconstruction funds at their disposal. Unless the Croatian government goes beyond the letter of agreements and begins to demonstrate a commitment to securing real human rights and protection for Serbian returnees, the log-jam is unlikely to be broken.

Cyprus
Chris Dammers

Cyprus represents one of the longest standing examples of displacement of people in the region, and one of the most static and intractable.

Greeks and Turks have been living together on Cyprus for more than four centuries, under Ottoman rule until 1878 and British rule until 1960. Turkish Cypriots comprise about 136,000 people, or 18 per cent of the population (1994 figures), with Greeks comprising almost all the remainder. The post-independence period from 1960 was dominated by Greek nationalist politicians, many of whom advocated unification with Greece. More than 20,000 Turkish Cypriots were displaced between 1963 and 1970 following intimidation and attack by Greek Cypriot troops and paramilitary forces.

Following a military coup engineered by the junta in Greece and ultra-nationalist Greek Cypriots in 1974, the Turkish invasion and occupation of northern Cyprus led to the southward displacement of about 200,000 Greek Cypriots, and the flight north of about 65,000 Turkish Cypriots, including most of those who had been displaced earlier. Ever since then, a cease-fire line divides the country in two, but since only Turkey recognizes the 'Turkish Republic of Northern Cyprus' proclaimed in 1983, displaced Cypriots, though frequently referred to as refugees, fall into the category of IDPs.

Despite some optimism in the mid-1980s when Turkish Cypriot leaders seemed prepared to make some concessions, and some progress with 'bi-communal' events and initiatives in recent years, the political stalemate has continued. Most displaced people are increasingly integrated into the surrounding society. The Turkish Cypriot authorities have consolidated the Turkish nature of the enclave through promoting immigration of Turks from Turkey.

The segregation of Greek and Turkish Cypriots is virtually complete; the tiny minorities of Greeks and Maronites (Christians of Lebanese origin) in the north, and Turks in the south have survived with difficulty. The number of Greeks in the north declined from 2000 in 1977 to fewer than 500 (mostly elderly) people in 1997. In the same period, the number of Maronites declined from 1000 to fewer than 200. Only about 100 Turkish Cypriots are believed still to be living in the south. The 'enclaved' Greek Cypriot and Maronite communities in northern Cyprus are subject to severe restrictions of movement and civil rights.

In 1996, there were violent disturbances along the buffer zone dividing the island, with several people killed and many more injured. Though 1997 was calmer, and diplomatic initiatives continue, prospects for a settlement and the return of displaced populations do not seem much better.

Turkey
Kemal Kirisci

Since the early 1990s, traditional forms of migration from rural to urban areas have been accompanied by internal displacement caused by the violence surrounding the Kurdish problem in the eastern and southeastern provinces of Turkey. The inhabitants of large numbers of villages and hamlets have been compelled to migrate to urban centres in the region, or even to western parts of Turkey. This wave of internal displacement reached a peak in 1994/5 and since then has virtually ended. However, the ensuing economic, social and political problems remain, by and large, unaddressed.

The origins of internal displacement in

Turkey lie in the many decades of government policy that did not recognize the existence of a separate Kurdish identity in Turkey. After a long period of government efforts to assimilate the Kurds, in the 1960s a growing number of young Kurdish university students, often belonging to radical left-wing groups, began to agitate against what they called 'Turkish colonization of Kurdistan'.

In the 1970s, a number of Kurdish political groups became active and some resorted to the use of violence. One such group was the PKK (the Kurdistan Workers Party). In 1984, the PKK took up arms against Turkey and started a campaign of violence with the declared intention of establishing an independent Kurdish state. In 1987 the government declared emergency rule in 13 Kurdish populated provinces. Since then the confrontation between the PKK and Turkish security forces is generally believed to have claimed 27,000 lives. Large numbers of people have been displaced as a result of this violence.

At least three factors have caused internal displacement:

- the evacuation of villages by the military or security forces, allowed by the 1987 law. The government claimed that these evacuations were necessary because remote areas were difficult to protect against the PKK or because, willingly or unwillingly, they provided logistical support for the PKK. This is the most common push factor;
- pressure to leave by the PKK, which targeted 'non-revolutionary' villages that did not support the national liberation struggle; and
- insecurity resulting from being caught between the PKK and Turkish security forces. Villagers could be asked by the PKK to provide food and shelter, and then be harassed by security forces who failed to distinguish between those civilians who

support the PKK willingly and those who do so out of fear.

Two types of areas are particularly affected by internal displacement: those bordering Iraq and Iran, where PKK militants have found sanctuary and a base from which to launch attacks in Turkey; and rugged and remote mountainous areas where intense military clashes occurred between the PKK and Turkish security forces, especially during the 1993–95 period.

The magnitude of internal displacement in Turkey is unclear because of the difficulty of distinguishing between the migration resulting directly from the operations of the Turkish security forces and the PKK, and the migration that is a function of general, including economic, insecurity. In July 1996 the minister of the interior stated that approximately 330,000 people from 918 villages and 1700 hamlets had been evacuated from provinces under emergency law, while the Turkish Human Rights Association put the numbers of internally displaced people at around 2.5 million. Other reports have put the number of villages evacuated at 3000 and internally displaced people at 3 million. The government figure may be taken as a minimum figure for the internally displaced, while the latter two figures include both the forcibly displaced and those who have left their communities for a combination of economic and security reasons.

The affected provinces are among the most underdeveloped parts of Turkey. Provinces under emergency rule were also those with the lowest per capita annual income, ranging from Bitlis with US$ 662 to Diyarbakir with US$ 1485, both well under the Turkish average of US$ 2655.

Three patterns of migration can be identified:

- the majority of internally displaced people from the rural areas have moved into the nearest urban centres. Provincial capitals such as Batman, Diyarbakir, Hakkari, Sanliurfa and Van have been particularly affected;

- those internally displaced people with greater economic resources and the right contacts have moved further away to cities such as Adana, Gaziantep, Kahramanmaras and Mersin, outside the emergency law provinces; and

- many members of the middle class in the provincial cities have moved to western cities in Turkey such as Ankara, Antalya, Bursa, Istanbul and Izmir.

Following the internal displacement and migration since 1990, the distribution of Kurds within Turkey has changed significantly. A majority of Kurds now live outside the eastern and southeastern provinces. It has been suggested that Kurds now account for one-third of Istanbul's total population of approximately 12 million. The national census taken in December 1997 will reveal more complete data on the extent of internal displacement since 1990.

The short-term economic and humanitarian consequences of this massive migration have been disastrous. The already depressed regional economy has deteriorated even further. The cities have become overwhelmed with people swelling the ranks of the unemployed and stretching municipal services. Starvation is reported among the poorest of the internally displaced living in makeshift housing in the cities of eastern and southeastern Turkey. Villagers have been forced to slaughter their herds to finance their move into urban centres. The tourist industry has virtually disappeared from this locality. Furthermore, there has also been a flight of capital from the region as the relatively well-off have closed their businesses and small factories before moving to the west of Turkey. Inevitably, these developments have aggravated the employment situation and resulted

in further pressure for groups to migrate out of eastern and southeastern cities.

Government policy towards internally displaced people has been limited to the provision of food and materials for very basic housing. This inadequate assistance has tended to favour IDPs from Kurdish *ashiret* (tribes or clans) who have traditionally had good relations with the government, rather than those who have supported the PKK or remained neutral. In June 1997, the parliament formed a special commission to investigate the problems and consequences of internal displacement and make recommendations for possibilities of return to evacuated villages. However, by December 1997, the commission had not yet prepared its report. During the course of 1996 and 1997 the government permitted and assisted the return of the inhabitants of a small number of evacuated villages. At a more general level, the government has tried to solve the larger Kurdish problem by developing policies to revive the economy of the region. However, these economic policies have failed to materialize. The government is clearly expecting that in the long run the problem will be significantly alleviated by job opportunites created as a result of the southeastern Anatolian Development Project and expanded trade with Iraq.

One of the few positive outcomes of the crisis is that it has helped the mobilization of civil society in Turkey. A growing number of non-governmental organizations are addressing many aspects of the problems associated with internal displacement. Projects range from financing and organizing humanitarian assistance, to the economic and social empowerment of vulnerable groups such as women and children. Some of these projects have involved cooperation with international NGOs as well as intergovernment organizations. A number of NGOs have also become actively involved in publicizing the problem and mobilizing business interests.

The military has considerably weakened the ability of the PKK to operate within Turkey. However, the many problems faced by the victims of internal displacement still remain broadly unsolved. The government has still not demonstrated a clear will to enable at least some of them to return to their villages. The question of return is highly political. Kurdish nationalist groups are keen to see internally displaced people return to their villages, while many of the government or non-government economic and humanitarian projects, by their very nature, seem to favour integration into new communities. Another problem is that Turkish NGOs suffer from lack of expertise in finding international funding for their projects, which significantly slows down reconstruction and return.

The government continues to ignore the larger Kurdish question, which lies behind the internal displacement. Although now and then some form of cultural autonomy for Kurds is discussed among politicians and the public, as recently as September 1997 the president argued that Turkey did not have a Kurdish problem but a problem of terrorism. Such an approach continues to put emphasis on military measures. The problem is also aggravated by the instability in northern Iraq as well as the Syrian government's support for the PKK.

Since 1985, a paramilitary force of 'village guards', drawn exclusively from loyal *ashirets*, and now numbering more than 60,000, has been used ostensibly to defend villages from PKK attacks. Complaints about the abuse of this system have been increasing over the last five to six years. If the calls by members of parliament and some members of the government for the dissolution of the village guards are put into effect, this might give the Kurds in the eastern and southeastern parts of Turkey more confidence in the government. This in turn could ease the pressure to migrate out of the area.

Another hopeful sign is that with a decline in the activities of the PKK and an increase in trade with Iraq, the region's economy is slowly but surely picking up, alleviating some of the massive problems of unemployment. However, in the meantime, most of the hundreds of thousands of internally displaced people are still a long way from having their daily problems resolved.

Notes on Contributors

Shahram Akbarzadeh completed his PhD on central Asian politics and writes on contemporary issues of the region.

Iain Beattie has worked for the UNDP's Regional Bureau for Africa and at the International Rescue Committee. He is currently working at the UN's Special Unit for Microfinance.

Jon Bennett is director of the Global IDP Survey, a project of the Norwegian Refugee Council. He is also a research associate at the Refugee Studies Programme, University of Oxford.

Roberta Cohen is the co-director of the Brookings Institution Project on Internal Displacement in Washington DC and coauthor of *Masses in Flight: The Global Crisis of Internal Displacement* (Brookings, 1998).

Chris Dammers is an independent consultant and writer on international development and human rights issues, based in Oxford.

Mark Davidheiser works for the International Rescue Committee in New York.

Francis Deng is the UN Secretary-General's Special Representative for internally displaced persons. He is also a co-director of the Brookings Institution Project on Internal Displacement, Washington DC.

Laurel Fain worked as a reproductive health adviser to the International Rescue Committee in Sudan. She is now continuinig her studies at Harvard University.

Janie Hampton has worked chiefly in Africa and has written 12 books about international development. She has also edited journals and been a producer with the BBC World Service.

Art Hansen works for the International Rescue Committee in New York.

Anuradha Harinarayan is a senior research assistant at the Feinstein International Famine Center at Tufts University, Massachusetts, USA.

Ana Maria Harkins is the programme officer for Asia and East Africa at the International Rescue Committee. She has also worked in the former Soviet Republic of Georgia and undertaken research for the Smithsonian Institution and the International Women's Tribune Center.

Pamela Harris has worked with refugees from Laos, Vietnam, Cambodia and Burma.

William Hayden is a graduate student at the Fletcher School of Law and Diplomacy, Tufts University, USA, and was formerly the researcher for the International Helsinki Federation for Human Rights, Vienna, Austria.

Gordon Hutchison is the director of Project Counselling Service in Costa Rica. PCS is an international consortium that works with IDPs all over Latin America.

Okechukwa Ibeanu's doctoral research was on the state and population in Nigeria. He now lectures at the Centre for Advanced Social Science in Port Harcourt, Nigeria.

Inforpress Centroamericana is a publishing and research company in Guatemala City. It publishes the weekly *Central America Report* in Spanish and English.

Kemal Kirisci is a visiting associate professor at the Department of Political Science, University of Michigan, USA.

Stephanie Kleine-Ahlbrandt works at the UN High Commission for Human Rights in Geneva, and has previously worked in human rights in Rwanda, Bosnia and Hercegovina.

James Kunder is Special Adviser to UNICEF.

Louise Ludlam-Taylor is currently doing an LLM in public international law at the University of Leiden, the Netherlands. She has worked for Médicins sans frontières Holland in the Ivory Coast and Burundi, and for MSF Canada as executive director.

William Maley is a research associate at the Centre for Middle Eastern and Central Asian Studies at the Australian National University. He has recently edited *Fundamentalism Reborn? Afghanistan and the Taliban* (London: Hurst & Company, 1998).

Bronwen Manby is a researcher for Human Rights Watch, London. She works in the Africa division with responsibility for South Africa.

Laura J Marks is the programme officer for West and southern Africa at the International Rescue Committee in New York.

Maxmillan Martin is an environmental journalist working in India.

Chariza T. Medina-Salgado is the coordinator for research, documentation and publication for the Ecumenical Commission for Displaced Families and Communities in the Philippines.

Ophelia Mendoza is director for research and evaluation of Community and Family Services International, in Manila, Philippines.

Omprakash Mishra is the coordinator of the Centre for Refugee Studies at Jadavpur University, Calcutta, India. He was the head of the department of International Relations at Jadavpur University.

Erin Mooney works for internally displaced people at the Centre for Human Rights in Geneva.

Geofrey Mugumya is the settlement officer in charge of refugee integration for the government of Uganda.

Patrick Mullen worked with MSF (Belgium) in Rwanda in 1994 and with the UN World Food Programme in Burundi and former-Zaire between 1995 and 1998.

Binaifer Nowrojee is the counsel at Human Rights Watch in New York and has particular responsibility for Africa.

Margaret Okole is assistant editor of the *Journal of Refugee Studies*, based at the Refugee Studies Programme, University of Oxford. For ten years she worked at the University of Nsukka, Nigeria.

Ana Maria Rebaza is the director of Suyasan, an NGO that supports projects for internally displaced women in Peru.

Steve Redding works for the International Rescue Committee in new York.

Bamanyirwe Aimé Sangara was a research assistant at the Refugee Studies Programme, Oxford and is currently programme coordinator for Social Trends in Contemporary Africa at the Africa Centre, London.

Sumit Sen is a Rhodes scholar and PhD candidate at the London School of Economics, where he is researching international refugee law in South Asia.

Susanne Schmeidl is an independent writer and researcher in the demographics of refugee migration and early warning of humanitarian disasters. She has most recently worked for the UNHCR in Geneva.

Martin Stein is a postgraduate student in the Department of International Relations at Yale University, USA. He was China field coordinator of Volunteers in Asia (a non-political NGO), and a researcher for the International Crisis Group.

Paul Stubbs is a researcher in Croatia for the Globalism and Social Policy Programme, a collaboration between the University of Sheffield, UK and STAKES, Helsinki, Finland.

Patty Swahn is the International Rescue Committee country director for Sudan, based in Khartoum. Previously she worked for IRC in Rwanda, and for the Office of Foreign Disaster Assistance at USAID.

P V Unnikrishnan is an Oxfam research fellow in India, focusing on disasters, refugees and conflicts.

Koenraad van Brabant worked with a humanitarian agency in Sri Lanka and is now a research fellow at the Overseas Development Institute in London.

Alex Vines is a researcher with Human Rights Watch, London, working for the Africa Division and the Arms Project.

Shyla Vohra works for the International Organization for Migration in Geneva.

UN Guiding Principles on Internal Displacement

In response to a request of the UN Commission on Human Rights to develop an appropriate normative framework for the protection and assistance of the internally displaced, the Representative of the Secretary-General on Internally Displaced Persons has prepared these Guiding Principles on Internal Displacement in collaboration with international legal experts and in consultation with UN agencies and other organizations, international and regional, intergovernmental and non-governmental. The Guiding Principles were submitted by the Representative to the Commission on Human Rights at its fifty-fourth session.

(UN document E/CN.4/1998/53/Add.2)

Guiding Principles on Internal Displacement

Introduction: *Scope and Purpose*

1. These Guiding Principles address the specific needs of internally displaced persons worldwide. They identify rights and guarantees relevant to the protection of persons from forced displacement and to their protection and assistance during displacement as well as during return or resettlement and reintegration.

2. For the purposes of these Principles, internally displaced persons are persons or groups of persons who have been forced or obliged to flee or to leave their homes or places of habitual residence, in particular as a result of or in order to avoid the effects of armed conflict, situations of generalized violence, violations of human rights or natural or human-made disasters, and who have not crossed an internationally recognized State border.

3. These Principles reflect and are consistent with international human rights law and international humanitarian law. They provide guidance to:

(a) The Representative of the Secretary-General on Internally Displaced Persons in carrying out his mandate;

(b) States when faced with the phenomenon of internal displacement;

(c) All other authorities, groups and persons in their relations with internally displaced persons; and

(d) Intergovernmental and non-governmental organizations when addressing internal displacement.

4. These Guiding Principles should be disseminated and applied as widely as possible.

Section I –
General Principles

Principle 1

1. Internally displaced persons shall enjoy, in full equality, the same rights and freedoms under international and domestic law as

do other persons in their country. They shall not be discriminated against in the enjoyment of any rights and freedoms on the ground that they are internally displaced.

2. These Principles are without prejudice to individual criminal responsibility under international law, in particular relating to genocide, crimes against humanity and war crimes.

Principle 2

1. These Principles shall be observed by all authorities, groups and persons irrespective of their legal status and applied without any adverse distinction. The observance of these Principles shall not affect the legal status of any authorities, groups or persons involved.

2. These Principles shall not be interpreted as restricting, modifying or impairing the provisions of any international human rights or international humanitarian law instrument or rights granted to persons under domestic law. In particular, these Principles are without prejudice to the right to seek and enjoy asylum in other countries.

Principle 3

1. National authorities have the primary duty and responsibility to provide protection and humanitarian assistance to internally displaced persons within their jurisdiction.

2. Internally displaced persons have the right to request and to receive protection and humanitarian assistance from these authorities. They shall not be persecuted or punished for making such a request.

Principle 4

1. These Principles shall be applied without discrimination of any kind, such as race, colour, sex, language, religion or belief, political or other opinion, national, ethnic or social origin, legal or social status, age, disability, property, birth, or on any other similar criteria.

2. Certain internally displaced persons, such as children, especially unaccompanied minors, expectant mothers, mothers with young children, female heads of household, persons with disabilities and elderly persons, shall be entitled to protection and assistance required by their condition and to treatment which takes into account their special needs.

Section II – Principles Relating to Protection from Displacement

Principle 5

All authorities and international actors shall respect and ensure respect for their obligations under international law, including human rights and humanitarian law, in all circumstances, so as to prevent and avoid conditions that might lead to displacement of persons.

Principle 6

1. Every human being shall have the right to be protected against being arbitrarily displaced from his or her home or place of habitual residence.

2. The prohibition of arbitrary displacement includes displacement:

(a) when it is based on policies of apartheid, "ethnic cleansing" or similar practices aimed at/or resulting in altering the ethnic, religious or racial composition of the affected population;

(b) in situations of armed conflict, unless the security of the civilians involved or imperative military reasons so demand;

(c) in cases of large-scale development projects, which are not justified by compelling and overriding public interests;

(d) in cases of disasters, unless the safety and health of those affected requires their evacuation; and

(e) when it is used as a collective punishment.

3. Displacement shall last no longer than required by the circumstances.

Principle 7

1. Prior to any decision requiring the displacement of persons, the authorities concerned shall ensure that all feasible alternatives are explored in order to avoid displacement altogether. Where no alternatives exist, all measures shall be taken to minimise displacement and its adverse effects.

2. The authorities undertaking such displacement shall ensure, to the greatest practicable extent, that proper accommodation is provided to the displaced persons, that such displacements are effected in satisfactory conditions of safety, nutrition, health and hygiene, and that members of the same family are not separated.

3. If displacement occurs in situations other than during the emergency stages of armed conflicts and disasters, the following guarantees shall be complied with:

(a) A specific decision shall be taken by a State authority empowered by law to order such measures;

(b) Adequate measures shall be taken to guarantee to those to be displaced full information on the reasons and procedures for their displacement and, where applicable, on compensation and relocation;

(c) The free and informed consent of those to be displaced shall be sought;

(d) The authorities concerned shall endeavour to involve those affected, particularly women, in the planning and management of their relocation;

(e) Law enforcement measures, where required, shall be carried out by competent legal authorities; and

(f) The right to an effective remedy, including the review of such decisions by appropriate judicial authorities, shall be respected.

Principle 8

Displacement shall not be carried out in a manner that violates the rights to life, dignity, liberty and security of those affected.

Principle 9

States are under a particular obligation to protect against the displacement of indigenous peoples, minorities, peasants, pastoralists and other groups with a special dependency on and attachment to their lands.

Section III –
Principles Relating to
Protection During
Displacement

Principle 10

1. Every human being has the inherent right to life which shall be protected by law. No one shall be arbitrarily deprived of his or her life. Internally displaced persons shall be protected in particular against:

    (a) Genocide;

    (b) Murder;

    (c) Summary or arbitrary executions; and

    (d) Enforced disappearances, including abduction or unacknowledged detention, threatening or resulting in death.

Threats and incitement to commit any of the foregoing acts shall be prohibited.

2. Attacks or other acts of violence against internally displaced persons who do not or no longer participate in hostilities are prohibited in all circumstances. Internally displaced persons shall be protected, in particular, against:

    (a) Direct or indiscriminate attacks or other acts of violence, including the creation of areas wherein attacks on civilians are permitted;

    (b) Starvation as a method of combat;

    (c) Their use to shield military objectives from attack or to shield, favor or impede military operations;

    (d) Attacks against their camps or settlements; and

    (e) The use of anti-personnel landmines.

Principle 11

1. Every human being has the right to dignity and physical, mental and moral integrity.

2. Internally displaced persons, whether or not their liberty has been restricted, shall be protected in particular against:

    (a) Rape, mutilation, torture, cruel, inhuman or degrading treatment or punishment, and other outrages upon personal dignity, such as acts of gender-specific violence, forced prostitution and any form of indecent assault;

    (b) Slavery or any contemporary form of slavery, such as sale into marriage, sexual exploitation, or forced labour of children; and

    (c) Acts of violence intended to spread terror among internally displaced persons.

Threats and incitement to commit any of the foregoing acts shall be prohibited.

Principle 12

1. Every human being has the right to liberty and security of person. No one shall be subjected to arbitrary arrest or detention.

2. To give effect to this right for internally displaced persons, they shall not be interned in or confined to a camp. If in exceptional circumstances such internment or confinement is absolutely

necessary, it shall not last longer than required by the circumstances.

3. Internally displaced persons shall be protected from discriminatory arrest and detention as a result of their displacement.

4. In no case shall internally displaced persons be taken hostage.

Principle 13

1. In no circumstances shall displaced children be recruited nor be required or permitted to take part in hostilities.

2. Internally displaced persons shall be protected against discriminatory practices of recruitment into any armed forces or groups as a result of their displacement. In particular any cruel, inhuman or degrading practices that compel compliance or punish non-compliance with recruitment are prohibited in all circumstances.

Principle 14

1. Every internally displaced person has the right to liberty of movement and freedom to choose his or her residence.

2. In particular, internally displaced persons have the right to move freely in and out of camps or other settlements.

Principle 15

1. Internally displaced persons have:

   (a) The right to seek safety in another part of the country;

   (b) The right to leave their country;

   (c) The right to seek asylum in another country; and

   (d) The right to be protected against forcible return to or resettlement in any place where their life, safety, liberty and/or health would be at risk.

Principle 16

1. All internally displaced persons have the right to know the fate and whereabouts of missing relatives.

2. The authorities concerned shall endeavour to establish the fate and whereabouts of internally displaced persons reported missing, and cooperate with relevant international organizations engaged in this task. They shall inform the next of kin on the progress of the investigation and notify them of any result.

3. The authorities concerned shall endeavour to collect and identify the mortal remains of those deceased, prevent their despoliation or mutilation, and facilitate the return of those remains to the next of kin or dispose of them respectfully.

4. Grave sites of internally displaced persons should be protected and respected in all circumstances. Internally displaced persons should have the right of access to the grave sites of their deceased relatives.

Principle 17

1. Every human being has the right to respect of his or her family life.

2. To give effect to this right for internally displaced persons, family members who wish to remain together shall be allowed to do so.

3. Families which are separated by displacement should be reunited as quickly as possible. All appropriate steps shall be taken to expedite the reunion of such families, particularly when children are involved. The responsible authorities shall facilitate inquiries made by family members and encourage and cooperate with the work of humanitarian organizations engaged in the task of family reunification.

4. Members of internally displaced families whose personal liberty has been restricted by internment or confinement in camps shall have the right to remain together.

Principle 18

1. All internally displaced persons have the right to an adequate standard of living.

2. At the minimum, regardless of the circumstances, and without discrimination, competent authorities shall provide internally displaced persons with and ensure safe access to:

    (a) Essential food and potable water;

    (b) Basic shelter and housing;

    (c) Appropriate clothing; and

    (d) Essential medical services and sanitation.

3. Special efforts should be made to ensure the full participation of women in the planning and distribution of these basic supplies.

Principle 19

1. All wounded and sick internally displaced persons as well as those with disabilities shall receive to the fullest extent practicable and with the least possible delay, the medical care and attention they require, without distinction on any grounds other than medical ones. When necessary, internally displaced persons shall have access to psychological and social services.

2. Special attention should be paid to the health needs of women, including access to female health care providers and services, such as reproductive health care, as well as appropriate counseling for victims of sexual and other abuses.

3. Special attention should also be given to the prevention of contagious and infectious diseases, including AIDS, among internally displaced persons.

Principle 20

1. Every human being has the right to recognition everywhere as a person before the law.

2. To give effect to this right for internally displaced persons, the authorities concerned shall issue to them all documents necessary for the enjoyment and exercise of their legal rights, such as passports, personal identification documents, birth certificates and marriage certificates. In particular, the authorities shall facilitate the issuance of new documents or the replacement of documents lost in the course of displacement, without imposing unreasonable conditions, such as requiring the return to one's area of habitual residence in order to obtain these or other required documents.

3. Women and men shall have equal rights to obtain such necessary documents and shall

have the right to have such documentation issued in their own names.

Principle 21

1. No one shall be arbitrarily deprived of property and possessions.

2. The property and possessions of internally displaced persons shall in all circumstances be protected, in particular, against the following acts:

    (a) Pillage;

    (b) Direct or indiscriminate attacks or other acts of violence;

    (c) Being used to shield military operations or objectives;

    (d) Being made the object of reprisal; and

    (e) Being destroyed or appropriated as a form of collective punishment.

3. Property and possessions left behind by internally displaced persons should be protected against destruction and arbitrary and illegal appropriation, occupation or use.

Principle 22

1. Internally displaced persons, whether or not they are living in camps, shall not be discriminated against as a result of their displacement in the enjoyment of the following rights:

    (a) The rights to freedom of thought, conscience, religion or belief, opinion and expression;

    (b) The right to seek freely opportunities for employment and to participate in economic activities;

    (c) The right to associate freely and participate equally in community affairs;

    (d) The right to vote and to participate in governmental and public affairs, including the right to have access to the means necessary to exercise this right; and

    (e) The right to communicate in a language they understand.

Principle 23

1. Every human being has the right to education.

2. To give effect to this right for internally displaced persons, the authorities concerned shall ensure that such persons, in particular displaced children, receive education which shall be free and compulsory at the primary level. Education should respect their cultural identity, language and religion.

3. Special efforts should be made to ensure the full and equal participation of women and girls in educational programmes.

4. Education and training facilities shall be made available to internally displaced persons, in particular adolescents and

women, whether or not living in camps, as soon as conditions permit.

Section IV – Principles Relating to Humanitarian Assistance

Principle 24

1. All humanitarian assistance shall be carried out in accordance with the principles of humanity and impartiality and without discrimination.

2. Humanitarian assistance to internally displaced persons shall not be diverted, in particular for political or military reasons.

Principle 25

1. The primary duty and responsibility for providing humanitarian assistance to internally displaced persons lies with national authorities.

2. International humanitarian organizations and other appropriate actors have the right to offer their services in support of the internally displaced. Such an offer shall not be regarded as an unfriendly act or an interference in a State's internal affairs and shall be considered in good faith. Consent thereto shall not be arbitrarily withheld, particularly when authorities concerned are unable or unwilling to provide the required humanitarian assistance.

3. All authorities concerned shall grant and facilitate the free passage of humanitarian assistance and grant persons engaged in the provision of such assistance rapid and unimpeded access to the internally displaced.

Principle 26

Persons engaged in humanitarian assistance, their transports and supplies shall be respected and protected. They shall not be the object of attack or other acts of violence.

Principle 27

1. International humanitarian organizations and other appropriate actors when providing assistance should give due regard to the protection needs and human rights of internally displaced persons and take appropriate measures in this regard. In so doing, these organizations and actors should respect relevant international standards and codes of conduct.

2. The preceding paragraph is without prejudice to the protection responsibilities of international organizations mandated for this purpose, whose services may be offered or requested by States.

Section V – Principles Relating to Return, Resettlement and Reintegration

Principle 28

1. Competent authorities have the primary duty and responsibility to establish conditions, as well as provide the means, which allow internally displaced persons to return voluntarily, in safety and with dignity, to their homes or places of habitual residence, or to resettle voluntarily in another part of the country. Such authorities shall endeavour to facilitate the reintegration of returned or resettled internally displaced persons.

2. Special efforts should be made to ensure the full participation of internally displaced persons in the planning and management of their return or resettlement and reintegration.

Principle 29

1. Internally displaced persons who have returned to their homes or places of habitual residence or who have resettled in another part of the country shall not be discriminated against as a result of their having been displaced. They shall have the right to participate fully and equally in public affairs at all levels and have equal access to public services.

2. Competent authorities have the duty and responsibility to assist returned and/or resettled internally displaced persons to recover, to the extent possible, their property and possessions which they left behind or were dispossessed of upon their displacement. When recovery of such property and possessions is not possible, competent authorities shall provide or assist these persons in obtaining appropriate compensation or another form of just reparation.

Principle 30

All authorities concerned shall grant and facilitate for international humanitarian organizations and other appropriate actors, in the exercise of their respective mandates, rapid and unimpeded access to internally displaced persons to assist in their return or resettlement and reintegration.

Bibliography

Compiled by Louise Ludlam-Taylor

Abdullahi, Ahmednasir M (1994) 'The Refugee Crisis in Africa as a Crisis of the Institution of the State', *International Journal of Refugee Law*, vol 6, no 4, Oxford: Oxford University Press
____ (1997) 'Ethnic Clashes, Displaced Persons and the Potential for Refugee Creation in Kenya: A Forbidding Forecast', *International Journal of Refugee Law*, vol 9, no 2, Oxford: Oxford University Press
African Rights (1995) *Sudan's Invisible Citizens: The Policy of Abuse against the Displaced People of the North*, London: African Rights
Aguilar Zinser, Adolfo (1991) *CIREFCA: The Promises and Reality of the International Conference on Central American Refugees*, Washington DC: Center for Immigration Policy and Refugee Assistance, Georgetown University
Allen, Tim (ed) (1996) *In Search of Cool Ground: War, Flight and Homecoming in Northeast Africa*, London: United Nations Research Institute for Social Development, Africa World Press and James Currey
Allen, Tim and Herbert Morsink (eds) (1994) *When Refugees Go Home, African Experiences*, London: James Currey
Amnesty International (1994) *Colombia: Political Violence, Myth and Reality*, London: Amnesty International Publications
____ (1996) *Peru: Human Rights in a Time of Impunity*, AMR 46/01/96, London: Amnesty International Publications
____ (1997) *Amnesty International Report 1997*, London: Amnesty International Publications
____ (1997) *Great Lakes Region: Still in Need of Protection: Repatriation, Refoulement and the Safety of Refugees and the Internally Displaced*, Report no AFR02/07/97, London: Amnesty International Publications
____ (1997) *Rwanda: Human Rights Overlooked in Mass Repatriation*, Report no AFR47/02/97, London: Amnesty International Publications
____ (1997) *Refugees: Human Rights Have No Borders*, London: Amnesty International Publications (see pp 42–7)
____ (1997) *Who's Living in My House? Obstacles to the Safe Return of Refugees and Internally Displaced People*, Report no EUR/ID, London: Amnesty International Publications
____ (1997) *Colombia Hacienda Bellacruz: Land, Violence and Paramilitary Power*, Report no 23/06/97, London: Amnesty International Publications
____ (1997) *Burundi: Forced Relocation: New Patterns of Human Rights Abuses*, AFR 16/19/97. New York: Amnesty International Publications
Anyang' Nyongo, Peter and Justus Abonyo Nyang'aya (1995) 'Comprehensive Solutions to Refugee Problems in Africa: Bilateral, Regional and Multilateral Approaches', *International Journal of Refugee Law*, special issue, Oxford: Oxford University Press

AVANSCO (1990) *Assistance and Control: Policies Toward Internally Displaced Guatemala*, Washington DC: Hemispheric Migration Project

Bakwesegha, Chris J (1995) 'The Role of the Organisation of African Unity in Conflict Prevention, Management and Resolution', *International Journal of Refugee Law*, special issue, Oxford: Oxford University Press

Barutciski, Michael (1996) 'The Reinforcement of Non-Admission Policies and the Subversion of UNHCR: Displacement and Internal Assistance in Bosnia Hercegovina (1992–94)', *International Journal of Refugee Law*, vol 8, nos 1/2, Oxford: Oxford University Press

Beller-Hann, Ildiko (1997) 'The Peasant Condition in Xinjiang,' *Journal of Peasant Studies*, vol 24, no 4, October, pp 87–112

Bennett, Jon (1997) 'Internal Displacement: Protecting the Dispossessed', *World Aid '96*, UK: The Winchester Group

____ (1997) 'NGOs and a New Government in Rwanda', in Bennett, J (ed), *NGOs and Governments: A Review of Current Practice for Southern and Eastern NGOs*, INTRA/ ICVA, Oxford

Bennett, J and M Kawatesi (1996) *Beyond Working in Conflict: Understanding Conflict and Building Peace*, Relief and Rehabilitation Network Paper 18, Overseas Development Institute, London

Benyani, Chaloka (1995) 'Internally Displaced Persons in International Law', unpublished thesis, available from Refugee Studies Programme Documentation Centre, Oxford

____ (1996) 'State Responsibility for the Prevention and Resolution of Forced Population Displacements in International Law', *International Journal of Refugee Law*, special issue, Oxford: Oxford University Press

Borgen, Jan (1994) *The Protection of Internally Displaced Persons by NRC: Platform, Concepts and Strategies*, Oslo: Norwegian Refugee Council

____ (1995) *Institutional Arrangements for Internally Displaced Persons: The Ground Level Experience. Report Commissioned by the United Nations Secretary-General's Representative on Internally Displaced Persons*, Oslo: Norwegian Refugee Council

Cernea, Michael M (1995) 'Understanding and Preventing Impoverishment from Displacement: Reflections on the State of Knowledge', *Journal of Refugee Studies*, vol 8, no 3, Oxford: Oxford University Press

Chalinder, Andrew (1998) 'Temporary Human Settlement Planning for Displaced Populations in Emergencies', *Good Practice Review*, no 6, RRN, Overseas Development Institute, London

CIAM (1994) *Hacia una Protección sin Discriminación de la Población Desplazada: Marco Jurídico y Organismos Internacionales, Regionales y Nacionales y las ONGs*, Managua: CIAM

Chimni, B S (1995) 'The Incarceration of Victims: Deconstructing Safety Zones', in N Al-Naumi and R Meese (eds) *International Legal Issues Arising under the United Nations Decade of International Law*, The Hague: Martinus Nijhoff

Christian Michelsen Institute (1997) *Conflict in Sri Lanka: The Human Rights Situation and the Refugees in Western Countries*, conference report, Bergen

CODEP UK (1996) *Beyond 'Working in Conflict': Understanding Conflict and Building Peace*, Relief and Rehabilitation Network Paper 18, London: Overseas Development Institute

Cohen, Roberta (1991) *Human Rights Protection for Internally Displaced Persons*, Washington DC: Refugee Policy Group

____ (1994) *International Protection for Internally Displaced Persons: Next Steps*, Focus Paper no 2, Washington DC: Refugee Policy Group

____ (1995) *Refugee and Internally Displaced Women: A Development Perspective*, Washington DC: The Brookings Institution/Refugee Policy Group Project on Internal Displacement

____ (1996) 'Protecting the Internally Displaced', in *World Refugee Survey 1996*, Washington DC: US Committee for Refugees

Cohen, Roberta and Jacques Cuenod (1995) *Improving Institutional Arrangements for the Internally Displaced*, Washington DC: The Brookings Institution/Refugee Policy Group Project on Internal Displacement

Cohen, Roberta and Francis M Deng (eds) (1998) *The Forsaken People: Case Studies of the Internally Displaced*, Washington DC: The Brookings Institution

____ (1998) *Masses in Flight: The Global Crisis of Internal Displacement*, Washington DC: The Brookings Institution

Cohen, Robin (ed) (1995) *The Cambridge Survey of World Migration*, Cambridge: Cambridge University Press

Colombey, J P (ed) (1995) *Collection of International Instruments and Other Legal Texts Concerning Refugees and Displaced*, Geneva: UNHCR

Cotran, Eugene (1995) 'The Establishment of A Safe Haven for the Kurds in Iraq', in N Al-Naumi and R Meese (eds) *International Legal Issues Arising under the United Nations Decade of International Law*, The Hague: Martinus Nijhoff

Cunliffe, S Alex and Michael Pugh (1997) 'The Politicisation of UNHCR in the Former Yugoslavia', *Journal of Refugees Studies*, vol 10, no 2, Oxford: Oxford University Press

Darcy, James (1997) 'Human Rights and International Legal Standards: What do Relief Workers Need to Know?', *Relief and Rehabilitation Network*, no 19, London: Overseas Development Institute

Davies, W (ed) (1998) *Rights Have No Borders*, Oxford: Global IDP Survey/Norwegian Refugee Council

Deng, Francis M (1993) *Protecting the Dispossessed: A Challenge for the International Community*, Washington DC: The Brookings Institution

____ (1993) *Comprehensive Study Prepared by Mr Francis Deng, Representative of the Secretary-General on Human Rights Issues Related to Internally Displaced Persons, Submitted Pursuant to Commission on Human Rights Resolution 1992/73*, UN Doc UN E/CN 4/1993/35, 21 January, Annexe contains Profiles of Displacement: Former Yugoslavia, Russian Federation, Somalia, Sudan and El Salvador

____ (1994) 'Internally Displaced Persons', *International Journal of Refugee Law*, vol 6, no 2, Oxford: Oxford University Press

____ (1994) *Internally Displaced Persons: An Interim Report to the United Nations Secretary-General on Protection and Assistance*, Washington DC: Refugee Policy Group/UN Department of Humanitarian Affairs

____ (1994) *Internally Displaced Persons: Report of the Representative of the Secretary-General, Francis M Deng, Submitted Pursuant to Commission on Human Rights Resolution 1993/95*, UN Doc E/CN 4/1994/44, 25 January, contains 'Profiles in Displacement: Sri Lanka'

____ (1995) *Internally Displaced Persons: Compilation and Analysis of Legal Norms: Report of the Representative of the Secretary-General, Francis M Deng, Submitted Pursuant to Commission on Human Rights Resolution 1993/95*, UN Doc UNE/CN 4/1995/CRP 1, 30 January

____ (1995) *Internally Displaced Persons, Report of the Representative of the Secretary-General, Mr Francis Deng, Submitted Pursuant to Commission on Human Rights Resolution 1993/95 and 1994/68*, UN Doc E/CN 4/1995/50, 2 February. Add 1, 2, 4: 'Profiles in Displacement: Colombia, Burundi, Rwanda'

_____ (1995) 'The International Protection of the Internally Displaced', *International Journal of Refugee Law*, special issue, Oxford: Oxford University Press

_____ (1995) 'Dealing with the Displaced: A Challenge to the International Community', *Global Governance*, vol 1, no 1, Boulder: Lynne Rienner

_____ (1995) 'The International Protection of the Internally Displaced', *International Journal of Refugee Law*, special issue, Oxford: Oxford University Press

_____ (1995) *Sovereignty, Responsibility and Accountability: A Framework of Protection, Assistance and Development for the Internally Displaced*, concept paper for The Brookings Institution/Refugee Policy Group Project on Internal Displacement, Washington DC: The Brookings Institution/Refugee Policy Group

_____ (1995) 'Frontiers of Sovereignty: A Framework of Protection, Assistance and Development for the Internally Displaced', *Leiden Journal of International Law*, vol 8, no 2

_____ (1996) *Internally Displaced Persons: Report of the Special Representative of the Secretary-General, Mr Francis Deng, Submitted Pursuant to Commission on Human Rights Resolution 1995/57*, UN Doc E/CN 4/1996/52, 22 February, Add 2, 'Conclusions of the Compilation and Analysis of Legal Norms'

_____ (1996) 'Curative Prevention: Breaking the Cycle of Displacement', in Kevin M Cahill MD, *Preventive Diplomacy: Stopping Wars before They Start*, New York: Basic Books and the Centre for International Health and Cupertino

_____ (1996) *Report of the Representative of the Secretary-General, Mr Francis Deng, Submitted to Commission on Human Rights Resolutions 1995/57 and Addendum: Profiles in Displacement: Peru*, UN Doc E/CN 4/1996/52/Add 1, 4 January

_____ (1996) *Profiles in Displacement: Tajikistan*, UN Doc A/51/483/Add 1, 24 October

_____ (1997) *Profiles in Displacement: Mozambique*, UN Doc E/CN 4/1997/43/Add 1, 24 February

_____ (1994) *Profiles in Displacement: Sri Lanka*, New York: UN Economic and Social Council

_____ (1995) *Compilation and Analysis of Legal Norms*, UN Doc E/CN 4/1996/Add 2, 5 December, Accessible on UNHCR Refworld URL: http://www.unhcr.ch/refworld/refworld.htm

Dieng, Adama (1995) 'Addressing the Root Causes of Forced Population Displacements in Africa: A Theoretical Model', *International Journal of Refugee Law*, special issue, Oxford: Oxford University Press

Duffield, Mark (1997) 'NGO Relief in War Zones: Towards an Analysis of the New Aid Paradigm', *Third World Quarterly*, vol 18, no 3, Abingdon: Carfax

Eade, Deborah (ed) (1996) *Development in States of War*, Oxford: Oxfam (UK/I)

EPICA and CHRLA (1993) *Out of the Shadows: The Communities of Population Resistance in Guatemala*, Washington DC: Ecumenical Program on Central America

Fleck, Dieter (ed) (1996) *The Handbook of Humanitarian Law in Armed Conflicts*, Oxford: Oxford University Press

Forced Migration Project (1997) *Protecting Eurasia's Dispossessed*, Forced Migration/ Soros Open Society Project, URL: http://www.soros.org/ fmpz/html/ ngp.html

Forsythe, David (1996) 'The International Committee of the Red Cross and Humanitarian Assistance: A Policy Analysis', *International Review of the Red Cross*, no 314, Geneva: International Committee of the Red Cross

Franco, Leonardo (1995) 'An Examination of Safety Zones for Internally Displaced Persons as a Contribution toward Prevention and Solution of Refugee Problems', in N Al-Naumi and R Meese (eds) *International Legal Issues Arising under the United Nations Decade of International Law*, The Hague: Martinus Nijhoff

Freedman, Paul (1995) 'International Intervention to Combat the Explosion of Refugees and Internally Displaced Persons', *Georgetown Immigration Law Journal*, vol 9, no 3, Washington DC: Georgetown University Law Centre

Gallagher, Dennis and Diller, Janelle M (1990) *CIREFCA: At The Crossroads Between Uprooted People and Development in Central America*, Working Paper no 27, Washington DC: Commission for the Study of International Migration and Cooperative Economic Development

Goodwin-Gill, Guy (1996) *The Refugee in International Law*, second edition, Oxford: Clarendon Press

Gowlland-Debbas, Vera (1996) *The Problem of Refugees in the Light of Contemporary International Law*, The Hague: Martinus Nijhoff

Hamid, Gamal (1997) *Population Displacement in Sudan: Patterns, Responses and Coping Strategies*, New York: Centre for Migration Studies

Hamilton, Claire, David Gibbon and Alice Kaudia (1997) *Participatory Basic Needs Assessment with the Internally Displaced Using Well-Being Ranking*, Contact: c/o gibbon@koshi.wlink.com.np

Harris, John (ed) (1995) *The Politics of Humanitarian Intervention*, London and New York: Pinters Publishers

Hathaway, James (1991) *The Law of Refugee Status*, Toronto: Butterworths (see pp 29–64)

Hein, Jeremy (1993) 'Refugees, Immigrants, and the State', *Annual Review of Sociology*, vol 19, pp 43–59

Helton, Arthur C (1994) 'UNHCR and Protection in the 90s', *International Journal of Refugee Law*, vol 6, no 1, Oxford: Oxford University Press

_____ (1996) 'The CIS migration conference: A Chance to Prevent and Ameliorate Forced Movements of People in the Former Soviet Union', *International Journal of Refugee Law*, vol 8, nos 1 and 2, Oxford: Oxford University Press

Higgins, Andrew (1998) 'On the Border of Despair: North Korea', *Guardian* (London), 14 March

Hoffman, Rainer (1996) 'Law of Refugees and Internally Displaced Persons', in *Law in Humanitarian Crisis*, Brussels: European Commission

Human Rights Watch (1996) *CIS: Refugees and IDPs in Armenia, Azerbaijan, Georgia, the Russian Federation and Tajikistan*, Report D807, London: Human Rights Watch

_____ America (1996) *Colombia: Military-Paramilitary Partnership and the US*, New York: Human Rights Watch

_____ (1997) *World Report 1997*, New York: Human Rights Watch

_____ Africa (1997) *Internally Displaced: The UNDP Displaced Persons Program in Kenya*, New York: Human Rights Watch

_____ Africa (1997) *Zaire: 'Attacked by All Sides'. Civilians and the War in Eastern Zaire*, Report no 9/1 (A), New York: Human Rights Watch

_____ (1997) *The Human Rights Watch Global Report on Women's Human Rights*, New York: Human Rights Watch

_____ Africa (1997) *Failing the Internally Displaced: The UNDP Displaced Persons Program in Kenya*, New York: Human Rights Watch

Immigration and Refugee Board Documentation Centre (1996) *Turkey: The Situation of the Kurds*, Ottawa: Immigration and Refugee Documentation Centre

International Committee of Internally Displaced Persons (chairperson Luke T Lee) of the International Law Association (1997) 'Draft Declaration of Principles of International Law on Internally Displaced Persons', *90 American Society of International Law Proceedings 224 (1996)*, Washington DC: American Society of International Law

International Centre for Ethnic Studies (1995) *The Bo-Atte massacre and the Kebetigollawa Refugee camp*, Colombo: International Centre for Ethnic Studies

International Council of Voluntary Agencies (1994) 'The Human Rights of Refugees and Internally Displaced Persons', *Humanitarian Affairs Series, no 6*, Geneva: ICVA

International Crisis Group (1997) *Going Nowhere Fast: Refugees and Internally Displaced in Bosnia*, ICG Bosnia Project Crisisweb, URL: http://www.intl-crisis-group.org/projects/bosnia/report/bh22main.htm

International Federation of the Red Cross (1996) *World Disaster Report 1997*, Oxford: Oxford University Press

International Law Association (1997) 'Draft Declaration of Principles of International Law on Internally Displaced Persons', in *90 American Society of International Law Proceedings 224 (1996)*, Washington DC: American Society of International Law

International Organization for Migration (1997) *Internally Displaced Persons: IOM Policy and Programmes*, Geneva: IOM

International Organization for Migration/ United Nations High Commissioner for Refugees (1997) *Report to the 1997 Steering Group Meeting in the Follow-Up to the CIS Conference*, Geneva: IOM/UNHCR

Kirisci, K and G Winrow (1998) *The Kurdish Question and Turkey*, London: Frank Cass

Kleine-Ahlbrandt, Stephanie (1996) *The Protection Gap: In the International Protection of Internally Displaced Persons: The Case of Rwanda*, Geneva: Graduate Institute of International Studies

Kunder, Jim (1996) *Building Towards Leadership: A Draft UNICEF Policy Paper on Internally Displaced Persons*, Geneva: UNICEF

Kwakwa, Edward (1995/6) 'Governance, Development and Population Displacement in Africa: A Call for Action', *African Yearbook of International Law, vol 3*

Lallah, Rajsmoor (1997) *Situation of Human Rights in Myanmar*, Report of the special rapporteur, UN Economic and Social Council E/CN 4/1997/64, February

Lambrecht, Curt (1996) *Response Systems of NGOs to Assistance and Protection of the Internally Displaced Persons*, Oslo: Norwegian Refugee Council

Langren, Karin (1995) 'Safety Zones and International Protection: A Dark Grey Area', *International Journal of Refugee Law, vol 7, no 3*, Oxford: Oxford University Press

Larkin, Mary Ann (1994) *Review of the CIREFCA Process*, UN Doc EVAL/CIREF/14 May

Larkin, Mary Ann et al (1991) *Repatriation Under Conflict in Central America*, Washington DC: Hemispheric Migration Project

Lavoyer, Jean-Philippe (1995) 'Refugees and Internally Displaced: International Humanitarian Law and the Role of the ICRC', *International Review of the Red Cross, no 305*, Geneva: ICRC

_____ (ed) (1996) *Internally Displaced Persons: Symposium Paper*, Geneva: ICRC

Lee, Luke T (1996) 'Internally Displaced Persons and Refugees: Toward a Legal Synthesis?', *Journal of Refugee Studies, vol 9, no 1*, Oxford: Oxford University Press

Lewis, Corinne E (1992) 'Dealing with the Problem of Internally Displaced Persons', *Georgetown Immigration Law Journal, vol 6, no 4*, Washington DC: Georgetown University Law Centre

Loughna, Sean (1998) *Forced Migration Review* (copublication of the Refugee Studies
    Programme, Oxford University, and the Global IDP Survey), March

Loughna, S and G Vicente (1997) 'Population Issues and the Situation of Women in Post-
    Conflict Guatemala', Working Paper, ILO Action Programme on Skills and
    Entrepreneurship Training for Countries Emerging from Armed Conflict, Geneva: ILO

McDowell, Chris (ed) (1996) *Understanding Improvishment: The Consequences of Development-
    Induced Displacement*, Providence: Berghahn Books

Machel, Graça (1996) *UN Study on the Impact of Armed Conflict on Children*, URL: http://www.
    unicef.org/graca/women.htm

MacFarlane, S Neil and Larry Minear (1997) *Humanitarian Action and Politics: The Case of
    Nagorno-Karabakh,* Occassional Paper no 25, Providence: Thomas J Watson Jr Institute for
    International Studies

Macrae, Joanna and Anthony Zwi (eds) (1995)*War and Hunger: Rethinking International
    Responses to Complex Emergencies*, London: Zed Books

Makanya, Stella Tandai (1995) 'Voluntary Repatriation in Africa in the 1990s: Issues and
    Challenges', *International Journal of Refugee Law*, special issue, Oxford: Oxford University
    Press

Maley, William (ed) (1998) *Fundamentalism Reborn? Afghanistan and the Taliban*, London:
    Hurst & Company

Maslen, Stuart (1996) 'The Implication of the 1996 Landmines Protocol for Refugees and the
    Internally Displaced', *International Journal of Refugee Law*, vol 8, no 3, Oxford: Oxford
    University Press

Mazrui, Ali A (1995) 'The African State as a Political Refugee: Institutional Collapse and Human
    Displacement', *International Journal of Refugee Law*, special issue, Oxford: Oxford University Press

Médecins sans frontières (1996) *World in Crisis: The Politics of Survival at the End of the 20th
    Century*, London and New York: Routledge

Mihalkanin, Ed (1993) 'Refugee Aid, Displaced Persons, and Development in Central America',
    in Robert F Gorman, *Refugee Aid and Development: Theory and Practice*, Westport:
    Greenwood Press

Minear, Larry et al (1994) *Humanitarian Action in the Former Yugoslavia: The UN's Role 1991–
    93*, Providence: Thomas J Watson Jr Institute for International Studies

Minear, Larry and Thomas Weiss (1993) *Humanitarian Action in Times of War*, Boulder and
    London: Lynne Rienner

_____ (eds) (1993) *Humanitarism across Borders*, Boulder and London: Lynne Rienner

_____ (1994) *Humanitarian Politics*, New York: Foreign Policy Association

_____ (1995) *Mercy under Fire: War and the Global Humanitarian Community*, Boulder: Westview

Mooney, Erin D (1995) 'Presence, ergo Protection? UNPROFOR, UNHCR and the ICRC in
    Croatia and Bosnia and Hercegovina', *International Journal of Refugee Law*, vol 7, no 3,
    Oxford: Oxford University Press

_____ (1996) 'Internal Displacement and the Conflict in Abkhazia', *International Journal on
    Group Rights*, vol 3, Amsterdam: Kluwer

_____ (1996/7) 'Conference Report: CIS Conference on Refugees and Migrants', *International
    Journal on Minority and Group Rights*, vol 4, no 1

Moore, Jonathan (1997) *The UN and Complex Emergencies: Rehabilitation in Third World
    Transitions*, Geneva: War-torn Societies Project (United Nations Research Institute for Social
    Development and the Programme for Strategic and International Security Studies).

Mugumya, Geofrey (1996) *Refugees/IDPs Participation in Mitigation of their Induced Environmental Problems: A Guide to Pertinent Features*, Kampala: Refugees Department, Ministry of Local Government

_____ (1997) *Uganda's Internally Displaced Persons: Towards A Durable Solution. A Practitioner's Perspective*, Kampala: Refugees Department, Ministry of Local Government

Mutua, Makauwa (1995) 'The Interaction between Human Rights, Democracy and Governance and the Displacements of Populations', *International Journal of Refugee Law*, special issue, Oxford: Oxford University Press

Nana-Sinkam, S C (1995) 'From Relief and Humanitarian Assistance to Socioeconomic Sustainability: Rehabilitation, Reconstruction and Development with Transformation as the Ultimate Solution', *International Journal of Refugee Law*, special issue, Oxford: Oxford University Press

Neefjes, Koos (1997) *Displacement and Environmental Change in the Great Lakes Region: Do We Need to Respond?*, Oxford: Oxfam UK/I

New York Times (1998) 'Ethnic Violence Flares Anew After Election in Kenya', *New York Times*, 31 January

Norwegian Refugee Council/Refugee Policy Group (1993) *Norwegian Government Roundtable Discussion on United Nations Human Rights Protection for Internally Displaced Persons (5–6 February 1993, Nyon, Switzerland)*, Washington DC: Refugee Policy Group

Office of the United Nations High Commissioner for Refugees (1994) *UNHCR's Operational Experience with the Internally Displaced Persons*, Geneva: Division of International Protection

_____ (1995) 'Issues and Challenges in International Protection in Africa', *International Journal of Refugee Law*, special issue, Oxford: Oxford University Press

Oloka-Onyango, Joe (1996) 'The Plight of the Larger Half: Human Rights, Gender Violence and the Legal Status of Refugees and Internally Displaced Women in Africa', *Denver Journal of International Law and Policy*, vol 24, nos 2/3, Denver: University of Denver, College of Law

Omar, Rakiya and Alex de Waal (1994) *Humanitarianism Unbound: Current Dilemmas Facing Multi-Mandate Relief Operations in Political Emergencies*, Discussion Paper no 5, London: African Rights

Ordoñez, Juan Pablo (1995) *No Human Being is Disposable: Social Cleansing, Human Rights and Sexual Orientation in Colombia*, Washington DC: Colombia Human Rights Committee, International Gay and Lesbian Rights Commission and Proyecto Dignidad por los Derechos Humanos en Colombia

Oxfam (UK/I) (1994/5) *Overview of the Situation of Displaced Persons in Puttalam District, Colombo*, Oxford: Oxfam

_____ (1996) *Listening to the Displaced: Conversations in the Vanni Region, Colombo*, Oxford: Oxfam

Painter, R (1996) 'Property Rights of Returning Displaced Persons: The Guatemalan Experience', *Harvard Human Rights Journal*, vol 9, Spring

Palwankar, Umesh (1994) 'Measures Available to States for Fulfilling their Obligation to Ensure Respect for International Humanitarian Law', *International Review of the Red Cross*, no 298, Geneva: ICRC

Paul, R (1996) *The Role of Non-Governmental Organizations in the Protection of Civilians Under Threat: Practical Considerations*, New York: Center for the Study of Societies in Crisis and the Jacob Blaustein Institute for the Advancement of Human Rights

Petrasek, David (1995) 'New Standards for the Protection of Internally Displaced Persons: A Proposal for a Comprehensive Approach', *Refugee Survey Quarterly*, vol 14, nos 1 and 2, Spring/Summer, Geneva: UNHCR/CDR

Plattner, Denise (1992) 'The Protection of Displaced Persons in Non-International Armed Conflicts', *International Review of the Red Cross*, no 291, Geneva: International Committee of the Red Cross

Plender, Richard (1995) 'The Legal Basis of International Jurisdiction to Act with Regard to the Internally Displaced', *International Journal of Refugee Law*, vol 6, no 3, Oxford: Oxford University Press

Prendergast, J (1996) *Frontline Diplomacy: Humanitarian Aid and Conflict in Africa*, Boulder: Lynne Rienner

Ramsbotham, Oliver and Tom Woodhouse (1996) *Humanitarian Intervention in Contemporary Conflict*, Oxford: Polity Press in association with Blackwells

Reiff, D (1997) 'Nagorno-Karabakh: Case Study in Ethnic Strife', *Foreign Affairs*, vol 76, no 2

Roberts, Adam (1996) *Humanitarian Action in War*, Adelphi Paper no 305, London: International Institute for Strategic Studies

Roch, M P (1995) 'Forced Displacement in the Former Yugoslavia: A Crime under International Law?', *Dickinson Journal of International Law*, vol 14, no 1, Carlisle

Rohde, D (1997) *A Safe Area: Srebrenica: Europe's Worst Massacre since the Second World War*, New York: Simon & Schuster

Ruiz, Hiram A (1995) 'Emergencies: International Response to Refugee Flows and Complex Emergencies', *International Journal of Refugee Law*, special issue, Oxford: Oxford University Press

_____ (1997) *Conflict and Displacement in Sri Lanka*, Washington: US Committee for Refugees

Sandoz, Yves (1995) 'The Establishment of Safety Zones for Persons Displaced within Their Country of Origin', in N Al-Naumi and R Meese (eds) *International Legal Issues Arising under the United Nations Decade of International Law*, The Hague: Martinus Nijhoff

Save the Children Fund (UK) (1996) *Preliminary Findings of Child-Focused Research with Displaced Communities: Colombo*, London: Save the Children Fund

Sen, Sumit (1997) *International Law of Internally Displaced Persons: The Role of UNHCR*, New Delhi: Universal Publishers

Smith, M (1994) *Ethnic Groups in Burma: Development, Democracy and Human Rights*, London: Anti-Slavery International

Sørensen, Birgitte Refslund (1996) *Relocated Lives: Displacement and Resettlement within the Mahaweli Project, Sri Lanka*, Amsterdam: Free University Press

_____ (1998) 'Self Help Activities Among Internally Displaced People', in Wendy Davies (ed) *Rights Have No Borders*, Oxford: Global IDP Survey/Norwegian Refugee Council

Steering Committee of Joint Evaluation of Emergency Assistance to Rwanda (1996) *The International Response to Conflict and Genocide: Lessons from the Rwanda Experience*, Copenhagen: Joint Evaluation of Emergency Assistance to Rwanda

Stravropoulou, Maria (1996) 'The Right Not To Be Displaced', *The American University Journal of International Law and Policy*, vol 9, no 3, Washington DC: The American University, Washington College of Law

Swain, A (1996) 'Environmental Migration and Conflict Dynamics', *Third World Quarterly*, vol 17, no 5, Abingdon: Carfax

Tishkov, V (1997) *Ethnicity, Nationalism and Conflict in and after the Soviet Union: The Mind Aflame*, London: United Nations Institute for Social Development, International Peace Research Institute and Sage Publications

Tolfree, David (1996) *Restoring Playfulness: Different Approaches to Assisting Children who are Psychologically Affected by War or Displacement*, Stockholm: Rädda Barnen

Turton, David (1997) *War and Ethnicity: Global Connections and Local Violence*, Rochester: University of Rochester Press

United Nations (1992) *Analytical Report of the Secretary-General on Internally Displaced Persons*, UN Doc E/CN 4/1992/23, 14 February

United Nations Development Programme (1997) *Human Development Report 1997*, New York: Oxford University Press

United Nations High Commissioner for Refugees (1969–98) *Report on UNHCR Assistance Activities and Proposed Voluntary Funds, Programmes and Budget*, Geneva, Switzerland: Executive Committee for of the High Commissioner's Programme

_____ (1993) *The State of the World's Refugees 1993–95: The Challenge of Protection*, Harmondsworth: Penguin Books

_____ (1993–96) *Populations of Concern to UNHCR: A Statistical Overview*, Office of the United Nations High Commissioner for Refugees: Food and Statistical Unit, Divisions of Programmes and Operational Support

_____ (1994) *Protection Aspects of UNHCR activities on behalf of Internally Displaced Persons*, UN Doc EC/1994/SCP/CRP.2, 4 May

_____ (1994) *UNHCR's Operational Experience with Internally Displaced Persons*, Geneva: UNHCR

_____ (1995) *The State of the World's Refugees 1995–97: In Search of Solutions*, Oxford: Oxford University Press

_____ (1996) *International Legal Standards Applicable to the Protection of Internally Displaced Persons: A Reference Manual for UNHCR Staff*, Geneva: Division of International Protection, UNHCR

_____ (1996) *Official Report of People of Concern Workshop: Internally Displaced and War-Affected Populations: Conceptual, Legal and Operational Challenges*, Geneva: UNHCR/CDR

_____ (1996) *Refugees: Focus – The Internally Displaced*, vol 103, I –1996, Geneva: UNHCR

_____ (1996) *The CIS Conference on Refugees and Migrants*, European Series, vol 2, no 2, Geneva: UNHCR

_____ (1997) *The State of the World's Refugees 1997–98: A Humanitarian Agenda*, Oxford: Oxford University Press

US Committee for Refugees (1996) (Jeff Dumtra) *From Coup to Coup: Thirty Years of Death, Fear and Displacement in Burundi*, Washington DC: US Committee for Refugees

_____ (1996) (Hiram Ruiz) *Go Home/Stay Put: Tough Options for Displaced Peruvians*, Washington DC: US Committee for Refugees

_____ (1996) *The People in Between: Sri Lankans Face Long-term Displacement as Conflict Escalates*, Washington DC: US Committee for Refugees

_____ (1969–96) *World Refugee Report*, Washington DC: US Committee for Refugees

_____ (1997) *Conflict and Displacement in Sri Lanka*, US Committee for Refugees, Washington DC: US Committee for Refugees

US Department of State (1980 to early1990s) *World Refugee Report*, Washington DC: US Department of State van Brabant, K (1996) *Banned, Restricted or Sensitive: Working with the Military in Sri Lanka*, London: Relief and Rehabilitation Network, Newsletter, vol 5, nos 4–6

_____ (1997) *The Coordination of Humanitarian Action: The Case of Sri Lanka*, London: Relief and Rehabilitation Network, paper no 23

van der Wijk, Dineke (1997) *The Human Side of Conflict: Coping Strategies of Women Heads of Household in Four Villages in Sri Lanka and Cambodia*, Paper, Oxford: Oxfam UK/I

Walker, P (1997) 'The IFRC', *RedR Newsletter*, no 42, Spring

Watson, Thomas J Jr (1994) *Humanitarian Action in the Former Yugoslavia: The UN's Role 1991–1993*, Washington DC: Institute for International Studies and the Refugee Policy Group

Weekly Guardian (1997) 'Save the Rhino but Kill the People', *Weekly Guardian*, 30 March

Weiss, Thomas and Jarat Chopra (1995) 'From Humanitarian Intervention to Humanitarian Space', in Gene Lyons and Michael Mastanduno (eds) *Beyond Westphalia? National Sovereignty and International Intervention*. Baltimore: Johns Hopkins University Press

Weiss, Thomas (1996) 'Nongovernmental Organizations and Internal Conflicts', in Michael E Brown (ed) *The International Implications of Internal Conflict*, Cambridge: MIT Press

Weiss, Thomas and C Collins (1996) *Humanitarian Challenges and Intervention: World Politics and Dilemmas of Help*, Boulder: Westview

Weiss, Thomas and Amir Pacir (1997) 'Reinventing UNHCR: Enterprising Humanitarians in the Former Yugoslavia 1991–1995', *Global Governance*, vol 3, no 1, Boulder: Lynne Rienner

Wilson, Kenneth B (1992) *Internally Displaced, Refugees and Repatriates from and to Mozambique*, Report no 1, Oxford: Refugee Study Programme

Wiseberg, Laurie (1997) 'Interview with Francis M Deng, Special Representative of the Secretary-General on Internally Displaced Persons', *Human Rights Tribune*, vol 4, nos 2–3, Geneva: UN Commission on Human Rights

World Vision (1996) *Displacement and Civil Society in Peru*, Milton Keynes: World Vision

This bibliography appears on our website: http//www.sol.no/nrc-no

Readers are requested to inform Global IDP Survey of any additional sources that can be included in regular updates.

Index